Philosophical Disputes in the Social Sciences

If you would like to receive regular news on Harvester Press publications, please just send your name and address to our Publicity Department, The Harvester Press Ltd., 17 Ship Street, Brighton, Sussex. We will then be pleased to send you our new announcements and catalogues and special notices of publications in your fields of interest.

Philosophical Disputes in the Social Sciences

EDITED BY

S. C. BROWN

Senior Lecturer in Philosophy, The Open University
and *Assistant Director of the Royal Institute of Philosophy*

HARVESTER PRESS. SUSSEX
HUMANITIES PRESS. NEW JERSEY

First published in Great Britain in 1979 by
THE HARVESTER PRESS LIMITED
Publisher: John Spiers
17 Ship Street, Brighton, Sussex

and in the USA by
HUMANITIES PRESS INC.,
Atlantic Highlands, New Jersey 07716

© Royal Institute of Philosophy 1979

British Library Cataloguing in Publication Data
Philosophy of the Social Sciences, *University of East Anglia,*
1977
Philosophical disputes in the social sciences.
1. Social sciences — Methodology — Congresses
2. Social sciences — Philosophy — Congresses
3. Objectivity — Congresses
I. Title II. Brown, Stuart III. Series 300'.1 H61

ISBN 0-85527-764-5

Humanities Press Inc.
ISBN 0-391-00933-8

Typeset by Inforum Ltd., Portsmouth
Printed and bound in Great Britain by
Redwood Burn Ltd, Trowbridge and Esher

Contents

Acknowledgements   vi
Introduction   vii

PART ONE
SOCIAL SCIENCE AND HUMAN COGNITIVE INTERESTS

1. Types of Social Science in the Light of Human
    Cognitive Interests   3
       by Karl-Otto Apel

2. Apel's 'Transcendental Pragmatics'   51
       by Peter Winch

3. Reply to Peter Winch   74
       by Karl-Otto Apel

PART TWO
CRITICAL THEORY AND ITS CRITICS

4. Technique, Critique and Social Science   89
       by Michael Lessnoff

5. Lessnoff's Critique of Critical Theory   117
       by David Papineau

6. Towards a Reconstruction of Critical Theory   127
       by Karl-Otto Apel

7. Reply to Papineau and Apel   140
       by Michael Lessnoff

PART THREE
RELATIVISM IN SOCIAL ANTHROPOLOGY

8. Pangolin Power   151
       by John Skorupski

9. World View and the Core   177
       by Mary Douglas

10. Our Philosopher Replies   188
       by John Skorupski

PART FOUR
TOWARDS A NON-RELATIVIST SOCIOLOGY OF THOUGHT

11. Material-Object Language and Theoretical
    Language: Towards a Strawsonian
    Sociology of Thought   197
    by Robin Horton

12. The Epistemological Unity of Mankind   225
    by Martin Hollis

13. Reply to Martin Hollis   253
    by Robin Horton

PART FIVE
THE RELATIVITY OF POWER

14. Power in Social Theory:
    A non-Relative View   243
    *by Michael Bloch, Brian Heading and Philip
    Lawrence*

15. On the Relativity of Power   261
    by Steven Lukes

Index   275

ACKNOWLEDGEMENTS

The publisher and authors wish to acknowledge help and support of various kinds. A version of Chapter 1 first appeared in *SOCIAL RESEARCH* vol. 44, no. 3, Autumn, 1977. Michael Lessnoff pointed out some confusions in the original version of Chapter 5. Martin Hollis gave specific advice, many conversations, and, in collaboration with Bryan Heading, a Philosophy of Social Science Course, to the deep gratitude of the authors of Chapter 14. Bill Newton Smith and Charles Taylor made helpful criticisms of earlier drafts of Chapter 15.

Introduction

THE question underlying much philosophical discussion of the social sciences in the past has been whether they are indeed 'sciences'. That question does, of course, break down into a number of others, but these have served to fill up the agendas of discussions on this subject and to map out courses on the philosophy of the social sciences. To judge from the discussions at the Royal Institute of Philosophy conference on the Philosophy of the Social Sciences, held at the University of East Anglia in 1977, times have changed. Readers of this volume, which consists substantially of papers written for that conference, will not find the kind of 'looking over the shoulder' at the natural sciences which they may have come to expect. Perhaps this reflects the fact that most of the contributors are either sociologists, social anthropologists or political scientists and that the philosophers involved are ones whose interest in the social sciences is not merely an extension of their interest in the philosophy of science. This in turn was not, of course, an accidental outcome but something which was sought by the advisory panel which planned the conference, including Professor Ernest Gellner, Mr Martin Hollis, Professor Peter Winch, Mr Alan Ryan and Mr Quentin Skinner. The shift away from the traditional agenda of philosophy of the social sciences which is reflected in this volume is thus, to some extent, prearranged.

If there is a hazard in departing from stock problems it is that the ensuing discussions may have little or nothing to do with one another. It is perhaps the more remarkable therefore that the discussions of this volume do have underlying concerns in common. Perhaps the most prominent of these is

vii

the set of issues raised by talk of the 'objectivity' of the social sciences. These may be couched in terms of a set of problems which arise for what one may call 'social scientific realism'. According to that view there are objective regularities governing human social behaviour which are more fundamental than and independent of the conventions which may prevail in a particular society at a particular time. Theories in the social sciences are thus called upon to identify or construct a language which will be universally applicable in the description of human behaviour. Disputes between theories, according to social scientific realism, can in principle be resolved by further investigation of the social realities to which they are answerable. The social scientist is not concerned with making value judgements about such realities but only with identifying them and offering an explanation of them. The findings of the social scientist are to be fitted into a theoretical framework which is objective in three ways, namely, by being answerable to facts, by being universally applicable and by being value free. This view is sometimes known as 'positivism' but, since those positivists who are wedded to some form of verifiability principle are thereby committed to opposing scientific realism, it is confusing to talk about 'positivism' in this connection.

The 'objectivity' of the social sciences is not discussed in this volume in a holus-bolus way. None the less the discussions are concerned, directly or indirectly, with criticisms of the kind of objectivity claimed by social scientific realists. In the first part Professor Karl-Otto Apel calls in question the neutrality of the social sciences, and indeed of the sciences generally, by arguing that the type of understanding sought reflects certain value-laden cognitive interests. Professor Apel's paper is, in some respects, a development of the views associated with the 'Frankfurt School' of social theorists and, in particular, with Jürgen Habermas. This standpoint is criticised by Mr Michael Lessnoff in his substantive paper 'Technique, Critique and Social Science'.

The substantive papers in the remaining parts of the

volume are concerned with the other forms of scepticism I have mentioned about a scientific realist standpoint in the social sciences. They are identified as forms of 'relativism'. Although these papers can be seen as offering alternatives to relativism, it is misleading to imply that 'relativism' denotes a single set of doctrines, any more than 'scepticism' does. Just as one cannot understand a particular form of scepticism without knowing what standpoint it is directed against, so too, in my opinion one cannot understand a form of relativism without knowing what form of scepticism underlies it. This is something rather different in the case of relativism in social anthropology or in the sociology of thought from what it is in relation to the theoretical concepts used in political science. The scepticism involved is directed against different aspects of social scientific realism. These points are implicitly acknowledged by the contributors to the second part of this volume. John Skorupski's paper is directed in the first place towards the writings of Mary Douglas but ultimately, according to Professor Douglas, to Durkheim.

Skorupski critically examines the view that it is not possible to decide between competing 'world views' and hence that we can only talk of true and false statements with respect to a given world view. The 'core statements' of a world view are not properly speaking true or false at all. The conclusions of a relativist are commonly found unacceptable. But to silence him it is necessary to offer a positive account which can fend off his sceptical attacks. Professor Robin Horton offers the beginnings of such an account in his paper. He sets out to show that human concepts are not as variable from one culture to another as has sometimes been suggested. His programme, if it could be carried through, would provide a basis for a cross-cultural sociology of thought and thus provide an answer to the sceptical suggestion that there is no basis on which people from one culture can criticize the beliefs of those in another.

The topic of the final symposium arises out of the work of

x

Steven Lukes on power. It focusses on Lukes's contention that power is 'an essentially contested concept' and that it is, therefore, 'ineradicably value-dependent'. In their paper 'Power in Social Theory: A Non-Relative View', Michael Bloch, Bryan Heading and Philip Lawrence offer a critique of this position. Though the discussion is made particular to the concept of power, Lukes's view implies that other concepts which are fundamental to social theory, such as 'structure', are also essentially contested.

Although many of the contributors to this volume are concerned, in one way or another, with doubts about aspects of what I have called 'social scientific realism', it would be a mistake to suppose that those who criticize one aspect of this view are fellow-travellers with those who criticize other aspects. Though Professor Apel, for example, accuses social scientific realism of what he would perhaps prefer to call 'positivism', there is nothing in his paper which suggests that he sympathizes with any form of relativism. Equally Dr Lukes, if he would be happy to accept the term 'relativism' as applying to his views on power, is in no way committed to but indeed opposes the forms of relativism in social anthropology which are duscussed by Dr Skorupski and Professor Horton. There are separate issues involved. Just as Kant could be a 'transcendental idealist' and at the same time an 'empirical realist' so too Professor Apel can combine his 'transcendental pragmatics' with an otherwise realist philosophy of the social sciences. So, while the problems of social scientific realism provide some underlying unity to these discussions, none of the contributors is expressly concerned with taking sides for or against social scientific realism as a whole. That, indeed, is just as well, in view of the common experience of philosophers that the way to make headway in discussions is to narrow down the issues between the participants.

S.C. Brown

PART ONE

SOCIAL SCIENCE AND HUMAN COGNITIVE INTERESTS

1. Types of Social Science in the Light of Human Cognitive Interests
by Karl-Otto Apel

A. Philosophical presuppositions of the concept of cognitive interests

IT is not possible, within the framework of this paper, to explain, in all its implications, the conception of 'cognitive interests' or 'leading knowledge-interests' (*'erkenntnisleitende Interessen'*)[1]. It will instead be illustrated by its application to the problems of the philosophy of the social sciences. There are, however, a number of prevalent misunderstandings about the conception of 'cognitive interests'. Some preliminary remarks are therefore needed about its meaning and status in the context of philosophy of science generally.

1. The idea of cognitive interests, in my opinion, makes up the characteristic core of a philosophy of science that understands itself as an alternative to the so-called 'modern theory of science', i.e. to the neopositivistic conception of a logic of unified science. Tracing back the different questions and methods of science to different cognitive interests does indeed mean denying the claim to a unification of scientific methodology by logical reduction. But this does not mean denying the unity of science altogether. At this point the first misunderstanding has to be dissolved. This may be done, I think, by a distinction between the problematics of a differentiated constitution of the meaning of possible objects of experience, on the one hand, and the problematics of a discursive reflection upon the validity-claims of all results of scientific inquiry, on the other hand. The latter question cannot be settled without carefully taking into account the different meanings of validity claims.

3

Nevertheless it shows the ultimate unity of all sciences as lying in the universality of their truth-claims. These should be confirmed by a universal intersubjective consensus reached by discursive arguments. It might be claimed that, just by taking into consideration the differeniated meaning-constitution as a presupposition of different scientific methodologies, it might be possible to ascertain the unity of all scientific truth claims. This might even be claimed about methods whose (scientific) truth-claim is often rejected — as, for instance, psychoanalysis or hermeneutic text-interpretation.

2. After this first preliminary remark it becomes possible to cope with a second misunderstanding: if the leading interests of knowledge are to be considered as conditions of the possibility of the meaning-constitution of possible objects of experience then they may obviously not be simply equated with external motivations which may promote or even corrupt scientific enterprises. Whereas the latter interests are only to be considered as causes with regard to the possibility of scientific knowledge (although they might be reasons for the action of individual scientists) the leading knowledge-interests are not only and not primarily to be considered as causes of the factual performance of science but rather as reasons or normative conditions of the possibility of the methodical meanings of typically differentiated scientific questions (*Fragestellungen*). (Although it must and may easily be admitted that, in the long run, they fulfill also a causal or energetic function in the evolution of human knowledge in being the force behind at least part of the external motivations of scientific enterprises.) Therefore the leading knowledge-interests, in contradistinction to merely external motivations, are not (primarily) a topic for 'science of science', which, as an empirical social science, has to explore the external steering of science by its environments. They are, rather, a topic of a transcendental reflection upon those conditions of the possibility of human know-

ledge that were not taken into account by Kant's transcendental idealism which, in a sense, presupposes that a pure mind or consciousness could constitute such a thing as a world of cognitive interests as a topic of 'transcendental pragmatics' (of language) which comprises anthropology of knowledge.[2]

3. The preceding two remarks imply that the conception of cognitive interests cannot be defended within the framework of a pure 'logic of science' — often identified with modern theory of science in recent decades. Modern 'logic of science' — as it was primarily developed under the paradigm of 'Logical Empiricism', but also along the lines of a Popperian unified methodology — presupposes that all questions concerning the constitution of knowledge may be treated as questions concerning the empirical genesis of knowledge and hence (being questions of the empiric-pragmatic context of discovery, which may be separated from the genuine questions of a logic of science concern) the context of justification of knowledge. As against this already classical dichotomy we must insist on the thesis that the conception of leading knowledge-interests belongs to the extended context of the Kantian and Husserlian question as to the transcendental conditions of the possibility of a constitution of meaningful objects of experience.

This question, concretized as it is by the conception of knowledge-interests as normative conditions of the possibility of meaning-constitution, may not be answered within the empiric-pragmatic 'context of discovery' but rather in the context of a transcendental-pragmatic reflection upon the internal connections between possible experiences, possible ways of practical world-commitments and possible contexts of language-games. In other words, the conception of cognitive-interests is a topic of a transcendental-pragmatic supplementation or integration of the current 'logic of science'. It is, at the same time, a transformation of the

traditional transcendental theory of knowledge or epistemology.[3] As such it no longer takes the theoretical subject-
object-relation for granted but calls it into question as a relation that has to be mediated by practical commitment in
order to be a primordial sphere of typically different constitutions of meaningful objects of experience.

Hence, from the present point of view, the fashionable
talk about the 'theory-impregnatedness' of all experiential
data does not suffice in order to overcome the naïveté of Logical Empiricism. For, instead of taking theories for granted,
it is necessary first to ask for the conditions of the possibility
of the constitution of theories as possible systematizations of
synthetic achievements of cognition. This might be done
under the heuristic assumption that the different synthetic
achievements of the different sciences — e.g. causal explanation, functional explanation, understanding of good reasons (sometimes called teleological or rational explanation)
— are not intelligible as synthetic achievements of cognition, if they are to be reduced to a unitary logical model of,
say, deductive or inductive nomological explanation.[4] For
the synthetic achievements of cognition may be dependent
on the different categories of posing questions which again
may be considered as expressing different leading knowledge-interests.

4.   Now, after these general and abstract remarks concerning the meaning and function of the conception of leading
knowledge-interests it is time to introduce those three fundamental knowledge-interests that, in the opinion of Habermas and myself, must be presupposed in a systematic
account of the conditions of the possibility of the constitution of meaningful objects of human experience.

(a) the interest in controlling an objectified environmental
world
(b) the interest in communicative understanding
(c) the interest in critically-emancipatory self-reflection

I shall add only a few remarks, in the present context, to further characterize these three knowledge-interests:

(a): The first knowledge-interest may be called practical in the sense of being related to technical praxis — in a wide sense. But this does not mean that as a leading interest of knowledge, as it is presupposed for instance in physics, it should assimilate the methodological structure of science to that of technique or even technology in the usual sense. It does, however, imply that the possibility of experimental physics by the categorical and technical device of its posing questions to nature is mediated, so to speak, *a priori* through the possibility of their nomological insights being transformed into technological if-then-rules, to be integrated into instrumental schemes for goal-directed actions. The interest in controlling an objectified environmental world may, however, be sublimated, and as such it goes far beyond its manipulative paradigm, comprising e.g. all theoretical objectifying of world-pictures[4] and even being presupposed in our present attempt at laying out leading knowledge-interests philosophically, in a very abstract model of their structure. In German this wide range of controlling knowledge may be expressed by the term '*Verfügungswissen*'.

(b): The second knowledge-interest may be called practical in a sense close to the Aristotelian term 'praxis' because in its origin it is not restricted to meaning-understanding and interpretation, in the abstractive sense of, say, modern philology, but comprises the interest of 'coming to agreement' with other people in human interaction. The wide scope of this interest may be explained by the Wittgensteinian insight that children could not learn the meanings of words if they did not learn to use them at the same time as coming to agreement with other members of the language community about paradigmatical evidences of experience and about paradigmatical rules of behaviour. The German word '*Verständigung*' encompasses both the understanding of meaning and the coming to agreement, and by this ambiguity it is

capable of expressing the whole concern of the second knowledge-interest by the term '*Verständigungs-Interesse*'.

(c): The third leading knowledge-interest may be called
practical in the sense of being related to an evolutionary or
revolutionary praxis of changing the human quasi-nature,
be it that of individuals or of the society, as a consequence of
a process of enlightenment, i.e. of overcoming inner constraints or compulsions by critical self-reflection.

This does not mean that the problems of eliminating socio-
political constraints are simply identical with the problems
of self-liberation by critical-emancipatory reflection. But it
does imply that a strategical-political praxis of changing
socio-political structures may be justified as emancipatory
if, and only if, it may be considered as a consequence of the
overcoming of inner constraints of a pseudo-nature by critical self-reflection, in contradistinction to those types of
social engineering which are based instead on a manipulative utilization of reified structures of social relations.

Concerning these three fundamental knowledge-interests I would claim that they can be systematically grounded
as normative conditions of the possibility of meaningful
experience within the framework of a transcendental pragmatic (of language-games). This implies the further claim
that all conceivable internal, meaning-constitutive knowledge-interests may be derived, in a sense, from the three
fundamental knowledge-interests or from possible typical
combinations or dialectical mediations of them. In this context it might be heuristically supposed that, on the one hand
and in one sense, all three leading internal interests are presupposed in all methodological forms or types of scientific
inquiries but that, on the other hand and in another sense,
certain types of science (in their constitutive questions and
methodical devices) are paradigmatically determined by
just one of the three fundamental interests. Moreover it
might be supposed that there are typical figures of thought-
constituting methodological devices that might be derived

from different types of combinations or dialectical mediations of the three fundamental knowledge-interests.

This, then, is what I want to show in this paper about the 'social sciences', this term being understood in a very broad sense such as *quasi*-physicalistic 'behavioural sciences' and *quasi*-biological 'system-theories' might be subsumed under that label, as well as, for instance, *historical-hermeneutical 'Geisteswissenschaften'* and *historico-critical* social sciences, in the sense of, say, sociological critique of institutions and of ideology and in the sense of psychoanalysis. Being broadly classified in this way, the social sciences provide a particularly favourable field of demonstration for the conception of knowledge-interests. For the fact is that the same human society may become an object of knowledge according to very different methodological perspectives. This fact, in my opinion, confirms the thesis that neither a pure logic of science nor an ontology of the essential regions of possible objects of knowledge, in the preKantian sense (e.g. in the sense of Neo-Thomism, or of N. Hartmann, or of orthodox dialectical materialism), is able to do justice to the inter-relationship between the structure of being and the normative conditions of possible constitution of meaningful objects of human experience, and hence of methodical questions of the sciences in the broadest sense of this word.

B. Introduction of the complementarity-thesis and the thesis of dialectial mediation between understanding and explanation as fundamental constellations of knowledge-interests and methodological figures of thought.

As a vantage-point for all further explorations of *a priori* constellations of knowledge-interests as a basis for methodological distinctions in the philosophy of science I want to introduce what I have called the '*complementarity-thesis*'[6]:

The phenomenon I have in mind is sometimes described in

such a way that it seems even to provide a new argument for the conception of unified science. Thus, e.g. it is argued in this way: On the one hand, it can be shown that no so-called 'hermeneutician' (*'Geisteswissenschaftler'*) may 'understand' a text without understanding, in a sense, the objective matters dealt with in that text, such as art, religion, law, or, in a classical text of the history of science, nature. On the other hand, it can also be shown that no natural scientist can explain the phenomena of nature in nomological terms without understanding the theories and hypotheses of his colleagues and, before that, the texts of the teaching tradition of his discipline. Hence it is argued that 'understanding' and 'explanation' must not be separated, as is done in the tradition of W. Dilthey, and that a methodological distinction along these lines is untenable or at least fruitless.

Now, the first thing to do here is to reject the rhetorically suggested identification of making a distinction between with separating or even tearing asunder understanding and explanation. After this clarification it can easily be recognized that the well-understood distinction of Dilthey between understanding and explanation has already been presupposed by the above-sketched argument. This becomes immediately clear if that argument is confronted with those accounts of understanding as they are given from the point of view of neopositivistic reductionism, as for instance by C. G. Hempel[7] and Th. Abel.[8] For these latter accounts do not speak of a reciprocal presupposition of understanding and explanation, as is done — and rightly so — in the above sketched argument. They try to show that the function of understanding may be reduced to a prescientific, i.e. only psychologically relevant, heuristic device in the service of discovering explanatory hypotheses of nomological sciences. Compared to these attempts to deny the necessity of a proper methodical function of cognition by understanding, the argument (above sketched) even provides the phenomenological evidence for the opposite view. For it might be explicated as follows:

1. Even physicists cannot explain regularities of nature nomologically without presupposing at the same time another type of knowledge, viz. communicative understanding. This other type of knowledge might be considered as prescientific from the point of view of the actual knowledge-interest of the physicist. Nonetheless it might eventually be mediated by hermeneutical methods and thus acquire the status of a special kind of research, following its own leading interest, as is testified e.g. by the new discipline of a history of (natural) science. This phenomenon (of complementarity) obviously shows the genuine origin and function of hermeneutic understanding and interpretation as it is, in principle, not to be replaced by or reduced to nomological explanation, because it is, in principle, presupposed by all kinds of explanation.

2. On the other hand, the fact that all communicative understanding presupposes some knowledge about the objective matters in question, only illustrates the impossibility of conceiving communicative understanding in terms of an objectifying knowledge on a special level of the subject-object-relation.

For as understanding is, in principle, embedded in the intersubjective communication about some objective matters in the world, it cannot be replaced and 'scientized' by just describing and eventually explaining certain objective processes to be observed in our communication partners, e.g. in their verbal behaviour, or in products, such as utterances or texts. For the actions, utterances and texts of our partners can only fulfil their function within communication so long as they are only expressive vehicles or media of the meaning-intentions that are to be understood. Even these meaning-intentions should not be classified primarily as isolated psychological phenomena, but as meaning-*claims*, truth-*claims*, rightness-*claims* and implicit sincerity-*claims*[9] in the context of a communication about some objective matter. As soon as this embedding of understanding within the context of communication about something is disregarded by abstractive classifying and objectifying of special features of the communication-media, the communicative understanding begins to dissolve itself. This shows itself in a massive form if we, in the middle of communication, try to objectify our partners, i.e. their utterances or their verbal behaviour, as topics say of phonetics or phonology or even psycholinguistics or sociolinguistics. Even those types of hermeneutics, developed within the framework of historico-philological objectivism, that classify meaning-claims as special entities (e.g. as so called '*Sinngebilde*'), by abstraction from *truth-claims*, and/or normative rightness-claims — even they are, in a sense, mutilations of the integral phenomenon of communicative understanding, although they might be considered as methodically abstractive mediations of the integral process of communicative understanding.[10] Hence it may be said that hermeneutic understanding as a proper method of knowledge is not allowed to loosen itself from the leading interest of improving the inter-subjective communication by instead objectifying that communication or its parts as a topic of a strictly observational description or even explanation.[11]

On the other hand, it can be shown by a thought-experiment that a complete replacement of intersubjective understanding by methods of objectifying descriptions and explanation would abolish even the possibility of objectifying descriptions and explanations, and hence its own possibility. If one lone scientist reduced not only nature but also all his possible communication-partners to mere objects of observational description and explanation, this solitary man could not achieve any knowledge at all because he would be deprived of language-communication as a condition of the possibility of meaningful and valid knowledge.

From these considerations we may derive the following thesis: Understanding and explanation, as it now turns out, are complementary forms of knowledge corresponding to complementary leading knowledge-interests. That is to say, they

(a) supplement each other within the whole household of human knowledge, so to speak, and at the same time,
(b) they exclude each other as different interests or intentions of asking questions, and,
(c) for both reasons, they cannot be reduced to each other.

By this complementarity-thesis we have fixed a first, ideal-typical constellation of possible methods of knowledge, according to a corresponding constellation of leading interests. This fundamental polarized constellation might serve as a first orientation for a further ideal-typical differentiation of possible methods of human knowledge.

Focussing now on the social sciences, in a broad sense, we may apply the point of view of the complementarity-thesis in a twofold way. First we may, in the light of that thesis, look for criteria for distinguishing between common presuppositions of all social sciences, on the one hand, and natural sciences, especially physics, on the other. Secondly, we may try, in the light of the same thesis, to find criteria of a methodological differentiation within the social sciences themselves, say between those of them that spring from a quasi-physicalist interest in nomological explanation of objectified social processes and those that methodically incorporate and elaborate on the hermeneutical interest in improving or re-establishing communicative understanding between different contemporary language-games and sociocultural forms of life, or between those of the present and those of the past.

The first way of looking at things may show that the ontological differences between the entities made the object of science, e.g. between human beings capable of intentional actions and communication with the scientists and mute physical things, are still to be considered as a reason for methodological differentiation of knowledge; i.e. they are to be considered as a factor that cannot be eliminated by the knowledge-interests on the side of the scientists. On the contrary, this factor already favours certain corresponding cognitive interests at the level of object-constitution and resists, or even definitely limits the realization of certain other cognitive interests.

The second way of looking at things, on the other hand, may show that the leading cognitive interests are indeed normative conditions of the possibility of object-constitution and thus far are reasons for a methodological differentiation of knowledge — not only in conformity with certain correspondences between kinds of interests and kinds of ontological entities, but also, to a certain extent, in spite of them; e.g. insofar as the same human beings or the same activities of the human society may become the object or topic of very different types of methodological approaches corresponding to different cognitive interests.

Now, as I said, both these considerations to do with the relationship between the nature of being and object-constitution according to leading knowledge-interests will be applications of the complementarity-thesis. They are, that is to say, only concerned with the two complementary knowledge-interests: in controlling objectified processes, on the one hand, and in communicative understanding, on the other. In order to show the function of the third leading cognitive interest, viz. that of critical-emancipatory self-reflection, we shall have to supplement the complementarity-thesis itself by that of a dialectical mediation between communicative understanding and a quasi-naturalistic explanation. This methodological figure of thought may be shown, I think, to correspond to an intrinsic constitution of human nature as well as to an ethical demand concerning an interest of man in himself, i.e. of critical-emancipatory self-knowledge. It may be considered as the characteristic methodological device of the *critical*-reconstructive social sciences, including sociological critique of ideology and institutional self-alienation of man, as well as psychoanalysis.

C. Criteria of methodological differences between natural science and social science in general (corresponding to the complementarity of knowledge-interests in as far as it corresponds to a difference in the nature of being).

Regarding the differences between natural science and social science in general that are constituted both by the nature of being and by the complementarity of knowledge-interests corresponding to the nature of being, the following criteria might be offered.

1. A fundamental precondition of the constitution of nature as an object of experimental explanatory physics in the modern sense is, I think, defined by the possibility of a complete objectification of nature with regard to the presupposed epistemological subject-object-relation,[12] whereas all social sciences, even those that provide the basis for social technology, are only allowed to perform certain secondary methodological objectifications but should not totally objectify their human subject-objects, lest they are lost as intentional objects of knowledge.

This may be elucidated as follows: For modern physics it was a precondition of its definitive constitution as science at the beginning of the seventeenth century that all kinds of sympathetic-communicative and teleological understanding of nature were definitely renounced (or dispensed with). Only this renunciation of understanding could release nature as a world of mechanical corpuscular motions, and that is to say, as an object of explanation according to causal laws. Precisely this renunciation of understanding, however, should not constitute the intentional object of social science, not even in the case of quasi-physicalistic behavioural sciences. These sciences must indeed try to objectify or reify human activities, in order to make them into objects of quasi-nomological explanations as a basis for social technology.

The reason why not even quasi-physicalistic empirical social sciences should totally objectify human behaviour in the sense of a complete renunciation of understanding is brought out by a further criterion for a necessary distinction between the methodology of all social sciences and that of natural science.

2.   Natural science as explanatory science must renounce every kind of communicative and teleological understanding because it must suppose that the regularities of nature are not rules (or even norms) which may be followed or not, or followed in a false way, by nature as a subject of (teleological) action, but that they are laws determining the behaviour of natural objects in the sense of causal or statistical necessity.

Methodological consequences of this presupposition concerning the object-constitution may be formulated in the following theses:

(a) the natural sciences must impose law-hypotheses on nature from the outside, and can only test them by communication-free observations;

(b) observed deviations of the behaviour of nature from the regularities exhibiting the hypothetical laws must, in principle, be considered as falsifications of the law-hypotheses; (notwithstanding the fact that, according to present insights, anticipated by P. Duhem and H. Dingler, it is in many cases extremely difficult to make out whether the observed deviations from the supposed regularities are in fact indications of alternative ruling laws or only indications of disturbing marginal conditions);

(c) so-called 'sign-experience' may constitute the experiential data of natural science only as experience of symptoms or 'indices' (in the sense of C. S. Peirce, i.e. expressing a causal connection of natural phenomena) but in no case as communicative experience of symbols (in the sense of signs expressing intentions being constituted by meaning-conventions).

In contradistinction to this situation, the social sciences are, in principle, to be considered as sciences confronted with a 'subject-object'. That is to say, they must, at least in a first approach, suppose that there are regularities constitutive for the specific character of their objects. These regularities must be considered as rules or norms followed more or less intentionally (although not necessarily in a conscious way) by human subjects of actions. That means also that they might not be followed, or in exceptional cases they might be incorrectly followed.

Methodological consequences of this necessary presupposition concerning the object-constitution may be formulated in the following theses:

(i) The social sciences cannot restrict themselves to imposing hypothetical regularities from outside onto their objects and to testing these hypotheses by communication-free observation. For they cannot, in principle, infer from an observed correspondence between a regularity imposed from outside and observed behaviour, that the regularity is a 'rule', followed by the objects as subjects of actions. The imposed regularity can always, in principle, be made so complicated that it must fit the observed behaviour (not to speak of the heuristical impossibility of discovering rules of social behaviour, such as the so called 'institutional facts', just by observation in the light of nomological theories, i.e. without presupposing communicative understanding).

(ii) Just as little as the social sciences may infer the existence of rules from observed correspondence of imposed regularities and observed behaviour, may they infer, from observed deviations of human behaviour from supposed regularities, that these regularities do not express a valid rule usually followed or even a norm that is valid although it is not often followed.

(iii) Hence it follows that the social sciences must insist on the presupposition that their hypotheses concerning rules of behaviour must rest on an understanding that, in principle, could be proved valid by a participation of the scientist in that rule-game ('language-game' in the wide sense of Witt-

genstein) which he must suppose as context of the hypothetical rules.

(iv) This involves, among other things, that all knowledge
of social science, in contradistinction to knowledge of natural science, is in a twofold way mediated by language, or
even in a twofold way mediated by theories — by the language-game and the theory of scientists and, besides that, by
the language-game, and sometimes even by the theory, in
the light of which human subject-objects understand their
own rule-following behaviour. Hence the decisive achievement of cognition must in this case consist in the methodical
bridging of the two language-games, or even theories, by
communicative understanding. It will be tested, in principle, by communicative participation in supposed language-
games.

As illustrations of the criteria so far expounded of a fundamental difference between natural science and social
science we may mention some examples. The following
examples refer to those cases of explanatory social science
that may be considered as methodologically limiting cases in
the sense of quasi-natural science but none the less must fulfil the methodological requirements thus far expounded for
all social sciences:

(*a*) Mathematical linguistics, in the sense of N. Chomsky's
generative-transformational grammar, may claim to provide a nomological-explanatory theory for human language-
universals and linguistic competence by deriving the restrictions of possible grammars to be generated by man from a
biological law of human nature. Nevertheless, as a social
science, whose experiential data are delivered by human
speech-acts and texts, generative linguistics has also to
understand and to reconstruct in a normatively correct way
those rules of grammatical sentences that competent native
speakers may be able to reconfirm as rules on the basis of
their intuition (notwithstanding the difficulties caused by
possible misunderstandings between the linguists and the

native speakers).[13] N. Chomsky even assumes explicitly that
the linguist must reconstruct precisely that grammar which
previously has been unconsciously constructed by the
competent speaker himself. This would mean that even
explanatory linguistics as a limiting case of social science
proves the methodological thesis that all knowledge of
social science must in a twofold way be mediated by language, or even by theory. What I have said thus far about
Chomsky's linguistic theory seems to hold good also for
other proposed explanatory theories of human competences, say of logico-mathematical, cognitive, communicative and role-taking competences of man.[14] Nomological
explanations, if they should be possible at all on the basis of
supposed biological programmes, must, in all these cases, at
least be combined with normative reconstructions. These,
in turn, have to be proved as correct by communicative
understanding between the social scientist and his 'subject-
object' (which sometimes may be the scientist himself).

(*b*) Another limiting case of social science, that nevertheless
illustrates the criteria expounded so far, is represented by
those behavioural sciences that owe the laws and antecedent
conditions of their quasi-nomological explanations to logical transformations of maxims, aims and beliefs into a so-
called 'volitional-cognitive causal-complex', by which
behaviour seems to be determined. It is also required in this
case, as a matter of principle, that whether or not someone
has correctly understood the presupposed maxims, aims and
beliefs can be tested by communication — e.g. by questions,
interviews, etc. This hermeneutical presupposition cannot
be considered, following C. G. Hempel, purely as a matter
of psychological-heuristic relevance, i.e. as being, in principle, dispensable. For the contrary is shown by every case
where the hermeneutical presupposition of understanding
people's mentality cannot be taken as a matter of course,
e.g. in the case of economic projects in developing coun-
tries.

Nevertheless, the results of quasi-nomological behavioural science — e.g. explanations and predictions of consumers' behaviour under certain situational conditions — look like results of natural science and may indeed be considered as a limiting case of social science. The reason for this fact becomes intelligible in the light of a further general criterion of the difference between social science and natural science:

3.   Pure natural science, i.e. physics, need not deal with the world as history in a proper sense. By this I do not mean that there is no dimension of irreversibility, and hence of a history of nature, to be dealt with by physics. It is true, I think, that physics has to deal with irreversibility in the sense of the second principle of thermodynamics, i.e. in the sense of the increase of entropy. But, in this very sense of irreversibility, physics may suppose nature's being definitely determined concerning its future and thus having no history in a sense that would resist nomological objectification.

Contrary to this, social science — in as far as it is concerned, on principle, with the history of the human society — must presuppose history in a structural sense that resists nomological objectification. For it must not only suppose irreversibility — in the sense of a statistically determined process — but irreversibility, in the sense of the advance of human knowledge influencing the process of history in an irreversible manner. (It is amazing, in my opinion, that Karl Popper, having noticed that the future evolution of science cannot be predicted, in principle, because of the self-determination of this process mediated by reflection,[15] does not draw the further consequence that this reflective self-determination of the historical progress of science be considered as the very paradigm of the relationship between history and socio-historical knowledge in the proper sense — as precluding, in principle, the reproducibility of antecedent conditions in historically relevant social experiments.[16] It seems to me that he shrinks back from this consequence — which indeed leads to a dialectical questioning of the separation of subject and object in socio-historical knowledge — because he wishes to save the basic presupposition of his unified methodology of science according to which no difference, in principle, exists between experiments concerning conditioned predictions in the case of nature and in the case of human history.)

I think that there is in fact a crucial symptom or indicator in favour of the assumption that experiments concerning conditional predictions are not possible with respect to history in that sense in which they are supposed to be possible in physics, viz. as repeatable experiments with respect to isolated systems of causal or statistical connections, i.e. as comparable tests of predictions presupposing, in principle, the reproducibility of initial — or antecedent — *conditions*. The crucial indicator against this possibility in the case of socio-historical knowledge is provided, I think, by Merton's theorem concerning 'self-fulfilling' and 'self-destroying' prophecy. For the point of this theorem seems to lie in systematically precluding or preventing system-isolation — in the very fundamental sense of a separation of the object-system and the subject-system of knowledge — by the understanding and reactive self-application of conditional predictions by the human subject-objects of those predictions.[17]

In this context it also becomes clear why, or in what sense quasi-nomological behaviour science — e.g. explanations and predictions of consumers' behaviour — is to be considered as a limiting case of social science in the sense of quasi-natural science. For the reliability of the results of these sciences in fact depends on the possibility, to be secured under certain conditions, of eliminating, at least for some time, the cognitive realization and reactive self-application of conditional predictions by the human subject-objects of those predictions. Now, such an elimination, establishing and stabilizing a quasi-physicalistic subject-object-relation, corresponds indeed to the leading interest of objectifying and explanatorily accounting for human behaviour as a basis for social engineering or social-technology. Thus, from this point of view (of knowledge-interest), the limiting-case character of quasi-nomological behaviour sciences is made intelligible.

At the same time, however, it also becomes clear that the crucial objection to the possibility of experiments concerning conditional predictions in socio-historical knowledge is not rebutted by the existence and results of those quasi-nomological behavioural sciences. For their very existence as a limiting case is obviously made possible only by a certain denaturization of the characteristic structure of the historical process of human society. This denaturization should not be considered as the paradigm case to be realized by elimination of all effects (in the sense of Merton's theorem), as the so called modern theory of unified sciences seems to suggest. In order to realize that this suggestion is either absurd or dangerous in a moral and political sense, one has to imagine concretely what it would mean to establish and stabilize a subject-object-relation that would be undisturbed, so to speak, by Merton-effects in the case of historically relevant predictions and experiments of sociology.

It would not suffice, in this case, to transitorily withdraw information from those persons made the objects of predictions and experiments. But it would be necessary to have the greater part of human society precluded from relevant communication with the knowing subjects of social knowledge in the long run, say by deprivation of higher education and by similar means of practical suppression. In other words: the society to be objectified in this way as a quasi-isolated system would have to be excluded from the proper process of history represented by the knowing subjects of (social) knowledge who are able to communicate on the proper level of the process of history. But even such a splitting of human society into manipulated and manipulators would not secure the possibility of experiments concerning conditional historical predictions. For, not to speak of the creative abilities of the manipulated objects of changing their behaviour, there has to be a sphere of unreduced reciprocal communication and hence of possible Merton-effects left over among the scientist-technocrats themselves. This at least would be a realm of an unelaminable *subject-object-dialectics* preventing all controlled experiments concerning conditioned socio-historical predictions.

Now this result of our thought-experiment raises the question whether the establishment of a subject-object-relation that would be undisturbed by Merton-effects may be reasonably postulated at all as an epistemological paradigm for social science, as it is in fact to be postulated for natural science. The answer to this question from the point of view of our complementarity-thesis seems to be clear enough, after all that has been said: Quasi-nomological behavioural science resting on experiments concerning conditioned predictions may only be considered as a limiting case of social science in the sense of quasi-natural science brought about by the leading knowledge-interest of having a basis for social technology. But this means that this type of social science is itself still to be categorized and reflectively controlled by another type of social science, whose epistemological paradigm is not a quasi-physicalistic subject-object-relation undisturbed by Merton-effects but rather a kind of scientific mediation of the society's self-reflection as a communication-community in the making. Its cognitive interest would not be that of controlling objectified human behaviour for purposes of social-engineering or steering but rather meta-control and integration of all measurements of social technology and administrative planning into 'dialogical planning' according to the regulative principle of discursive deliberations of a communication-community.[18]

The subject-object-dialectics of a human sphere of unrestricted communication, as far as I can see, may be characterized in Mertonian terms along the lines of two extreme possibilities. In the case of 'undisturbed co-operation' there would be a steady process of self-fulfilling prophecy based on a steady fulfillment of reciprocal expectations of behaviour by the process of human interaction. In the case of 'disturbed co-operation' there would be a transition to a process of self-destroying prophecy, based on constant thwarting and thereby frustrating of expectations. Now in this case there are again two possible ways of coping with the problems. First there is the way into social engineering based on grounding one-sided expectations concerning people's behaviour by the subjects of planning on quasi-nomological explanations and conditional predictions. The subjects of planning in this case must be interested in eliminating Merton-effects by establishing a quasi-physicalistic subject-object-relation with respect to people's behaviour. The other possibility consists in discursive deliberation with the aim of re-establishing the state of reciprocal fulfilling of behavioural expectations on a higher level of co-operation through consensus-formation about aims and means of social praxis. (The difficulties of following this last way exclusively are well known. In fact it contradicts the western market-system of economy as well as all types of bureaucratic socialism. It even seems to contradict people's inclination to strategic forms of interaction and their need for institutional relief from participation in political decision-making. Nevertheless it seems to me that the way of organizing co-operation on the basis of discursive deliberation constitutes the main road of democracy and freedom as it is demanded by the ethics of human communication. Hence it seems to me also to provide the vantage-point and regulative principle for a philosophical understanding and assessment of the different functions of possible types of social science.)

It should be pointed out, in this context, that there are normative-analytical social sciences, e.g. decision-theory and games-theory, that should not only be considered as means of social technology concerning steering-measurements but at the same time also as argumentative aids for dialogical planning, i.e. for finding inter-subjective agreements concerning aims and norms to be answered for by the social community as subject of social technology. Normative-analytical social sciences make up the turning point, so to speak, in a transition from the leading interest of technological disposition of objectified processes on the basis of nomological explanation to communicative understanding about norms and aims of common undertakings of human praxis on the basis of their conditions of possible realization.

It has to be added, however, that *normative analytical* social sciences should not be considered as the only aid for communicative understanding about possible norms and aims of human praxis, as still has to be shown.

D. Criteria of methodological differences between types of social sciences, corresponding to a complementarity of knowledge-interests within the framework of social science in spite of the apparent unity of human nature.

By these latter considerations we have already performed a transition from the point of view of illustrating the criteria of a fundamental difference between social science and natural science in general to the point of view of a differentiation between types of social science in the light of the complementarity of leading knowledge-interests. I shall now try to expound some criteria relating to this possibility.

1. The first criterion was already implicitly put forward by our claim that a certain methodological abstraction from the dialectical structure of human history and socio-historical knowledge is the condition of the possibility for quasi-nomological behaviour sciences. This criterion is supported, I think, by W. Dray's thesis that it is impossible in principle to provide nomological explanations as a basis for predictions for historical events in the full sense of this word.[19]

The point of Dray's thesis may, in this context, be stated as follows: 'Because'-sentences of historical explanation, in contradistinction to 'because'-sentences of the quasi-nomological behavioural sciences cannot be reduced to nomological sentences of the form 'always if . . . then'. The reason for this impossibility is that historians, in contradistinction to behavioural scientists, are not allowed to refer their explanations by 'because'-sentences to quasi-laws and antecedent conditions of a habitual social behaviour within the context of a social system that is itself still to be understood as relative to a certain period or region of history. Instead of presupposing such methodological abstractions, historians must explain historical events in the light of the whole of history to be considered as open to the future in principle. Now, if they would claim nomological explanations of events in the light of all history, i.e. with regard to all possible historical situations and to all possible human reactions to those situations, they would have to face the following dilemma: *Either* they would have to cautiously restrict their nomological premisses to propositions that would be so general and hence trivial that they would not be falsifiable and hence would not present relevant explanatory hypotheses; *or* they would have to provide nomological premisses that would contain definite descriptions and even proper names for all historical subjects (individual and collective) and for all their particular circumstances in life. In this case they would not have achieved a nomological explanation either, but at best they would have postulated the historical necessity, in principle, of the historical events, as in the proposition: 'In all cases where a ruler acts in the same way as Louis XIV did, and does so under the same conditions as the French king, he would necessarily lose his popularity at the end of his life, as Louis XIV in fact did.'

Now in this context W. Dray suggested that historical explanations, as they, in fact, can be provided, are not to be distinguished from so-called 'rational explanations' or good reasons-essays by which the actions of people can be understood and even justified as reasonable with respect to their aims and maxims, given the situational circumstances as they were understood by the actors themselves. This suggestion has been confirmed and enforced in a sense by G.H. von Wright's thesis that so called 'rational' or, as he says, 'teleological' explanation, i.e. understanding actions as rational in the sense of Aristotle's practical syllogism, might be considered as the equivalent, in the case of the social sciences, of nomological causal explanations.[20] Now, I think that the claim of this thesis is ambiguous, and that the whole debate, following this claim, between G.H. von Wright and the defenders of C.G. Hempel's thesis, on whether so called rational or teleological explanation may be logically transformed into causal explanations, can only be settled if the point of view of cognitive interests is brought to bear on it.[21]

For if the cognitive interest is in fact directed to winning explanatory controlling knowledge, as must be presupposed for quasi-nomological behavioural sciences, then it is, in fact, possible and even necessary to transform those reasons for actions we can understand (i.e. aims, maxims and beliefs concerning situational circumstances) into a volitional-cognitive complex that is supposed to work as a quasi-cause in the context of a quasi-causal explanation. The crucial argument for this proHempelian view is provided by the fact that, if we are interested in achieving explanatory knowledge concerning human behaviour that might provide a basis for social technology, then we will not satisfy ourselves with having understood those good reasons that could justify some action as reasonable. We shall insist on ascertaining which intelligible (good or bad) reasons might be considered as causally effective reasons, and that is to say, as quasi-causes in the case of the behaviour to be controlled by explanation and conditional prediction. Even in this case, however, the possibility of quasi-nomological explanation is dependent, I think, on the above-mentioned abstraction from history, as is tacitly pre-supposed in so-called behavioural sciences. For, in the case of Dray's so-called historical (causal) explanations, the logical transformation of the understanding of causally effective reasons into covering-law explanations suggested by Hempel cannot be performed, as Dray and von Wright have shown. The utmost to be reached here along the lines of so called rational or teleological explanation is a Hegelian *ex-post* suggestion of the intelligible necessity of the historical events, i.e. a surragatory explanation, which cannot be transformed into testable predictions, in principle. Hence it follows that history, from the point of view of the leading interest in controlling objectified processes, is both more ambitious and less efficient as explanatory knowledge than behavioural science.

However, in the light of our approach, the interest in controlling objectified processes is not the only and not even the characteristic cognitive interest underlying the social sciences and particularly underlying history. In the case of human actions, especially of historically significant actions, we are indeed also interested in finding out whether the actions in question can be understood and eventually justified as following good reasons. In this respect Dray was right in emphasizing the structural difference between nomological explanation or a good reasons-essay; and G.H. von Wright was right to support this differentiation by his subtle analysis of 'teleological explanations' as understanding on the basis of a practical syllogism. In this case, however, we do not wish primarily to find out the 'effective' reasons but rather the 'good reasons', i.e. the intelligible and justifiable reasons for action. Hence we are not primarily interested in nomological explanation at all but rather in a normative-hermeneutic reconstruction of human actions along the lines of an internal reconstruction of history as an enterprise of man to be justified by man. I therefore suggest, in the light of the complementarity-thesis, that we do not speak of explanation at all in these cases but rather of understanding good reasons or purposive-rational understanding, as M. Weber suggested, or of internal reconstruction of history as it was proposed by I. Lakatos in the context of the paradigmatical debate around the relation between history of science, in the sense of T. Kuhn, and normative philosophy of science.[22]

2. Now, by our confrontation of quasi-nomological social sciences with normative-hermeneutic or reconstructive social sciences, we have already touched upon a further criterion for distinguishing not only between social science and natural science but, moreover, between different types of social science. The new criterion to be introduced is familiar, since the days of M. Weber, as that of the necessity for value judgements, denied by Weber. To deal with this question from the point of view of our approach, I first have to introduce a distinction which was not, as far as I can see, sufficiently reflected upon in the classical discussion. The distinction to be introduced refers to the difference *between* (a) evaluating actions or institutions in the light of those rules or norms that are constitutive for the actions or institutions as describable facts of the socio-historical world, and (b) evaluating the very rules or norms by which the actions or institutions are constituted. The first kind of evaluation is indeed always presupposed in order to understand and to describe the facts of the socio-historical world. To that extent it constitutes a further criterion of the general difference between all social sciences, on the one hand, and natural science on the other. The second kind of evaluation, on the contrary, has been heavily contested since the days of M. Weber, since it, in fact, presupposes a principle of normative Ethics not to be derived from empirical facts.[23]

In the light of our approach — i.e. of the thesis of complementarity between the interest in accounting for factual regularities as a basis for technological praxis, and the interest in communicative understanding as a basis for praxis, in the sense of coming to intersubjective agreements about goals and norms — the difference between the two kinds of evaluation recommends itself as a basis for a differentiation between types of social science. For it seems intelligible that abstaining from evaluation of rules of action or institutions as acceptable norms is called for, and to that extent legitimized, in all cases where our interest in controlling, even in a very sublimated form, is the necessary condition for the possibility of the very constitution of the object of possible knowledge. This concerns not only the case of quasi-nomological social sciences that make up the basis for social technology but also certain important aspects of historical inquiry. It even concerns those methodical abstractions from the question of truth-claims and rightness-claims of texts that accompanied the constitution of philological hermeneutics in the nineteenth century, i.e. since the days of Schleiermacher and August Boeckh. But let us have a closer look at the internal connection between the abstention from value judgements and the leading knowledge-interest in these different paradigms of social science.

In the case of the quasi-nomological behavioural sciences it is fairly clear that abstention from evaluating rules as norms is required because the 'rules' here are interesting not as possible confirmations or alternatives to those rules we have to accept ourselves as obligatory norms for our life but only as supposed regularities or quasi-laws of a behaviour to be accounted for by quasi-nomological explanations. Hence abstention from value-judgements is in this case a normative condition of the possibility of the object-constitution, precisely as in the case of the explanatory natural sciences. By this statement, especially by using the phrase 'normative conditions of the object-constitution', we have, however, pointed to the fact that both cases of a value-free cognition — i.e. that of explanatory natural sciences and that of social sciences restricting their value-judgements to understanding actions as correct or incorrect rule-following behaviour — are not value-free in the sense of being just pure knowledge without an underlying 'interest' that *a priori* constitutes the 'meaning-value' or the 'life-significance' of the possible results of knowledge with respect to the future of human life-praxis. For even abstention from value-judgements is a normative condition of the possibility of nomological natural science and of quasi-nomological social science precisely for the reason that we have an interest, that may be normatively grounded itself, in the value of nomological and quasi-nomological knowledge as a basis of technological ordering of the environmental world in the widest sense.

This also gives a first hint of how to understand certain features of value-free cognition even in the case of history and of philology (although in these cases the interest in ordering does not have the last word). Thus it need not be denied that, for example in history, we have a certain interest in ordering a connection of events into a process to be objectified in the framework of the chronological time that is also the framework of objectifying natural history. In so far as this is the case, historians are obliged and entitled to reduce their questions as to the 'meaning' of historical events to the question as to the 'effects' of these events within a certain objectified time-space of history to be demonstrated by value-free judgements.[24] In a similar way, abstaining from evaluating the validity-claims of texts in the case of *hermeneutic philology* may be understood as a requirement of objectifying and presenting the very meaning to be understood before any attempt at forming a judgement on the validity-claims of the texts. It should be conceded that, in this sense, an interest in ordering and objectifying is inherent in all human striving for knowledge, not excluding our present attempt to present types of social science.

This concession to objectivism of course, does not yet show the place of history and philology in the light of a possible differentiation of types of social science. Rather, the point of this differentiation is dependent on the presupposition that the leading interest of controlling objectified processes is only constitutive for a limiting case of social science. Indeed, history and hermeneutic philology, although they necessarily comprise abstractive procedures of value-free objectifications, cannot, in contradistinction to the quasi-nomological behavioural sciences, be understood as being essentially constituted by the leading interest of controlling objectified data. Corresponding to this difference is the fact that abstractive procedures of value-free objectifications in history or (even) in hermeneutic philology have another function or place-value within the framework of their disciplines, as value-free descriptions and explanations have in the framework of behavioural science.

Thus I would defend the thesis that value-free objectifications of meanings (or meaning-intentions), in the case of the hermeneutic philologies, do not primarily or finally have the function of, say, progressively collecting and ordering those very different objectified meanings in an 'imaginary museum', so to speak. They have, rather, the function of providing a methodological mediation for a normatively 'applicative' understanding[25] which puts itself at the service of inter-subjective understanding in the broader sense of coming to an agreement or consensus *about validity-claims*. This is equally true both in the context of contemporary interactions between men or social groups on a planetary level and in the context of coming to terms with our cultural traditions in the sense of a critical re-examination whose results are themselves to be integrated into the attempts of communicative agreements between contemporaries.

An important argument against the possibility of isolating the methodical function of objectifying meaning-intentions by abstraction from validity-claims lies, I think, in the fact that in many cases the progress of understanding the meaning itself is not so much dependent on philological abstraction but on the competence of the interpreters to form a judgement concerning a possible justification of the validity-claims of difficult texts. Classical examples supporting this thesis are provided e.g. by the history of science, from the days of Tartaglia's reconstruction of Archimedes' teachings on hydrostatics, which the humanist philologians could not understand, up to the present discussions about an internal reconstruction of the history of science that would have to critically understand the historical documents, under the regulative principle of separating the justifiable modes of thought from those that cannot be justified but are eventually to be 'explained' by external motives.

Regarding the historical objectifications of events within the framework of chronological time and corresponding reduction of the meaning of historical events to its effects, I would defend the thesis that these methodical procedures again do not have the function of replacing and sparing a 'valuative understanding' of the (individual) meaning-value or significance of historical events, but rather have the function of questioning our prescientific prejudices concerning their significance by providing a scientific mediation for better-grounded evaluations of the significance of historical events. For so much seems evident: If the individual meaning or rather significance of a so-called object of historical inquiry such as a person or a work of art or an institution or an epoch is to be understood and elucidated by history, which is hardly to be denied, then the historian can no longer abstract from also evaluating the goal-directed intentions of actions and of whole policies, and from evaluating also the validity-claims or legitimation-claims of whole institutions or even socio-cultural forms of life. Such an evaluative understanding of individual significance in the widest sense cannot reduce the horizon of its criteria to that part of history which can be methodically objectified thus far as a connection of causes and effects within the framework of chronological time. It has, rather, to assess the meaning and significance of the single phenomenon from the perspective of history as a whole, including the open horizon of the future, still to be realized by human praxis. At the same time it has to reorganize and to slightly correct our project of the total horizon of history by understanding the individual meaning and significance of the particular phenomenon under study.

This consideration, of course, implies the thesis that the so-called 'hermeneutic circle' defines not only the methodological procedure of pure meaning-exploration but involves also a corresponding procedure of reciprocal presuppositions and corrections of evaluative prejudices. This view in fact contains a crucial argument against the conception of a methodological and even epistemological separation between a so-called prescientific evaluating perspective, lying at the ground of all selections of relevant historical topics and even data, and, on the other hand, a value-free procedure of scientific historical inquiry. The argument against this conception, implied in the structure of the hermeneutical circle, rests on the fact that evaluative pre-understandings of meanings cannot be separated from the historical-hermeneutic process of improving and deepening this very understanding of meanings, as external motivations of nomological explanations, by evaluative assessments of their significance, can, in fact, be separated from the methodical procedure of explanatory science. In contradistinction to this paradigm of modern logic of science, the paradigmatic claim of the hermeneutic circle may be explicated by the postulate of a continuous pervasion of all methodical stages of the reciprocal correction of understanding the whole of history, and interpretative understanding of individual meanings, by the prescientific value-perspective that makes this whole hermeneutical process possible, in order to purge itself by this very process.

It has to be noted, however, that, in my opinion, the purifying effect of the hermeneutic circle with respect to our value-judgements — the deepening of humanity through understanding humanity, as it has been called — is dependent on the possibility that the prescientific value-perspective enclosed in our preconception of history can be made explicit and justified, in principle, by an ethical foundation of the humanities. In this case the deepening of humanity by understanding humanity must not only be based on hypothetical justifying actions, habits, and institutions, or, correspondingly, on learning from the great texts of our cultural traditions, but also on criticizing all traditions in the light of those norms whose content we must try to display to our imagination through hermeneutic understanding of human history. If an intersubjectively-valid, ethical foundation of the value-judgements of the humanities should be impossible, then the effect of the 'hermeneutic circle', i.e. the moral issue of understanding all cultures and traditions of present-day humanity, might, rather, amount to paralysing all moral responsibility, as the development of relativistic historism in the nineteenth and twentieth century has shown. It is, I think, from this relativistic historism and the corresponding attitude of defeatism with regard to a possible foundation of ethics that the most important motive for defending value-free cultural sciences has sprung. Abstention from value-judgement is considered as the only way of securing intersubjective validity in the field of the humanities. This would indeed be true if a rational foundation of intersubjectively-valid, ethical norms were impossible.[27]

From the point of view of our approach (to the normative conditions of the possibility of different types of social science), however, it is by no means sufficient to discuss the problem of value-judgements only by answering the questions as to their avoidability or unavoidability. More important is the question whether there should be — or ought to be — evaluative social science. We have already suggested a possible answer to this question in the light of the complementarity-thesis, insofar as we have postulated a critical-reflective control of the results of the quasi-nomological behavioural science and their technological applications by other types of social science. This reflective control should have a compensatory function, so to speak, with respect to the danger of technocratic manipulation or at least of a decrease of majority brought about by the inevitable tendency of quasi-nomological behavioural science and social technology towards an establishment and stabilization of a quasi-physicalist subject-object-relation not to be disturbed by Merton-effects. Whereas these social sciences are in fact supplementing the power of man over nature, provided by natural science, by increasing the potential power of men over men, the complementary and compensatory function of hermeneutical social sciences constituted by the leading interest in communicative understanding should be directed towards the shaping and continuous reshaping of an educated, critical and competent public opinion.

E. Criteria of methodological differences between types of social science in the light of the critical-emancipatory knowledge-interest

At this point, however, where we are looking for a compensation of social-technological power of manipulation by another type of social science, we must reflect upon the fact that the complementarity-thesis rests on an idealization which is necessary, but not sufficient, for an understanding of the whole scope of possible cognitive interests underlying different types of social science. The idealization involved in the complementarity-thesis has its paradigm in the esoteric community of scientific investigators and, moreover, in the esoteric community of argumentative discourse, where the communication-partners must consider each other as pure subjects of thought and speech and hence as limiting cases of the objectifiable world, so to speak. They are thereby anticipating an ideal situation where only two complementary cognitive interests would be justified, viz. the interest in controlling (by explanation and prediction) an objectified environmental world and the interest in communicative understanding between the co-subjects of argumentative discourse. Now, this idealization disregards or embezzles, so to speak, the fact that human beings interacting in social relations are in no case those pure co-subjects of understanding presupposed in the esoteric situation of argumentative discourse.

What I have in mind now is not, as we have already noticed, simply the fact that the human subjects of thought and speech can also be made the objects of quasi-nomological behavioural science. This fact by no means contradicts the ideal complementarity-situation, since, in any case of an objectification of human behaviour there has to be pre-supposed a community of co-subjects of science that corre-sponds to the anticipated ideal of a pure communication-community. This very anticipation, however, is, at the same time, a necessary presupposition of arguing and a counterfac-tual presupposition that contradicts at least the present state of human self-understanding and hence of communicative competence. For even as subjects of understanding we are not (or not yet) transparent to ourselves, and our speech is not the pure expression of our intentions by public symbols as intersubjective vehicles of unambiguous meanings. Rather, we are, as subjects of understanding, more or less alienated from ourselves, and from our self-understanding, and our speech is ambiguous insofar as it always expresses both connotations that cannot be unambiguously expressed by individual speakers, because there self-understanding in terms of public language underlies idiosyncratic restric-tions, and connotations that cannot be expressed by public language at all.

By these two dimensions of speech-ambiguity due to speech-restriction I tried to suggest two dimensions of human self-alienation (due to splitting off unconscious moti-vations and hence ex-communicated meanings): one con-cerning the individual person and his or her communicative competence, and one concerning the society as a communi-cation community that functions as the subject of the public conventions of language-games and hence of a public world — and self-understanding of men. Although these two dimensions of self-alienation are to be considered as interconnected, their overtly pathological aspects have been first noted separately in two quite different, and initially rather antagonistic new disciplines of human science, viz. Freudian psychoanalysis on the one hand and Marxist critique of ideology on the other hand. In the pres-ent context I want to suggest that these two disciplines should be understood under the common label of critical-reconstructive social science and that their methodological approach may be explicated by tracing it down to a common leading interest in knowledge, i.e. to the interest in critical-emancipatory self-reflection. I want to show that, corresponding to this peculiar leading knowledge-interest there is a peculiar methodological figure of thought underlying both psychoanalysis and critique of ideology as it is part of a critical socio-historical reconstruction of the state of society.

Now, in the context of our present approach it is no matter of course that a peculiar knowledge-interest and methodological figure of thought has to be postulated to account for so called· 'critical-reconstructive' social sciences. Rather the necessity of this postulate has to be shown by confronting the approach of critical-reconstructive social science with that of quasi-physicalistic behavioural science and hermeneutical science of communicative understanding.

(For reasons of space I cannot elaborate here on the special problematics of quasi-biologistic functionalistic systems-theory, although I am convinced that it makes up an irreducible methodological approach to social science that must not be neglected in our age of the ecological crisis, but has to be accorded its appropriate place in relation to the other types of social science, from the point of view of its underlying knowledge-interest.[27])

I can be rather brief, I think, in defending the thesis that critical reconstructive social science cannot be reduced to quasi-physicalist behavioural science, or, more loosely and generally, to so-called empirico-analytic social science, in the sense of the unified logic or methodology of science. The propagators and absolutizers of that type of social science have often shrewdly remarked that neither psychoanalysis nor critique (in the sense of Marx) fits in with the methodological standards of an experimentalistic, nomological-explanatory science. One example of such a standard is the requirement that consequences be yielded in the form of conditional predictions to be tested by repeatable experiments based on observations by exchangeable observers, etc. (Thus Karl Popper, at the beginning of his career in Vienna, came to distinguish Marxism and Freudian psychoanalysis as pseudoscience from Einsteinian physics as a paradigm of science, giving rise to possible falsifications by yielding risky testable consequences.[28] Very similar criticism was directed against Marxism and psychoanalysis along the lines of a Carnap-Hempel-Nagel-logic of unified science.[29]) It almost goes without saying that I cannot see much sense in defending both types of critical-reconstructive social science against reproaches that rest on a systematic disregard of the rise of the leading questions of different sciences from different leading knowledge-interests. The usual issue of the scientistic defences of Marxism and psychoanalysis at best represents a bad approximation to the prestige-paradigm of (quasi-natural) science at the cost of the characteristic features of a critical reconstructive project of inquiry, springing from an interest in emancipatory self-reflection.

Thus it seems intelligible from what we have said about the impossibility, in principle, of testing by repeatable experiments nomological explanations in history (i.e. history of the human species and life-history of single persons) that neither the Marxist conception of historical necessity nor the Freudian quasi-causal explanations of neurotic symptoms within the context of a life-history should be conceived of as applications of universal laws and special marginal conditions to explaining and predicting certain classes of observable phenomena to be tested by exchangeable observers in repeatable experiments. The crucial significance of explicative interpretations of ambiguous symbols in psychoanalysis, as well as in the critique of ideology (from the critique of religious myths to that of the myths of everyday life in late capitalism and state-socialism), may suggest, from the outset, that critical-reconstructive social science is concerned with improving or re-establishing communicative understanding rather than with nomological explanation. It is clear, even from a Carnapian point of view, that all kinds of explication of the meaning of symbols are different, in principle, from explanation according to laws, since an unambiguous system of symbols is already presupposed for nomological explanation.

At this point, it seems as if critical-reconstructive-social science were to be understood along with the hermeneutic sciences, and from the point of view of the leading interest in communicative understanding, being complementary to the interest in explanatory and predictive control of objectified processes. This point of view has indeed inspired some important philosophical reinterpretations of Freudian psychoanalysis, especially within the framework of hermeneutic phenomenology. Humanistic reconstructions of Marxism or NeoMarxism in western Europe have also been more or less influenced by hermeneutical points of view. It is hard to contest that hermeneutical procedures, similar to text-interpretation, play a crucial role in the context of psychoanalysis. More precisely: since psychoanalysts try not only to interpret the ambiguous meanings of everyday language and of religious and poetical texts, but, moreover, so-called dream-texts, and even neurotic symptoms, as a paralanguage of bodily expressions, it may seem that they differ from normal hermeneuticians (interpreters) only by going even further than the realm of traditional text-interpretation, widening, so to speak, the program of hermeneutics into that of 'Depth hermeneutics' (*'Tiefenhermeneutik'*).

It might seem plausible, at this stage of our discussion, to redefine the whole business of hermeneutics by supposing that not just communicative understanding of symbols but rather interpreting of ambiguous symbols is the task of hermeneutics, whereas unambiguous symbols of artificial formalized languages of logics and mathematics and even symbols of everyday language, rendered unambiguous by the pragmatical context of understanding, do not pose problems for hermeneutics. The latter distinction was indeed introduced by W. Dilthey,[30] who emphasized that methodical-hermeneutical understanding can only constitute itself where the meanings of delivered texts, works or institutions have become unintelligible; and the redefinition of hermeneutics in terms of interpretation of ambiguous symbols was proposed by P. Ricoeur.[31] Hence it seems plausible that psychoanalysis might be considered as the very paradigm of *hermeneutics*.

However, for reasons still to be explicated, I cannot follow this suggestion, that would involve a merely bipolarized or complementaristic architectonics of epistemology. I do not wish to renounce the distinction made by Dilthey between purely logical and pragmatical understanding, on the one side, and methodical-hermeneutical on the other.[32] But I do not think that the ambiguity of symbols as it is presupposed in psychoanalysis should be considered as the paradigm for hermeneutics in general. The reason for questioning this latter suggestion is provided by the fact that the ambiguity of symbols in psychoanalysis is not only a topic of *hermeneutic interpretation* but at the same time also the object of quasi-causal and quasi-functional explanation in terms of a quasi-nomological theory of energetic processes.[33] Such processes are excluded from hermeneutic understanding by the fact that split-off motives for compulsive behaviour are, so to speak, renounced.

Here there appears to be a methodological analogy between psychoanalysis and neo-Marxist critical reconstruction of social history, insofar as the latter must also presuppose causally determined, reified processes of a human pseudo-nature, in order to supplement historical hermeneutics and to mediate, so to speak, a deeper understanding of human history, through a quasi-naturalistic explanation of the causally determined reified processes. In both cases the critical analyst must go behind the whole sphere of communicative understanding; that is to say, he must not only try to render dark and ambiguous texts intelligible by meaning interpolations of a philological kind; but he must rather change his attitude to the human utterances insofar as he interpolates meanings that are not supposed to be accessible to the (intentional self-understanding of the) subjects of the interpreted utterances. In doing so the analyst at least partially 'suspends' the relation of communicative understanding between himself and his subject-object and replaces it by the subject-object-relation of quasi-naturalistic explanation.

This attitude, which is characteristic and indispensible for the critical-reconstructive social sciences, is excluded, so it seems to me, by the idea of pure hermeneutics and is indeed abhorred by the typical hermeneutician for good reasons. Hermeneuticians must stick to the heuristic idea that human utterances and texts, works of art, religion, philosophy and science, are sources of a possible disclosure of valid truth and hence subjects of learning to the interpreter. The systematic tension between this attitude and that of the critical social sciences becomes immediately clear if one reflects on the fact that psychoanalysts and critics of ideology must also presuppose a communicative understanding among themselves. In this context an interpretation of texts, such as those by Freud and Marx of their own critical tradition, is different, in principle, from that understanding of ambiguous symbols which is mediated by a quasi-naturalistic phase of causal explanation, and nevertheless may be mediated and improved by hermeneutical methods in the usual sense. By this reflection the methodological point of the complementarity-thesis is re-established by the back-door of critical social science.

At this point in our deliberations, one might think that the methodical structure of the critical social sciences must, after all, be very similar to that of the quasi-nomological behavioural sciences, in view of the fact that in both cases the relation of communicative interaction and understanding is partially suspended in favour of a quasi-naturalistic objectification and explanation. However, within the framework of the approach we have developed so far, this conjectured analogy proves to be hasty and superficial. For it does not take into account the very different constellations of the leading knowledge-interest and hence of the methodological figures of thought in both cases.

In the case of quasi-nomological behavioural science the leading interest is directed to control over objectified and predictable processes as the final result of the whole procedure of inquiry. Corresponding to this interest, the proper aim of knowledge is quasi-nomological explanation as a basis for social-technology, whereas communicative understanding of reasons for human actions is only a heuristic means, although an indispensable one, for reaching explanatory hypotheses. Thus the methodological figure of thought is characterized by a dialectical mediation of explanatory knowledge through communicative understanding.

The contrary is true in the case of a critical-reconstructive social sciences, as in psychoanalysis and critique of ideology. In this case, the leading knowledge-interest is not directed to control of objectified processes, but to deepening of self-understanding by critical-emancipatory self-reflection. Hence the proper aim of the methodical procedure is not to achieve quasi-nomological knowledge of human behaviour. But quasi-causal explanation is, on its side, only a heuristic means of deepening human self-understanding. Hence the methodological figure of thought corresponding to the leading knowledge-interest of critical social science is characterized by a dialectical mediation of human self-understanding, and thus also of communicative understanding, through quasi-naturalistic causal-explanation.

In order to show that this outcome of our analysis is not only a lofty play of construction but actually opens an epistemological and methodological dimension that is inaccessible, in principle, to a pure logic of science, one should reflect upon the different role played by self-reflection of the human subject-objects of science in both cases. In the case of quasi-nomological behavioural science relevant self-reflection of the subject-objects in the sense of self-application of conditioned predictions can only disturb, in the sense of Merton's paradox, the subject-object relation presupposed by controllable experiments. Therefore it has to be eliminated as far as possible for methodological reasons, as we have pointed out already. On the other hand, in the case of critical social science, particularly in the paradigmatical case of psychoanalysis, self-reflection on the side of the human subject-objects of knowledge is intentionally provoked for methodological reasons, because it is the very vehicle of the dialectical mediation of deepening self-understanding through quasi-causal explanation of split-off reified compulsive processes.

In this case *reflective self-application* of the explanatory theory to the effect of changing the behaviour of the human subject-objects of inquiry is not only no obstacle but, on the contrary, is intended as the very therapeutic aim of the analysis, which is, at the same time, a test of the truth-claim of the analysis. For, when the therapy is entirely successful the very causes of compulsive behaviour which were supposed by quasi-causal explanation, are eliminated, with the aid of the reflective-self-application of that explanation by its subject-object. This effect is not considered as a self-destroying prophecy of a conditional prediction but rather as a self-applicative verification of the truth-claim of the analysis.

Facing this remarkable inversion of the methodological device of behavioural science by psychoanalysis, and imagining that this methodological figure of thought might, in principle, also hold good in the case of a possible sociological critique of ideology connected with a critique of social institutions, one might come to the conclusion that critical social science is the very counterpart of quasi-nomological behavioural science, — a counterpart that might also fulfil a compensatory function with respect to the danger of a technocracy based on manipulative conditioning of behaviour.

Notes

[1]   See J. Habermas, *Erkenntnis und Interesse*, Frankfurt a.M.: Suhrkamp

1968; eng. transl., *Knowledge and Human Interests*, Boston: Beacon 1971. See also K.-O. Apel, 'Szientistik, Hermeneutik, Ideologiekritik', in *Wiener Jahrbuch f.Philos. 1* (1968), 15-45 (shortened version in *Man and World, 1* (1968), 37-63); repr. in Apel *et alii, Hermeneutik und Ideologiekritik*, Frankfurt a.M.: Suhrkamp 1971, also in Apel (1973); cf. further K.-O. Apel, 'Communication and the Foundation of the Humanities', in *Acta Sociologica 15* (1972), No. 1, 7-26; expand. version in *Man and World, 5* (1972), 3-37. - Cf. to this topic J. Habermas' 'Nachwort' in the second edition of *Erkenntnis und Interesse*, Frankfurt a.M. 1973, and *Materialien zu Habermas' 'Erkenntnis und Interesse'*, (ed.) W. Dallmayr, Frankfurt a.M.: Suhrkamp 1974.

2   Besides the above-mentioned (in note 1) works, cf. the following programmatic essays: K.-O. Apel, 'Programmatische Bemerkungen zur Idee einer "transzendentalen Sprachpragmatik"', in *Studia Philosophica in Honorem Sven Krohn*, (ed.) T. Airaksinen *et alii*, Turku: Annales Universitatis 1973, 11-36 (also in *Semantics and Communication*, ed. by C.H. Heidrich, Amsterdam/London: North-Holland Publ. Co. 1974, 81-108); K.-O. Apel, 'Zur Idee einer transzendentalen Sprachpragmatik' in *Aspekte und Probleme der Sprachphilosophie*, (ed.) J. Simon, Freiburg i.Br.: Alber 1974, 283-326; K.-O. Apel, 'Sprechakttheorie und transzendentale Sprachpragmatik sur Frage ethischer Normen' in *Sprachpragmatik und Philosophie*, (ed.) K.-O. Apel, Frankfurt a.M.: Suhrkamp 1976; K.-O. Apel, *Transcendental Semiotics and the Paradigms of First Philosophy*, in Philosophic Exchange, 2/4 (1978), 3-24.

3   Cf. K.-O. Apel, *Transformation der Philosophie*, two volumes, Frankfurt a.M.: Suhrkamp 1973, especially the essays in vol.2 (Engl. trans. forthcoming, Routledge and Kegan Paul).

4   This thesis is supported, it seems to me, by the aporetic result of the lengthy discussion about the adequacy of the Hempel-Oppenheim model of causal explanation. For it turned out that neither the deductive nor the inductive version of the model is capable, in principle, of yielding criteria to distinguish between genuine nomological and causal explanations, providing relevant real grounds, and mere rational groundings, e.g. inferences from predictively relevant or even irrelevant symptoms or from pseudo-laws. Cf. on this topic M. Scriven 'Explanation and Prediction in Evolutionary Theory', in *Science 130* (1959), 477-82; W. Stegmuller, *Wissenschaftliche Erklarung und Begrundung. Probleme und Resultate der Wissenschaftstheorie und Analytischen Philosophie*, Vol. 1, Berlin: Springer 1969, 761 ff.; W.C. Salmon, 'Statistical Explanation' in *Statistical Explanation and Statistical Relevance*, ed. by W.C. Salmon, Pittsburgh 1970, 29-87. — From the viewpoint of a Kantian epistemology that makes a sharp distinction between causes and reasons one may hold *a priori* that a logico-semen-

tical explication that abstracts from all subjective categorial conditions of the possibility of experience cannot account for causal explanation as an achievement of synthetic cognition concerning objective connections of events in a space-time world of experience. Our approach goes beyond Kant insofar as it postulates different leading knowledge-interests as transcendental pragmatic background of the categories as view-points for posing questions. cf. K.-O. Apel, *Die 'Erkläven: Verstehen' — Kontroverse in Transcendental-pragmatischer Sicht*, Frankfurt a.M.: Surkamp, 1979.

5   Cf. M. Heidegger, 'Die Zeit des Weltbildes', in M. Heidegger, *Holzwege*, Frankfurt a.M.: Klostermann 1950, 69-104.

6   See K.-O. Apel, 'Szientistik, Hermeneutik, Ideologiekritik', *loc. cit.*, and 'Communication and the Foundation of the Humanities', *loc. cit.*

7   See C.G. Hempel, 'The Function of General Laws in History', in *The Journal of Philos. 39* (1942) and C.G. Hemple/P. Oppenheim, 'Studies in the Logic of Explanation', in C.G. Hempel, *Aspects of Scientific Explanation*, New York: The free Press (1965).

8   See Th. Abel, 'The Operation called "*Verstehen*"', in *Readings in the Philosophy of Science,* (ed.) H. Feigl and M. Brodbeck, New York 1953.

9   Cf. J. Habermas, 'Wahrheitstheorien', in *Wirklichkeit und Reflexion*, Festschrift für W. Schulz, Pfullingen: Neske 1973; Cf. J. Habermas, 'Vorbereitende Bemerkungen zu einer Theorie der Kommunikativen Kompetenz', in J. Habermas/N. Luhmann, *Theorie der Gesellschaft oder Sozialtechnologie*, Frankfurt a.M.: Suhrkamp 1971.

10 Cf. H.-G. Gadamer, *Wahrheit und Methode*, Tübingen 1960, p. 162 ff.

11 It is, of course, possible to understand hermeneutics (i.e. '*hermeneutike techne*' or '*ars interpretandi*', as it was called in the Greek and Latin tradition) as a kind of technology (of understanding) thus presupposing a technical knowledge-interest. But from this it does not follow that hermeneutic understanding, the improvement of which is the purpose of hermeneutics as a technology, must itself presuppose a technological knowledge-interest. This confusion, it seems to me, underlies the chief argument of H. Albert against the methodological autonomy-claim of hermeneutics with respect to its subject. Cf. H. Albert, 'Hermeneutik und Realwissenschaft', in H. Albert, *Pladoyer für kritischen Rationalismus*, München 1971, 106-149, and H. Albert, 'Transzendentale Träumereien', Hamburg: Hoffmann u. Campe 1975, pp. 46 ff.

12 This is true with regard to classical physics in the sense of objectifying an independent realm of events as determined by strict causal laws; it is true also with regard to microphysics, I think, in the sense of objectifying the behaviour of ensembles of particles as determined by statistical laws.

13 Cf. K.-O. Apel, 'Noam Chomsky's Sprachtheorie und die Philoso-

phie der Gegenwart', in *Jahrbuch des Instituts für Deutsche Sprache*, Mannheim 1972, also in Apel, *Transformation der Philosophie, loc. cit.*, vol. 2, 264-310.

14   Cf. the extrapolation of Chomsky's approach into the idea of a special type of competence-reconstructive sciences in J. Habermas' recent papers (see under note 8) and especially in his 'Was heisst Universalpragmatik?' in *Sprachpragmatik und Philosophie, loc. cit.* (see note 2).

15   Cf. e.g. K.R. Popper, *The Poverty of Historicism*, sec. ed., London: Routledge & Kegan Paul, 1960, preface.

16   Arguing against the 'antinaturalistic' version of 'historicism', Popper seems to have forgotten his strongest argument against 'pronaturalistic historicism'; for he suggests that the situation concerning the variability of experimental conditions in the case of piece-meal social experiments is not different, *in principle*, from that in natural science, such that the variability of antecedent conditions might, *in principle*, be deducible from universal laws, although one can never be sure — neither in natural science nor in social science — that a supposed regularity is in fact a universal law (cf. K.R. Popper, *loc. cit.*, III; 25 and 26). Contrary to this, the problem seems to me to consist in the question whether it is possible *a priori* to expect that the alterations of historical situations (and hence of experimental conditions) by way of the very process of the growth of knowledge can be derived from universal laws and boundary conditions without thereby postulating the absurd possibility of a science predicting its own growth of knowledge.

17   It has to be noticed in this context that Robert K. Merton in his famous discussion of 'self-fulfilling prophecy' in his book *Social Theory and Social Structure* (rev. ed. New York: The Free Press of Glencoe 1957, 421-36) is far away from being aware of the fundamental epistemological implications of his topic. He seems to consider it as a special prescientific 'object-phenomenon' of social science which does not raise fundamental methological questions but, rather, may be eliminated, even as a social phenomenon, through enlightenment on the basis of social science. I think indeed that the phenomenon of self-fulfilling or self-destroying prophecy cannot be thoroughly recognized as an epistemological problem from the vantage point of an 'analytic' philosophy of science that does not reflect upon the subject-object-relation of scientific cognition but rather takes it as a matter of course that in social science too the object can be kept separated from the subject of cognition.

18   Cf. P. Lorenzen/O. Schwemmer, *Konstruktive Logik, Ethik und Wissenschaftstheorie*, Mannheim: B.I.-Wissenschaftsverlag 1973, and O. Hoffe, *Strategien der Humanität. Zur Ethik öffentlicher Entscheidungspro-*

zesse, Freiburg/München: Alber 1975.

19   Cf. W. Dray, *Laws and Explanation in History*, Oxford: University Press, 1957.

20   Cf. G.H. von Wright, *Explanation and Understanding*, Ithaca, N.Y.: Cornell University Press 1971.

21   Cf. to the following K.-O. Apel, 'Causal Explanation, Motivational Explanation and Hermeneutic Understanding. Remarks of the recent stage of the Explanation-Understanding Controversy', in *Contemporary Aspects of Philosophy*, (ed.) G. Ryle, Stocksfield: Oriel, 1976, and my book announced in note 4.

22   Cf. especially I. Lakatos, 'History of Science and its Rational Reconstructions', in *Boston Studies in the Philosophy of Science*, VIII (1971), 91-136.

23   Cf. my critical examination of J. R. Searle's meta-critique of the critique of the 'naturalistic fallacy' in K.-O. Apel 'Sprechakttheorie und Begrundung ethischer Normen' in *Konstruktionen versus Positionen*, Festschrift fur P. Lorenzen, (ed.) K. Lorenz, Berlin: W. de Gryter 1979, vol. II, 37-106.

24   Cf. to this perspective e.g. K.-G. Faber, *Theorie der Geschiechtswissenschaft*, Munchen: Beck, 1971, pp. 165 ff.

25   Cf. H.-G. Gadamer, *Wahrheit und Methode, loc. cit.*, pp. 290 ff.

26   For an attempt to cope with the problem of an ethical foundation of the humanities cf. my essay 'Das Apriori der Kommunikation-gemeinschaft und die Grundlagen der Ethik', in K.-O. Apel, *Transformation der Philosophie, loc. cit.*, vol. 2, pp.358-436, and K.-O. Apel, 'Sprechakttheorie und transzendentale Sprachpragmatik zur Frage der ethischen Normen', in *Sprachpragmatik und Philosophie, loc. cit.* (see note 2).

27   The leading cognitive interest underlying quasi-biological system-analysis as a type of social science seems to me to be different from that underlying quasi-physicalistic behavioural science in that it does not simply aim at controlling causal processes, say by conditioning behavioural responses, in the service of means-ends planning (i.e. social engineering) but rather aims at understanding the means-ends rationality of human planning itself as integral part of the functional organization of a social system that has to ensure its survival by maintaining its identity in relation to its environment. The most important consequence of the quasi-biological viewpoint of system-analysis seems to consist in a new attitude towards nature as environment of the human social system as a whole. Instead of considering the relationship between nature and man merely in the light of the relation between controllable linear causal processes and isolated means-end-rationality of intentional actions we have to learn to consider social systems, e.g. agricultural, industrial, and settlement-sys-

tems, as parts of natural (ecological) systems whose objective-teleological structures must not be disturbed by the subjective teleology of human goal-directed activities. In this context the ecological crisis forces us, for the first time in human history, to take into account the problem of survival of the unitary human social system on a planetary scale.

This last fact yields the best vantage-point, I think, for considering the relationship between quasi-biological system-analysis as a type of social science and the specific humanistic types of social science, whose approach is guided by the hermeneutic and the critical-emancipatory knowledge-interest. On the one hand, it amounts to a new version of the naturalistic fallacy if the point of view of sociological systems-theory is expanded as far as to comprise functionalistic accounts of a possible legitimation of human validity-claims (such as *meaning*-claims, *truth*-claims, and *rightness*-claims of scientific or philosophical arguments); the reason for the shortcomings of such an absolutization of the functionalistic point of view obviously lies in the fact that humans, being capable of the subjective teleology of purposive actions, may call into question, on principle, all kinds of objective system-teleology, even that of the human ecological survival-systems, and must, at least formally, transcend all functionalistic dependence on concrete system-teleology by the universal validity-claims of their thoughts (e.g. the truth-claims of their insights into functionalistic system-structures). Thus communicative understanding between men, at least on the level of discourse, cannot be reduced to an object of functional analysis within system-theory, and the normative standards of critical-emancipatory self-reflection, and hence of reconstructive legitimation of social institutions, cannot be reduced to standards of functionalistic adaptions to the requirements of a survival-system. Hence also the concrete historical evolution of human institutions that underly the claim of legitimation cannot be 'explained' as 'nothing but' adaption to functionalistic requirements of system-formation. Nevertheless, on the other hand, it can be shown that, as survival of some kind of social system is a necessary precondition of human emancipation, i.e. of realization of the ideal communication-community within the real human society, so functionalistic adaption to certain requirements of a system-structure, e.g. 'reduction of complexity' (N. Luhmann), is a necessary precondition of effectiveness even on the level of scientific and philosophical cognition and discourse.

From this it seems to follow that a special methodological figure of dialectical mediation between quasi-biological system-theory (or its underlying knowledge-interest) and hermeneutic and critical reconstructive social science (or their underlying knowledge-interests) has to be postulated, in order to cope with the problem of social history as a continuation of biological evolution on a new level. And one might even conjecture, on a quasi-hegelian line of heuristics, that the postulate of dialectical mediation between systems-theoretical requirements and demands of emancipation with regard to understanding a historical situation of human society marks the regulative principle for an optimal realization of both underlying interests of knowledge with regard to that very praxis.

This, in a very rough sketch, seems to me to be the upshot of the controversy between J. Habermas and N. Luhmann (cf. their discussion-volume *Theorie der Gesellschaft oder Sozialtechnologie — Was leistet die Systemforschung?*, Frankfurt a.M.: Suhrkamp 1971); it is suggested also by the succeeding works of Habermas, as e.g. his *Legitimation Crisis*, Boston: Beacon Press 1975, and *Zur Rekonstruktion des Historischen Materialismus*, Frankfurt a.M.: Sahrkamp 1976.

28 Cf. K. R. Popper, *Conjectures and Refutations*, London: Routledge and Kegan Paul 1963, pp.34-35; and Autobiography of Karl Popper, in P.A. Schilpp (ed.), *The Philosophy of Karl Popper*, La Salle (Ill.); The Library of Living Philosophers, Inc. 1974, Vol. I, p.32.

29 Cf. e.g. Ernest Nagel, 'Methodological issues in psychoanalytical theory', in *Psychoanalysis, Scientific Method and Philosophy*, (ed.) Sidney Hook, New York 1959, pp.36-56, and M. Scriven, 'The experimental investigation of psychoanalysis', *ibid.*, pp.226-251.

30 See W. Dilthey, *Der Aufbau der Geschichtlichen Welt in den Geisteswissenschaften*, in *Gesammelte Schriften*, VII, pp.210 ff.

31 See P. Ricoeur, *De l'interpretation. Essai sur Freud*, Paris: Editions de Seuils, 1965.

32 Cf. W. Dilthey, *loc. cit.*

33 Also P. Ricoeur (*loc. cit.*) emphasizes the 'energetic' aspect of psychoanalysis and conceives of it as an argument against the surrender of psychoanalysis to the exclusive competence of a phenomenological type of hermeneutics, postulating instead a 'dialectical' approach to Freud. Thus the difference between his approach and my sketchy one seems to be only a difference of epistemological architectonics, which, in my case, is based on the conception of three leading knowledge-interests. -Cf. on this point of view also J. Habermas' account of psychoanalysis in *Erkenntnis und Interesse, loc. cit.*, III, 10 and 11.

2. Apel's 'Transcendental Pragmatics'
by Peter Winch

PROFESSOR Apel has written a paper which is both elaborate in structure and densely packed with material. It would be impossible for me to discuss all the important and complex issues which he raises and I shall not attempt to do so. I shall begin by setting out, in my own words, what I take to be the main lines of his argument. Then I shall make some comments on points in the argument which strike me as both crucial and also either obscure or doubtful.

1 Apel's argument

Apel's conception of 'cognitive interests' on which many points in the argument turn, does not belong to an attempted sociology or psychology of inquiry. It has to be understood, rather, as part of an account of 'concept formation' in an epistemological sense. The account is fundamentally anti-empiricist. Human discourse is not to be conceived as a speaking and asking of questions about subject matters the understanding of which is just derived or abstracted from observation and experience; it is expressive of fundamental interests or concerns. These concerns themselves play an essential role in shaping the concepts which enter into a man's understanding of the subject matter to which he is addressing himself. For example, if I am confronted with something which I take to be a sort of mechanical device and enquire into how it works, I must make a distinction between its correct operation and various ways in which it can go wrong. (I 'must' do this in the sense that, if I do not, I am no longer understanding it as a mechanical device.) But this notion of a 'correct' operation presupposes a background of human activities in the context of which the

51

machine may be used; and those activities in their turn are what they are by virtue of the human interests and concerns which they express. If, for instance, the object in question is a clock, it has a part to play in human time-keeping activities and those activities themselves can be understood only in the light of the kind of importance which time-keeping has in human life. Unless I come to the object prepared to ask the kind of question which springs from the human interest in time keeping, I shall not be able to conceive it as a clock and shall not be in a position to investigate 'how it works'.

Following Habermas, Apel distinguishes three fundamental categories of 'cognitive interest':

(i) the interest in manipulation and control of the environment;

(ii) the interest in communication with other human beings;

(iii) the interest in freeing oneself from constraints in the way of understanding oneself and communicating with others.

The distinction between (i) and (ii) is used to differentiate the conceptual structures and methodologies of, on the one hand, natural science (which deals with natural laws) and social science (which deals with normative rules) and, on the other hand, different kinds of social science — those which focus directly on normative rules and those which are 'quasi-naturalistic' ('quasi', because their naturalistically-studied regularities presuppose an underlying rule-governed structure). These distinctions destroy the conception of the 'unity of science' advocated by positivist and Popperian philosophies of science. But Apel hopes to introduce a new conception of the unity of science based on interest (iii), which is to be expressed in a 'critical-emancipatory' social science standing in a dialectical relationship to the naturalistic establishment of laws and the hermeneutic elucidation of normative rules.

An essential feature of this conception is what Apel calls 'complementarity'. His discussion of this notion has some striking parallels with the argument with which Socrates confronts the Sophists in Plato's *Gorgias*. Socrates argues that the use of language cannot be explicated solely in terms of the Sophists' naturalistic conceptions of 'success' and 'failure' in an attempted manipulation of one's hearers' reactions, since the kind of manipulation which is in question rests on 'understanding of what the speaker says'. We need, therefore, a distinction between understanding and misunderstanding (or failing to understand), a distinction which cannot be expressed in naturalistic terms. The notion of understanding requires on the one hand a reference to the subject matter which is being spoken of and on the other hand reference to a communicative relation between speaker and hearer which has an irreducibly normative structure. In similar fashion Apel argues that the pursuit of natural science presupposes a communicative relationship between scientific investigators; and the communicative relationship between natural scientists presupposes reference to a natural order which provides the subject matter of their communication. But communication involving mutual understanding cannot be taken as a matter of course; it will frequently require the use of special techniques developed by specialised study — hermeneutical study. Further, more purely theoretical study of what human communication consists in cannot itself be purely naturalistic. It is not denied that naturalistically conceived regularities may be revealed by the study of communicative behaviour, but the significance of these regularities as having to do with 'communicative' behaviour will always require reference to rules and standards which have a normative, and not merely a naturalistic, character.

Notions like truth and validity play an important part in the normative structure of communicative relationships. If I hear somebody say something, or read what somebody has written, it can be asked whether I 'understand' what he says (writes) and also whether I find it 'acceptable': for instance, whether I accept what he asserts as true, what he argues as valid, the standards to which he appeals as legitimate or appropriate. Furthermore, the intelligibility to me of what somebody says is not completely independent of my finding it, in this broad sense, acceptable; even though, of course, it is perfectly possible over a wide area to understand someone without agreeing with him. On the one hand, to understand what somebody says is to recognize it as presenting me with the question whether I find it acceptable or not. And on the other hand to the extent to which I find absolutely nothing which I can accept as true, valid or appropriate in somebody's words, it is not clear that I should have understood those words as expressing an intelligible communication at all. Such considerations tempt Apel into a stronger conception of the unity of the sciences than what is involved in the 'complementarity thesis' as I have so far expounded it: 'as lying in their universal truth claims to be reconfirmed by a universal intersubjective consensus to be reached by discursive arguments'. He thus firmly dissociates himself from the relativistic tendencies which are often characteristic of 'hermeneutical' ways of thinking and takes up a position in what he calls a 'transcendental pragmatics', which claims to find a rebuttal of relativism in certain universal 'conditions of the possibility of human knowledge'. Amongst those conditions Apel gives prominence to the idea of a universal consensus about the truth of claims which enter into intersubjective discussion. Exactly what status we are to give this idea seems to me highly problematic; since this lies at the heart of the difficulties I have with Apel's position, I shall postpone discussion of it until I come to say what these difficulties are.

The obstacles which stand in the way of full intersubjective understanding cannot all be dealt with by 'hermeneutical' methods. Such methods are fully adequate only in what is really an ideal-typical situation, where we are dealing with 'an esoteric community of scientific investigators' in which 'the communication-partners must consider each other as pure subjects of thought and speech'. This is a situation in which each participant can fully grasp his own thought and express it in language fully accessible to all the other participants. But the real world of 'human beings interacting in social relations' is not like that. In this world we are 'more or less alienated to ourselves', in that factors outside our immediate voluntary control restrict and destroy our ability to articulate our thought clearly. These factors may be either psychological or sociological in nature. We can free ourselves from them only through becoming clear about what has occasioned them and this requires investigation of a quasi-causal, not merely hermeneutical, kind. Apel (following Habermas) sees psycho-analysis and Marxist 'critique of ideology' as prototypes of such investigation. They use investigation of causes in the service of emancipating men from obstacles to mutual, and self-understanding. They thus correspond to the third of the 'cognitive interests' with which Apel starts, an interest which turns out to be related to the other two roughly in the way a Hegelian 'synthesis' is related to 'thesis' and 'antithesis'. It is in terms of this relationship that we are to understand the 'unity of the sciences'.

2 Some difficulties

Most of what Apel writes in this paper about 'complementarity' seems to me right as well as important. I shall say no more about the many things with which I agree, but focus attention on features of his position about which I have misgivings.

Apel notes, and deliberately exploits, the ambiguity in the German word *'Verständigung'* as covering the idea both of 'understanding the meaning' of what someone has said and also 'coming to agreement' with him. Of course, 'coming to agree' in its turn encompasses a variety of different cases, but here I am concerned, in the first instance, with coming to agree with someone that what he says is *true*. Apel refers, in this connection, to the arguments by which Wittgenstein tries to show that there is an important internal connection between understanding someone's meaning and being in agreement with his judgements. The *locus classicus* is Wittgenstein's *Philosophical Investigations*, I.§§241/242:

> 'So you are saying that human agreement decides what is true and what is false?' ... It is what human beings *say* that is true and false; and they agree in the *language* they use. That is not agreement in opinions but in form of life.
>
> If language is to be a means of communication there must be agreement not only in definitions but also (queer as this may sound) in judgements. This seems to abolish logic but does not do so. ... It is one thing to describe methods of measurement, and another to obtain and state results of measurement. But what we call 'measuring' is partly determined by a certain constancy in results of measurement.

It's important to see that Apel's position is significantly different from Wittgenstein's on this question. Wittgenstein stresses a distinction between 'agreement in judgements' and 'agreement in opinions'. Agreement in 'judgements' is important, on his view, because it enters into what he calls 'agreement in form of life'. His treatment of this question is highly complex and in this context I cannot discuss it in the detail it deserves. What matters for our purposes is the contention that any disagreement in 'opinions' rests on a shared application of procedures the results of which are accepted as counting for or against the truth of such opinions; and that this is possible only insofar as those who apply such procedures by and large agree on the results obtained thereby. Wittgenstein does not make the further claim, at least not in the general form in which Apel seems to be making it, that the possibility of communication rests on the idea of an eventual agreement in all 'opinions'. In making this much larger claim Apel is following not Wittgenstein, but C.S. Peirce, who writes for instance in 'How to Make Our Ideas Clear':

> The opinion which is fated to be ultimately agreed to by all who investigate is what we mean by the truth, and the object represented in this opinion is the real. That is the way I would explain reality.

The movement of Apel's thought seems to be something like this. Serious discussion between people must have the aim of distinguishing truth from falsity. But the idea of truth cannot be separated from that of a general consensus, a general acceptance, after due investigation, of a given opinion. Therefore, serious communication must aim at, and presuppose the possibility of, such a consensus.

My dissatisfaction with this thesis relates to two prominent features of Apel's argument: his triadic classification of 'cognitive interests' and his 'transcendental' way of thinking.

I should want first to emphasize the enormous diversity, which is masked by Apel's triad, of interests which underly human attempts to understand themselves, each other and the world they live in. There are, let us agree, certain kinds of discussion for which the Peirce/Apel thesis looks plausible: discussions in which the participants do share the aim of reaching agreement in opinions and do suppose that this aim is achievable. I might even be willing to go further with Apel along his road and agree that in such contexts such a 'presupposition' is importantly connected with what we understand the opinions in question to mean and with the way we conceive their truth. I dare say, for instance, that this holds for discussions about what exactly is wrong with a motor car that will not start. I should hesitate to say, without considerable qualification, that it holds generally within the context of natural scientific investigation. One does not have to accept all Thomas Kuhn's claims to be impressed by the thought that the consensus of scientists is a fragile affair and that there is little reason to expect it to become less so in any future development of science. And if we look in other directions, towards philosophical or ethical discussions for instance, any thought of a possible universal consensus begins to look very unrealistic indeed.

Professor Apel would no doubt retort that this line of criticism is misconceived. He would argue, I think, that he is not concerned with how realistic the expectation of a possible universal consensus may or may not be in practice, since the presupposition he is speaking of is a transcendental presupposition. How should we understand this?

We might try saying as a first step that what is in question is the realizability 'in principle' rather than in practice of a universal consensus. It is something which is aimed at in any co-operative enquiry and, in order to be aimed at, it must be conceived as possible. This still leaves some difficulties unresolved. First, we must ask what is meant in this connection by 'possible in principle'. Second, there is some obscurity regarding to whom (or perhaps to what) the aim of a universal consensus is to be attributed. And third, we must try to understand the grounds for such an attribution.

Where should we look for the principle according to which the possibility of a universal consensus is to be conceived? There seem to be two alternatives. We might, in the first place, focus our attention on particular kinds of co-operative enquiry, taking each singly and asking what role, if any, the idea of an eventual universal consensus plays within it. Or we might, in the second place, attend rather to what is involved in co-operative enquiry and its concomitant discussion as such, whatever may be its particular subject matter, and ask in a general way whether the idea of an eventual universal consensus is essential to it.

I think it is reasonably clear that Apel takes the second of these directions and I will discuss what he has to say about it presently. But I should like to pause for a moment and consider some of the implications of the first alternative. Notice first that Apel's own general epistemological approach exploits the idea that there is an internal connection between the subject matter of an investigation or discussion and the form (expressive of certain 'interests') of a discussion appropriate to such a subject matter; and also that the direction of this connection is not that the subject matter simply determines the form of the investigation, but that the form of the discussion is at least an important factor in 'constituting' the subject matter. I think this is right. But Apel is prevented from following it up by the poverty of his conception of the human interests which may be expressed in a discussion.

Let us consider two contrasting examples. For the first one I will return to my previous case of a discussion concerning what is wrong with a car that will not start. Suppose that two mechanics discuss various possible defects. They may be undecided as to which of these is responsible for the failure, but they will certainly take it for granted that some determinable defect *is* responsible and they will expect to be able to discover it. If it should elude them they will investigate more closely and in almost all cases they will eventually find something. In the unlikely event of their being able to find nothing at all, they will still assume that something is indeed responsible and that it is discoverable. If one of them were to deny this, the other would have difficulty in understanding what he was talking about. This last is the crucial point. It is a feature of what we should be prepared to call understanding what is at issue in a case like this, that it should be taken for granted that there is a determinate answer which an investigation could uncover and that anyone competent to make such an investigation would agree on what its results showed to be wrong with the car.

Contrast that with the following case. People sometimes discuss the proper role of love and friendship in human affairs and express widely different and apparently irreconcileable opinions on the subject, which they support by arguments. There is, for instance, a very interesting essay by George Orwell on this subject in which he discusses, and vigorously rejects, Gandhi's idea that 'for the seeker after goodness there must be no close friendships and no exclusive loves whatever'.[1] Orwell understands and accepts Gandhi's contention that 'through loyalty to a friend one can be led into wrong-doing' for example. But, in opposition to Gandhi, he maintains that: 'The essence of being human is that one should not seek perfection, that one *is* sometimes willing to commit sins for the sake of loyalty, that one does not push asceticism to the point where it makes friendly intercourse impossible, and that one is prepared in the end to be defeated and broken up by life, which is the inevitable price of fastening one's love upon other human individuals'.

I think it would hardly do justice to the nature of Orwell's disagreement with Gandhi to say that he regards Gandhi's view as 'mistaken' (if this is understood in anything like the sense of Apel's 'universal truth claims').

It is not as if he attaches no importance to the moral dangers that Gandhi sees as springing from close personal attachments. What he does is to point out corresponding dangers in Gandhi's position: the danger, for instance, of emotional aridity and isolation from one's fellows. What he says is not that Gandhi is mistaken but that Gandhi's 'other-worldly' and his own 'humanistic' ethics are incompatible.[2] Faced with this opposition, and conscious of the difficulties and problems inherent in either of these attitudes to life, he expresses his own attachment to the humanistic ideal.

Some people, either because of the pressure of circumstances or because of some inner drive, find themselves called on to make a definite choice between such opposing ideals. Gandhi seems to have been an example. Others are more ambivalent. Perhaps they find themselves involved in potentially dangerous personal attachments — and one needs to be extremely ruthless to avoid this entirely — but they also sometimes steer clear of them, because of the moral risks involved. If they are very lucky, they do not get into serious trouble. If they are less lucky they may find themselves faced with a choice. Such a choice may be made with greater or less clarity concerning its implications and a possible criticism of a man in such a situation is that he has taken insufficient pains to achieve clarity. People who do clarify their thoughts on such issues to the greatest extent that is humanly possible may still choose differently. And a man who chooses in one way need not think that anyone who in such a situation made a different choice would be mistaken. I mean that his choice does not logically commit him to such a judgement.[3] If he makes such a judgement he may be open to the charge of moral dogmatism; if he refrains from making it he may be open to the charge of undue 'permissiveness'. How far anyone thinks that such charges are justified will have to depend on his own judgement of the particular circumstances; and again, not everybody will reach the same conclusion.

I feel like saying that such a background of sometimes irresolvable diversity of outlook and judgement makes an essential contribution to our understanding of what such judgements *are*. That is to say, the nature of the discussions which give rise to these judgements presupposes precisely the reverse of Apel's 'universal truth claims to be reconfirmed by a universal intersubjective consensus'.

I am pretty sure that the position I have been sketching would attract Apel's charge of 'paralysing all moral responsibility', as a case of 'relativistic historism and the corresponding attitude of defeatism with regard to a possible foundation of ethics'. However, the word 'defeatism' is question-begging, implying as it does that one has half-heartedly given up the search for an intelligible and desirable goal. But what Apel seems to be after strikes me as not desirable and indeed not even intelligible. As I have tried to suggest, the very nature of the issues which are at stake in the sort of discussion I have described presupposes a diversity of opinion which is at odds with a 'foundation' of the sort Apel argues for. Perhaps we could imagine a possible human society in which things were different: where there were no such irreconcilable conflicts. But such a society would be one which just did not contain the possibility of issues of the sort which confront us. For myself, I would not regard such a society as desirable; on the contrary I should think it a great impoverishment of the potentialities of human life. Perhaps — I do not know — there would be less distress in such a society, but that does not have to be regarded as decisive. As Wittgenstein remarked:

> The human gaze has a power of making things precious; it makes them cost more too though.[4]

Is all this 'paralysing [to] all moral responsibility'? The boot is surely on the other foot. 'Moral responsibility' goes along with such notions as 'moral blindness', 'moral courage' and 'moral cowardice'. Serious moral choices involve risks: and not just risks to one's material well-being, but moral risks. The ways of thinking which lie behind such choices all bring their own characteristic difficulties with them. One form of moral blindness is to make such choices without investigating the peculiar risks to which one is thereby exposing oneself. Another is to be so impressed with the risks characteristic of one way of thinking that one does not see those characteristic of its alternative(s). This second form of blindness is fostered, it seems to me, by the conception of an eventual universal consensus on such issues. One exercises responsibility when one clearsightedly faces the risks. Eliminate the risks and you eliminate moral responsibility.

As I remarked earlier Apel does not, in arguing the point at issue, attend to any differences involved in the discussion of various kinds of subject matter which fall below the level of his triadic classification of 'cognitive interests'. He relies rather on what he takes to be essential features of serious intellectual discussion as such. Indeed he seems to think that these features transcend his triadic classification. That is to say, he takes *any* serious 'communicative' or 'emancipatory' interests, to presuppose 'universal truth claims to be reconfirmed by a universal intersubjective consensus'. This is an indispensible point in the construction of his edifice of a unified science. In arguing thus he has not taken seriously enough, I believe, the kind of consideration developed by Wittgenstein, in *Philosophical Investigations*, against the possibility of characterizing 'the essence of language': considerations which would take me too far afield to review here.

The direction of Apel's thought is something like this. A discussion is intellectually serious only if it is directed towards promoting the participants' understanding of the issues in dispute. For this to be possible the participants must recognize and submit themselves to common standards of argument. Otherwise there will be no genuine meeting of minds, no common understanding of what is at issue; and this is as much as to say that nothing will *be* commonly at issue. What we shall have will be a sophistical contest. But, he seems to go on, something which is genuinely a common standard of argument, when it is applied to determinate data, leads to determinate logical consequences (or at least fails to do so in a logically determinate way). But this must mean that there are in the offing certain conclusions which will have to be accepted as true by any group of people who honestly apply *these* standards of argument to *these* data.

Steps somewhat similar to those I have tried to reconstruct in my last paragraph are, I believe, essential to Apel's argument. They perhaps have a certain plausibility when stated in such an abstract general way. They are nevertheless illegitimate as a general characterization of everything we are entitled to call a serious intellectual discussion.

This can only be shown by attention to the details of various forms of discussion which are characteristic for different kinds of issue. The particular ways in which these diverge from Apel's model may be expected to vary from case to case. I must content myself here with referring again to my previous example of a familiar kind of discussion about the ethical significance of love and friendship in human life. The important question is this. Can there be no meaningful serious discussion between, say, a Gandhi and an Orwell which does not presuppose and is not directed towards an eventual agreement between them on the issues?

Well, in the first place, we cannot of course rule out *a priori* a shared desire to reach agreement, nor the possibility that such an agreement will in fact be reached, however remote that possibility may look in the case of the actual Gandhi and the actual Orwell. But though this is something we can gladly concede, it is not enough for Apel. For what if Gandhi and Apel recognize that any prospect of eventual agreement between them is no more than a pipedream. And what if, as intelligent, realistic men, they therefore do not enter the discussion with the aim of reaching agreement. Does this mean that, to this extent, there can be no meaningful discussion between them from which they may both learn? It looks *prima facie* as though Apel must make this inference.

But here we come against another difficulty in interpreting Apel's position, to which I alluded earlier. To whom, or to what, I asked, is the aim of a universal consensus to be attributed in his view? In the last paragraph I have raised questions about the implications of attributing various aims and beliefs to the participants in a discussion. Such attributions would, it seems, have to be settled empirically: it is surely a matter of fact whether or not a Gandhi or an Orwell enters a discussion with certain aims and beliefs. But Apel almost certainly wants to reject such empirical questions as irrelevant: the aims and beliefs that are at issue for him are a 'transcendental' presupposition. The grounds for attributing them are not empirical facts about the participants' psychologies, but are rather to be derived *a priori* from the very conception of a serious discussion.

To what then are we to attribute these aims and beliefs? Here we are faced with an uncomfortable dilemma. On the one hand it looks a bit high-handed and doctrinaire to ascribe them to the participants on *a priori* grounds in the face of all the empirical evidence. Perhaps then we should ascribe them not to the participants in the discussion, but to the discussion itself. But the difficulty with this alternative is that it is not clear what it means. What is it for a discussion to have aims and beliefs, especially if these are not thought of as in any way shared by the participants in it?

Perhaps we are to look at the matter in the following way: We *can* speak of the 'aim' of a discussion in cases where we have not established this by asking the participants what *their* aims are, but where we have rather read it off, as it were, from our understanding of the course the discussion has taken. It may well be that the participants themselves have not thought explicitly about their aims or formulated them to themselves. It may be that they would not be able to say, when asked, what their aims are, even after reflection. Nevertheless, the manner in which they engage in the discussion may still provide overwhelming grounds for saying they have certain aims. This evidence may even, in some cases, be so strong as to override any disclaimers they may make. We may feel that their way of participating in the discussion makes no sense unless they are assumed to have those aims; that their disclaimers can only be indicative of confusion on their part.

I think that considerations like these lead us much closer to the position Apel wants to maintain. But it is important to see that they do not yet lead us right into it. For they are still based on observation of the demeanour of the actual behaviour of participants in actual discussions. In a word, they would not be 'transcendental' considerations. Apel's argument does not rely on such evidence as this but, as we have seen, on alleged features of discussion 'as such'. So it would run something like this: It is a necessary condition of an activity's being properly called a serious intellectual inquiry, or discussion, that those who participate in it should believe that an eventual universal consensus on the truth or falsity of the propositions at issue in the inquiry, is at least conceiveable, and that they should be aiming at achieving it. Thus, to the extent that they lay claim to intellectual seriousness, they necessarily commit themselves to this belief and this aim. They may not be fully aware of this commitment, but it is possible to show them that it is implied by their claim to intellectual seriousness.

The most questionable feature of the argument seems to me clearly its initial premise. What reason does Apel have for his claim that serious intellectual discussion implies such a commitment to an eventual universal consensus? I think he would want to say that, without this, the participants are not genuinely putting forward their views for criticism by others but are, as it were, disingenuously withholding something in their private domain, as immune from criticism. But I do not believe that a claim like this can be settled by any abstract reflection on what we mean by expressions like 'discussion', 'inquiry', 'intellectual seriousness'. We have rather to look at how we do *apply* these expressions in particular cases. It is, after all, through learning to apply them in particular cases that we have mastered their meaning. And it is perfectly possible — indeed, it is to be expected — that their application will be controlled by rather different considerations in different kinds of case.

Reflections on cases like the dispute between a Gandhi and an Orwell can help to break the hold of Apel's picture. A discussion of such issues can show someone that the position he holds is subject to difficulties that he had not previously suspected. But it may also strengthen his conviction that the alternatives to his position are subject to at least equal difficulties. He may come to realize that there just is no position on such matters which does not have its own difficulties. Such a realization represents an advance in understanding. And I can see no good grounds for saying that an increase in understanding of this sort presupposes any belief that there must be some position on the matters under discussion which is free of difficulties of a kind which will make its adoption a risk. At the same time there may (or may not) be compelling reasons why he should nevertheless adopt *some* position. Indeed, to speak only apparently paradoxically, refraining from adopting a position may itself be a form of adopting a position: and one which, in its turn, carries its own risks with it. A discussion which leads to such an understanding of the situation may of course bring some of the participants to alter the positions which they originally brought to it. But there is no good reason to suppose that it either will, or ought to, lead them all to adopt the *same* position. For one thing, the general risks which attach to a given position may be more or less threatening to an individual man in his own particular circumstances. So we have to allow for the exercise of individual judgement and, as soon as we do so, the prospect of any universal consensus evaporates very quickly.

I turn now to another closely related part of Apel's argument. What his 'critical emancipatory' social science is to emancipate us from are constraints on free intellectual communication. He develops a model of such free intellectual communication in terms of what he calls 'the esoteric community of scientific investigators and ... the esoteric community of argumentative discourse, where the communication-partners must consider each other as pure subjects of thought and speech and hence as limit-instances of the objectifiable world, so to speak'. His procedure then is to ask in what respects the actual social world deviates from this model and what is required to make it approximate to the model more exactly.

In what sense are we to understand this community of argumentative discourse as 'esoteric'? I think Apel in fact wants to make two quite distinct contrasts here. (1) On the one hand there is a contrast between a 'transcendental' conception of such a community and the *actual* world in which scientists, philosophers and other enquirers carry on their work: a world in which enquirers are subject to ambition, fear, vanity and impressionability to the diverse character-traits of their fellow-inquirers. (ii) On the other hand there is a contrast between the actual world of intellectual inquiry and the wider social world to which this belongs, a world of multifarious interests other than those in inquiry.

Let me say something first about contrast (1). I am not altogether clear what it would be to regard someone else, a professional colleague, say, as a 'pure object of thought and speech', but I am quite sure that this is not how I do in fact regard those with whom I enter into philosophical discussion. I do not for a moment imagine, moreover, that I am in any way idiosyncratic in this respect. Those with whom we converse and dispute are human beings with their distinctive traits of character, histories, positions in society, personal entanglements, etc. It is true of course that most of these distinctive personal characteristics will not play a role in what we say to each other when we discuss a philosophical problem; what we shall each be interested in is what the other has to say relevant to that problem, and naturally what is of paramount importance here is the other's comprehension of and ability to express himself concerning the subject we are discussing, his honesty in argument and so on.

I say that these things will be of paramount importance. But this does not mean that they can be separated off from his other human characteristics. The point I want to make here is in many ways analogous to some remarks Wittgenstein made about the corporeality (and the distinctive corporeal characteristics) of measuring instruments. Comparing this case with the spatio-temporal character of linguistic utterances he writes:

> In this case too, you cannot say: 'A rule does measure in spite of its corporeality; of course a ruler which only has length would be the Ideal, you might say the *pure* ruler. No, if a body has *length*, there can be no length without a body — and although I realise that in a certain sense only the ruler's length measures, what I put in my pocket still remains the ruler, the body, and isn't the length.[5]

Just as what I put in my pocket, and what I lay against the object to be measured, is the body and not the length, so he with whom I converse is a man and not a pure subject of speech and thought. Furthermore, although all that is essential to a ruler 'as such' is that it should have length, its particular physical peculiarities are not irrelevant to its serviceability for measuring. For instance, sometimes a flexible instrument will be what is needed, sometimes one that is rigid; and so on. Something analogous holds concerning the conditions for profitable discussion of an issue by human beings. To speak autobiographically by way of example: I find myself, in my professional life, surrounded by many people of high intelligence, intellectual seriousness and honesty, and philosophical competence, with whom I nevertheless know that I shall never have a genuinely profitable philosophical discussion. This has to do, in ways which are often by no means clear, with the sort of people we are, our backgrounds, histories and personalities, and also with quite contingent features of the way we have come to know each other, the context in which we are placed, and so on. How important such factors are will vary from one case to another; and I expect that *different* factors will tend to be important in the context of different types of intellectual inquiry. I should for instance not expect the same kinds of factor to be characteristically prominent in intellectual relations between physicists as I would in the case of philosophers. But I do not believe that such factors can be completely abstracted from in considering the conditions under which profitable discussion can be carried on. It is only because they do vary so much from one context to another that we are subject to the illusion that they are really inessential to 'communication as such'. The fact of the matter is that there is *no such thing* as 'communication as such'. There is only communication between particular people in particular circumstances. And, as I have suggested, the distinction between profitable and unprofitable communication depends on wide varieties of different features of the particular cases.

It's very important to remember here — obvious as it may be — that it is only through learning to communicate — about different kinds of thing and with different kinds of people — that anyone comes to understand what communication *is*. And 'learning what communication is' cannot be separated from learning to distinguish between more or less successful communication: a distinction which takes many different forms and is subejct to many different conditions which are learnt in trying to communicate in a variety of contexts. We cannot arrive at an understanding of what they are *a priori*, by derivation, as it were, from a 'pure concept of communication', any more than we can arrive at an understanding of what type of ruler is going to be best fitted for measuring — in all cases — from a pure concept of measurement.

I have been looking at the relation between Apel's 'transcendentally' conceived 'community of investigators' and what goes on in actual communities of investigators. I want now, finally, to consider briefly what Apel thinks to be the relation between an esoteric community of investigators and the non-esoteric world of 'human beings interacting in social relations', a world in which investigating, in the sense in which this is something carried on by specialized professionals, is not the only or even the primary concern. I am genuinely puzzled about what Apel's thoughts are on this. What he actually writes, in his concluding section, suggests that the distinction between the esoteric and the exoteric communities consists in the fact that the latter, unlike the former, does not correspond to 'the anticipated ideal of a pure communication community'. This is because our speech and our understanding within this wider social world is subject to a variety of constraints which 'alienate' us from each other and from ourselves.

It is difficult to believe that Apel really intends what this suggests, although it seems to me that his conception of the 'emancipatory' role of critical social science does largely depend on the suggestion. I mean the suggestion that human communication at large is directed towards the same kinds of end and is to be judged by the same standards as professional communication between scientists and philosophers, differing from this only in respect of the fact that sociological and psychological constraints prevent it from achieving those ends with the same degree of success. But this is surely grotesque. Inquiry and discussion does of course have a place in social life outside 'scientific' contexts. But it is a relatively restricted place and, more importantly, it is not at all the same kind of thing as is scientific inquiry and discussion. Parents and children, husbands and wives, may discuss difficulties which affect their relationship and inquire into what has gone wrong. But the form taken by discussion and inquiry cannot be understood apart from the difficulties and problems peculiar to the relationship; and these are 'difficulties' and 'problems' in a sense which could hardly be elucidated simply by extrapolation from what is understood by these terms in scientific contexts. The relation between the 'communication' which takes place in such discussions and professional 'communication' between scientists is not that the former is of the same kind as the latter but takes place under the pressure of 'alienating' restrictions (which is not of course to deny that there may sometimes be such alienating restrictions.)

Furthermore, not all 'idiosyncratic restrictions' on communication can properly be understood as 'alienating'. This has to do with the irreducibly personal, individual character of many human relationships.[6] To see this, contrast the following two cases:

(a) The governing body of a university passes a resolution about the allocation of finances between different activities of the institution. This resolution is binding on the university's officers. It remains binding no matter who the officers may happen to be and throughout changes in personnel on the governing body. Its force depends on the public, institutional position of the persons involved.

(b) A man regards himself as under an obligation to respect the wishes expressed by his friend on a certain personal matter. The relation of 'friendship' is not of course

peculiar to these two men. But the force of the
obligation which is felt to exist will not characteristically depend solely, or even mainly, on an
abstractly conceived relation of friendship. It will
depend on the peculiarities of *this* relationship
between these two particular people.

What is more, it is characteristic of many close personal
relationships that there are many things which are *not*
expressed between the parties. — Think of Bulstrode's
silent 'confession' to his wife in George Eliot's *Middlemarch*
(Ch. 74).[7]

It was eight o'clock in the morning before the door
opened and his wife entered. He dared not look up at
her. He sat with his eyes bent down, and as she went
towards him she thought he looked smaller — he
seemed so withered and shrunken. A movement of new
compassion and old tenderness went through her like a
great wave, and putting one hand on his which rested
on the arm of the chair, and the other on his shoulder,
she said, solemnly but kindly —
'Look up, Nicholas'.
He raised his eyes with a little start and looked at her
half amazed for a moment: her pale face, her changed,
mourning dress, the trembling about her mouth, all
said, 'I know;' and her hands and eyes rested gently on
him. He burst out crying and they cried together, she
sitting at his side. They could not yet speak to each
other of the shame which she was bearing with him, or
of the acts which had brought it down on them. His confession was silent. Open-minded as she was, she
nevertheless shrunk from the words which would have
expressed their mutual consciousness, as she would
have shrunk from flakes of fire. She could not say 'How
much is only slander and false suspicion?' and he did not
say, 'I am innocent.'

It would be a great mistake, I think, to suppose that we

have here a suitable case for emancipation. There are relationships — and perhaps this is one — the depth and vitality of which is manifested precisely in the fact that there are things the parties do not and cannot say to each other. 'Cannot' in the sense that to do so would be a violation of the relationship. This certainly need not mean that there is anything 'wrong' with the relationship that a course of psycho-analysis, say, might put right.[8] A society, if we could conceive it, in which such idiosyncratic barriers to communication had been eliminated would be one in which the possibility of deep human relationships had also been eliminated. Perhaps some would regard such an 'emancipation' as progress. I should not.

Notes

1 'Reflections on Gandhi' in Vol. 4 of the Penguin *Collected Essays, Journalism and Letters of George Orwell*, pp.526-7. I am grateful to Cora Diamond for drawing my attention to this essay.
2 *Op. cit.* p.528.
3 See 'The Universalizability of Moral Judgements' in my *Ethics and Actions* (Routledge and Kegan Paul, 1972) for further discussion.
4 L. Wittgenstein, *Vermischte Bemerkungen* (Suhrkamp 1977), p.12.
5 *Philosophical Remarks*, V, § 48.
6 See Grete Henry-Hermann: 'Die Überwindung des Zufalls' in Minna Specht and Willi Eichler (eds.) *Leonard Nelson zum Gedächtnis*, Verlag 'Öffentliches Leben'.
7 I am grateful to Norman Malcolm for drawing my attention to this passage.
8 See Rush Rhees's discussion of Thomas Mann's *Mario und der Zauberer* in The Human World, No. 6.

3. Reply to Peter Winch
by Karl-Otto Apel

As Professor Winch has primarily commented on the background philosophy of my paper, i.e. on the conception of 'transcendental pragmatics', I shall try to comment briefly on some points where the implications of transcendental pragmatics differ in my account from what they are or are assumed to be according to Winch's suggestions.

To begin with Professor Winch's explication of my argument, it is not *my* contention that the third cognitive interest, by its 'dialectical relationship to the naturalistic establishment of laws and the hermeneutic eludication of normative rules', i.e. 'in the way of a Hegelian "synthesis"' of the other two, provides a new conception of the 'unity of science'. A somewhat similar conception, which included the idea of a dialectical unity of knowledge and interest and hence also an *Aufhebung* of traditional philosophy through a mediation of theory and praxis, was indeed presented by Habermas in his *Knowledge and Human Interests*. But he later (see his 'Introduction to the New Edition' of *Theory and Practice*, London, 1975 and especially his 'Afterword' to *Knowledge and Human Interests*, London/Boston, 1978) corrected his 'architectonics' (to use Kant's formulation) through the introduction of the distinction between *Erfahrungsapriori* (*a priori* of experience) and *Argumentationsapriori* (*a priori* of argumentation) which comes closer to my own conception.

According to this conception the methodological differentiation of possible scientific inquiries (in a very broad sense of the word 'scientific') is due to the self-differentiation of the *Erfahrungsapriori* according to the three cognitive interests as ultimate conditions of the possibility of different constitutions of experience. The *unity* of all types of scientific inquiry, on the other hand, is exclusively bound up with the *Argumentationsapriori*, which holds for all types of scientific inquiries in so far as they imply truth-claims or validity-claims which, in principle, call for a universal intersubjective consensus to be reached through argumentative discourse. This latter represents the philosophical instancy of validity-reflection with respect to all cognitive inquiries (and besides that also with respect to all rightness-claims of human actions and their conventional or institutional norms). It is, by its idealized conception, strictly distinguished from ordinary communication (i.e. symbolic interaction) in so far as it is unburdened from practical life-commitment, and hence also separated from strategical interaction which is interwoven with consensual inter-action in ordinary communication. Thus whereas argumentative discourse can be thought of as a discursive medium of epistemological validity reflection, it can no longer be thought of as a medium of experience-constitution because the latter is bound up with the practical life-commitment in so far as it is represented by human cognitive interests.

From this ideal-typical distinction (which, I think, cannot and need not correspond exactly to empirically discernible forms of discourse or communication in the sense of the ordinary use of language) the following two consequences may be derived:

(1) The dialectical relationships between the different cognitive interests — especially the dialectical mediation of hermeneutic understanding through naturalistic explanation in the case of a critical reconstructive social science which, in my account, may be schematized by a figure of thought that is the reverse of that provided by the heuristic mediation of quasi-nomological explanation through understanding of rules and reasons in the case of the quasi-naturalistic type of social science — do not constitute the unity of science, but rather illustrate the methodologically relevant differences between the cognitive interests. Thus they illustrate the self-

differentiation of the *Erfahrungsapriori* which is the polar-opposite to, but nevertheless presupposed by, the unity of science as it is represented by the argumentative discourse to which the truth-claims of all scientific inquiries are intrinsically submitted.

(2) Hermeneutic understanding, even in the broad sense of improving upon or making possible *Verständigung*, is not simply identical with pre-scientific understanding within the framework of ordinary communication. Nor is it identical with striving for consensus within the framework of argumentative discourse. (This was suggested in a way by Winch's equation of philosophy and (hermeneutic) social science in his *The Idea of a Social Science*. It also seems to be presupposed in his present discussion of my alleged transition from the ambiguous notion of *Verstandigung* to the postulate of a universal consensus that is to be reached through argumentative discourse.) It is true I think, that the notion of *Verständigung* suggests a practical continuum between the three things; and this intrinsic connection between them may, in fact, be exploited in the anti-reductionist twist of the complementarity-thesis. (It is exploited also in H.G. Gadamer's conception of 'hermeneutical philosophy' and in my own slightly different conception of 'transcendental hermeneutics'.)[1] The same intrinsic connection is obviously presupposed by the revolutionary request made by analytical philosophy of language, that in philosophical discourse we should first examine the meaning-claims of propositions before trying to reach a consensus about their truth-claims. This is even better illustrated, I think, by the later Wittgenstein's insight that both enterprises cannot be *completely* separated methodically, since there is no possibility of an understanding of meaning without a certain agreement about factual truth being already presupposed. Nevertheless, it is also possible and even necessary to bring to bear upon the notion of *Verständigung* two ideal-typical distinctions: the first is that between *Verständigung* within the frame-

work of ordinary communication and methodical understanding within the framework of a hermeneutic methodology; the second is between this empirical-hermeneutic understanding and Verständigung *qua* coming to consensus, within the framework of argumentative discourse *qua* validity-reflection, whether it be within the framework of science or within the framework of philosophical epistemology. Let me elucidate these distinctions:

(i) Firstly, there is the need for *Verständigung*, i.e. for the understanding of meanings to be already intertwined with reaching agreement about validity-claims (i.e. truth-claims, normative rightness-claims and veracity- or sincerity-claims) in ordinary communication (i.e. symbolic interaction). This consensual element of communicative understanding is even presupposed in those types of communication where strategic interaction is predominant, as in diplomatic and business negotiations. It is to this framework of ordinary communication that I would apply and also restrict what I take to be the Wittgenstein/Winch version of the consensus-presupposition, viz. the rather weak and vague contention, that those who successfully apply the procedures of communicative understanding must, by and large, reach agreement not only about meanings but also about all validity-claims (in the above sense). (This, by the way seems to me to correspond to Dilthey's conception of pre-hermeneutic, i.e. unproblematicized *pragmatisches Verstehen* ('pragmatic understanding'),[2] where, in Gadamer's terminology, a certain *'Einverständnis'* ('agreement') is always already presupposed. In the philosophy of rhetoric it is reflected by the device that the good orator can and must always start out not from true but from generally accepted premisses[3] that he also can consider to be true.)

(ii) Secondly, there is 'hermeneutic understanding' in the sense of a type of scientific inquiry (in the very broad sense of the word 'scientific') that springs from difficulties in ordinary communication, especially from crises in understanding cultural traditions. With respect to this enterprize I wish to maintain that, notwithstanding its abstractive methodical concentration on *meanings* (of rules and reasons etc.), it cannot completely separate its methodical aim from that of judging all the validity-claims of its subject-matter (i.e. texts, actions, institutions etc.) In other words, it cannot approach the fulfilment of its methodical aim to reach a consensus about human meaning-claims in the long run without at the same time approximating to the aim of reaching a consensus about human truth-claims and rightness-claims. This in turn presupposes, in my opinion, a long-range practical (ethically relevant) progress of humanity, as the subject of hermeneutic understanding, towards realizing the ideal of a communication-community. The reason for the interdependency of hermeneutic understanding and agreement about all validity-claims in the long run is, on the one hand, already suggested by the weak Wittgenstein/Winch version of the interwovenness of the understanding of meaning and consensus in ordinary communication, which is the life-basis of hermeneutic understanding. On the other hand, however, hermeneutic understanding as an enterprize of empirical science (in a wide and unusual sense of this word) underlies the 'regulative principle' of aiming at a complete understanding of meanings (and hence also of a complete consensus about truth-claims and rightness-claims). This means in fact that, in contradistinction to ordinary communication, it 'rests on the idea of an eventual agreement in all opinions' (P. Winch). I would like to make this statement more precise in terms of Kant's definition of an 'idea' as being a 'regulative principle' in view of the fact that 'nothing empirical' can correspond to it.

Thus, in my account, one has indeed to switch over from a Wittgensteinian to a Kantian (or rather Peircean) way of thinking in order to make the transition from a descriptive analysis of ordinary communication to a methodologically relevant epistemology of hermeneutic understanding as a branch of 'scientific' inquiry that includes the possibility of progress. It is true, though, that the entire notion of hermeneutic sciences ('*Geisteswissenschaften*') as potentially progressive, methodical types of inquiry is by no means as widely accepted as the corresponding conception of natural science. Thus H.G. Gadamer separates the idea of 'hermeneutics' from that of methodically progressive science altogether, and correspondingly admits of no more than adequate hermeneutic understanding in relation to one's own epoch or cultural form of life. This means that, in the long run of history, there is no understanding better but merely understanding differently ('*anders verstehen*'). This position seems to come closer to that of Wittgenstein and Winch. (Winch, inspired by Kuhn, even seems to question the idea of progressive natural science. But he does so by substituting empirical arguments concerning the 'fragility' of the factual 'consensus of scientists' for my transcendental arguments concerning the necessary presuppositions or normative postulates that are internally connected with the notion of scientific inquiry, and this is against his own previous concessions. I regret very much that I cannot here argue against Kuhn's and Feyerabend's quasi-empirical arguments against the reality of progress in natural science, especially against the problematic (if not confused) idea of 'incommensurability' of theories like those of Kepler, Newton, and Einstein. This idea seems to me to spring from a confusion between the 'semantic' structure of a theory in the narrow abstractive sense and the wider (transcendental-) pragmatic conception of the role of theories within the progress of scientific inquiry. This progress, as I see it, is evidenced already by the increase in technological power over nature.)

(iii) The solution of the problem as to whether the notion of a methodically progressive science that underlies the regulative principle of approximating universal consensus applies to a certain cognitive inquiry depends, in my opinion, upon its participation in the notion of 'argumentative discourse' (a dependency, by the way, that indicates the intrinsic relationship between the idea of empirical sciences and that of philosophy). Hence we are led to the third aspect of the vague and ambiguous ordinary language-idea of *Verständigung*. The paradigm of argumentative discourse is that necessarily philosophical discussion which has already been joined by those people who raise similar questions to Winch and myself. I would indeed claim that it cannot be thought of as meaningful and hence cannot be seriously applied to practice without presupposing, among other things, the possibility and necessity, in principle, of reaching a consensus about all kinds of validity-claims that may be brought forward by relevant speech acts. This means that the consensus can and must be reconfirmed, in principle, by an indefinite possible extension of the actual community of discourse, and hence approximates to the notion of a universal consensus (which is the transcendental-pragmatic explication of the idea of truth as a human idea that, in principle, can provide a critical re-interpretation of the traditional explications of truth in terms of correspondence and coherence, by having recourse to the possibility of argumentative agreement about both experiential and logical 'evidences' of correspondence or coherence).

This idea of a possible and necessary consensus cannot be refuted — as Winch attempts to do in the greater part of his comments — by pointing to all the serious factual difficulties that are faced in seeking to reach agreement. For this notion of consensus is corroborated, first of all, by the obvious fact that Winch himself is constantly trying to convince his audience of the correctness of his arguments, which is, of course, a quite appropriate attitude. This constant presupposing of possible assent which makes up the implicit performative claim of his contrary propositional claims shows, in my opinion, that he deviates from, or even abandons, the very *idea* of serious discussion or argumentative discourse, when he suggests the possibility of a discussion without maintaining, or after having given up, the presupposition of consensus as a possible aim of the discussion. In actual practice one may of course decide, on my account, that it is wise to give up or avoid a serious discussion in favour of mere conversation, after having recognized 'that any prospect of eventual agreement . . . is no more than a pipedream'.

Hence it does not follow from my approach, as Winch assumes, that people cannot arrive at the situation of being compelled to follow their own risky decisions in the face of the *factual* impossibility of coming to intersubjective consensus because of factually undecidable disputes of opinions or irreconcilable conflicts of normative maxims or evaluative attitudes. This maxim of Existentialism already follows from the fact that our life is 'finite' and hence all factual discussion must also be finite. On the other hand, all 'regulative ideas' in Kant's sense involve the idea of infinity. In the face of the intricate relationship between the finitude of all factual life-processes and the infinity involved in all transcendental postulates or regulative principles that are intrinsically connected with human validity-claims, one may, or rather must, maintain that the relationship between my approach and Winch's alleged counter-examples is not simply one of contradiction and hence of mutual exclusion but a much more complicated one. We might have to face here a 'dialectical tension' that we human beings simply have to cope with (in Hegel's sense of 'dialectical contradictions' that we must 'endure').

This type of answer is also suggested by Winch's question as 'to whom, or to what, the aim of a universal consensus [is] to be attributed'. The answer, in my account, is not that it is to be attributed 'to the discussion itself' instead of the participants, as Winch suggests. Rather, I would be inclined to answer that the aim of a universal consensus is to be attributed to the participants not in so far as they are finite individual persons but in so far as they bring forward and defend validity-claims and thus are in charge, as it were, or represent the 'transcendental subject' of argumentation (which in my account of a transcendental pragmatics of argumentative discourse can only be realized by an indefinite, ideal argumentation-community). Contrary to Winch's suggestion, there is no contradiction between this transcendental-pragmatic contention and the obvious supposition that participants in a discussion have different personal aims concerning their lives or that of their social groups.

Precisely this fact was illustrated to me in an unforgettable way by Winch's earlier statement that even within the framework of argumentative discourse we cannot abstract from the fact that we are individual persons with different historical backgrounds and aims (I am quoting from memory!). For, according to my interpretation of this assertion, the first 'we', in contradistinction to the second 'we', is appealing to the participants of the discourse not as individual persons (although individual persons are in fact addressed by the actual speech-act) but as members, so to speak, of that indefinite, ideal community of argumentation which we are in charge of, when we propose or defend or contest validity-claims. We cannot and need not separate the transcendental status of the participants from their empirical status but may and must nevertheless make a distinction between them. This remarkable situation is confirmed, I think, by the fact that we are sometimes well aware of the dialectical tension between, on the one hand, our being in charge of an infinite effort of judging validity-claims (especially truth-claims) and thus of belonging to an indefinite argumentation-community and, on the other hand, of our being finite beings, bound to (subject to) finite life-cycles, i.e. to becoming tired and finally having to die.[4]

In addition to this rather esoteric argument more exoteric ones might also be advanced, in order to show that the entire contra-position of personal aims and the aim of argumentative consensus must be mistaken. For it seems clear that the situation of a disparity (difference) of opinions, or even of a conflict of purposes, is the very reason for entering argumentative discourse in all cases where one wants to avoid serious quarrel. In actual practice, it is true, such a resort to arguments does not yet mean that the opponents intend to reach a universally valid consensus. They might instead wish to reach a favourable compromise or to persuade the other party to share their own position. But even in these types of discourse people must already, in a sense, be purporting to presuppose the possibility and necessity of reaching, through the power of arguments, a universally valid consensus about opinions and about generalizable interests or purposes. It was this fact, I suggest, that made it possible for the Greek philosophers to distil the idea of argumentative discourse, in the above sense, from the rhetorical discourse of the Sophists. At this crucial point it seems clear that the diversity of opinions or personal aims (as presupposed by the institution of argumentative discourse), does not logically prevent the participants in the discourse from entering it with a common intention that could be made explicit by a declaration something like this: 'Now, let us try to find out which of our different opinions, or even purposes, can be grounded through argumentative reasons that, as far as we can judge, can be assented to not only by us but by virtually all conceivable competent participants in the discourse'.

We should not leave out of account the fact that in the case of a practical (i.e. ethically relevant) discourse concerning the generalizability of interests or purposes the special problem of anticipating and taking into account the interests of all possibly affected persons comes into play. For instance, in present-day ecological-political discussions the interests of the next generations are at stake. But all these difficulties do *not* prove, as Winch supposes, that the idea of searching for universal consensus through argumentative discourse must involve an intrinsic tendency to suppress the individual peculiarities of persons or socio-cultural groups in favour of enforcing a uniform mass-society. On the contrary, since our present post-industrial planetary civilisation, for the first time in history, forces us to live together in the same boat, so to speak, argumentative discourse in the above sense provides the only possibility for rescuing and protecting as much as possible of the richness of personal and socio-cultural individualities. Precisely this is testified to by the numerous international conferences about every vital problem of humanity which we are informed about through the mass-media almost every day. For it is philosophically interesting, I suggest, that all these conferences today take the form of argumentative discourse. Their participants, notwithstanding their strong strategic purposes or, respectively, provisos, must at least *feign* the intention of solving the problems raised by conflicts on the basis of intersubjectively valid arguments in the above sense. Even if there should be argumentatively irreconcilable conflicts due to incommensurable forms of life, as Winch emphasises, we have to face the urgent task of providing a basis for co-existence, or mutual tolerance, by coming to consensus about more fundamental opinions, interests, or purposes. Thus, mutual tolerance and striving for consensus are *not* in contradiction with each other, and the ideal of an indefinite communication-community is *not* equivalent to the ideal of illiberal collectivism.

Furthermore, I cannot conceal my general impression that the post-Wittgensteinian tendency to fall back upon ultimate incommensurable paradigms or forms of life as a limit of rational argumentation may often amount to a precipitious and even irresponsible breaking off of serious attempts at *Verständigung*. In many cases the alleged incommensurability of life-forms can be dissolved by a careful inquiry into all the external and internal boundary-conditions of people's fundamental responses to their situations in life. Thus I should convince myself with the aid of ethnological information that the shocking custom of certain Arctic tribes of exposing their old, disabled people to starvation by leaving them with a last provision, may very well be understood (i.e. 'rationally explained' in the sense of W. Dray) under the presupposition of our own so called humane premisses *and* very different boundary conditions. Even in the case of Winch's example of the 'dispute between a Gandhi and an Orwell' I am far from being convinced that we must leave it by stating the imcompatibility between an 'other-worldly' and 'humanistic' ethics. The problem of coping with 'the moral dangers that Gandhi sees as springing from close personal attachments' and, on the other hand, the danger of 'emotional aridity and isolation from one's fellows' which is seen by Orwell, seems to me to be an 'intra-humanistic' moral problem. To mention here only one point of view, in the case of a public person like Gandhi or the Pope or, for that matter, Brezhnev, we will judge the pertinent decisions on different criteria than in the case, say, of a youngster like Romeo in Shakespeare's play. Notwithstanding the fact that everybody has to solve it for himself by ultimate decisions of conscience, such a problem is by no means inaccessible to rational arguments.

This much must suffice in defence of 'transcendental pragmatics' as a way of thinking. I am very sorry that, for lack of space, I cannot reply to Winch's second point concerning my account of the third cognitive interest. I have to concede that my 'derivation' of its necessity at the end of my paper was too short to avoid the misunderstanding that I might be supposing or envisaging the status of a 'pure subject of thought and speech' as the aim or regulative principle of emancipation. But the pertinent passage in my first treatment of this question is the following: 'The regulative principle of this commitment to inquiry (sc. of the interest in emancipation) would not eventually be something like the liberation of the mind from the body, or reflective *Aufhebung* of the material into the absolute idea, but rather the pure expression of the spiritual through its embodiment, i.e. 'humanization of nature' and 'naturalization of Man'.'[5]

Notes

1   Cf. my paper 'Szientismus oder transzendentale Hermeneutik' in R. Bubner *et alii* (eds.), *Hermeneutik und Dialektik*, Festschr. f. H.-G. Gadamer, Tübingen: J. C. B. Mohr, 1970, vol. I, p.105-44; English, trans. as 'Scientism or Transcendental Hermeneutics' in K.-O. Apel, *Towards a Transformation of Philosophy*, London/Boston: Routledge, 1979.

2   Cf. W. Dilthey, Gesammelte Schriften, vol. VII, p.207 ff.

3   Cf. Ch. Perelmann and L. Olbrechts-Tyteca, *Traité De L'Argumentation*, 2nd, ed. Bruxelles, 1970.

4   Cf. my paper 'Ist der Tod eine Bedingung der Möglichkeit von Bedeutung?', in *La Réflexion sur la Mort*, Athènes: Ecole Libre de Philosophie, 1977, p.122 ff. (repr. in J. Mittelstrass and M. Riedel (ed.), *Vernünftiges Denken*, Berlin/New York: De Gruyter, 1978, pp. 407-19.

5   Cf. K.-O. Apel, *Transformation der Philosophie*, *loc. cit.* vol. II, p.127.

PART TWO

CRITICAL THEORY
AND ITS CRITICS

4. Technique, Critique and Social Science
by Michael Lessnoff

IN recent years a good deal of attention has been devoted to the work of writers associated with the Frankfurt Institute of Social Research (the Frankfurt 'School'). In this article I shall consider the view of science and social theory developed by a group of these writers, from the 1930s up to the present. The writers in question, who belong to that part of the Marxist tradition relatively strongly influenced by Hegel, are Max Horkheimer, Herbert Marcuse, Jürgen Habermas, and (to a lesser extent) Theodor Adorno and the anonymous authors of a recent textbook produced by the Institute. In addition I shall discuss some recent work by English-speaking writers who seem to have been influenced to a greater or lesser degree by the Frankfurt School, or at least reproduce some of their characteristic themes.

The Frankfurt Institute was founded in Weimar Germany (in 1923), migrated from its homeland when Hitler came to power, found its way eventually to the U.S.A., and returned to Frankfurt after Hitler's defeat (though some of its members continued to live in the United States). This history is of some importance to the present theme. The point, simply, is that the social systems which the Frankfurt theorists have experienced — a disintegrating capitalist Republic, Nazi totalitarianism, later the uninhibited capitalism of the United States and the Federal Republic — they have not liked. No better have they liked the Stalinist and post-Stalinist systems they have seen developing in the U.S.S.R. Thus, all the social systems they have experienced or known they have considered bad. As Marxists, however, they have made their main target the highly 'rationalized' (in Max Weber's formal sense) modern capitalist system — what we may call 'bureaucratic capitalism'.

The position of the Frankfurt writers on science and social theory has been developed in opposition to a view which they usually call 'positivism' (sometimes 'scientism'). 'Positivism' is a vague term (and is indeed in danger of degenerating into a vehicle of indiscriminate abuse), but for present purposes it should be taken to be the view that, in the realm of human knowledge, the natural sciences (understood in a particular way, of which more later) take pride of place, and provide a model. This implies, first, that other fields of enquiry in which the natural science model is applicable, must apply it if they are to produce genuine knowledge; second, fields of enquiry where this cannot be done cannot produce real knowledge, or can at best produce knowledge of an inferior kind. Into the first category, in the positivist view, comes empirical social theory (social science); into the second fall metaphysics, and moral and other value-judgements. It follows that according to positivism social science must be value-free. Such, roughly, is the set of positions against which the Frankfurt theorists have directed their 'critical theory' (or 'critique'). Also among their targets, however, have been writers who can scarcely be called fully-fledged positivists, but who, in the Frankfurt view, have failed to free themselves from some important positivist errors — most notably, Max Weber and Karl Popper. In brief, the claim of the critical theorists is that both positivism itself and positivist social science (perhaps even natural science too) are conservative ideologies — in Western society, therefore, they are ideologies of bureaucratic capitalism.[1] This means, I take it, that these belief systems are at least partly false, and help to sustain the power of the capitalist ruling class over the rest of society. As ideologies they are, crudely, both false and immoral.

The Frankfurt critique of positivist social theory embraces two general claims, which I shall discuss in turn. First, a social theory modelled on natural science will be a *technical* science ('technique') and hence inherently manipulative — in the case of social science the objects of manipulation will be people, whereas in natural science they are non-human nature. Second, such a social theory becomes a *hypostratization of the actual*; that is, it confines social knowledge to description of what is the case, and rules out any consideration of what *will* be the case, what *could* be the case, or what *ought* to be the case — it even fails to *explain* what is the case, as distinct from describing it.

I now turn to the Frankfurt notion of science as technique. Let us first consider natural science. It is a platitude to say that natural scientific knowledge is often useful. If, however, those to whom it is useful have undesirable aims this usefulness also will be undesirable (Bertrand Russell came to believe that, such is the folly of the wielders of power in the world, the advance of scientific knowledge is on balance a misfortune and may yet prove a disaster). Correspondingly, if one sees modern society through Marxist spectacles, that is, as controlled by a capitalist ruling class whose interests are fundamentally opposed to those of the masses and indeed of humanity as a whole, then the usefulness of science must be disproportionately to the advantage of that ruling class, it must serve them as a weapon of exploitation, and to that extent be undesirable. This is indeed the view of the Frankfurt theorists, but if their theory went no deeper than this it would be of little interest.

According to the theory, however, there is a deeper affinity between science and capitalism. In the first place, both are characteristic developments of the modern world and manifestations of what Weber called 'rationalization', that is, the increasingly self-conscious, systematic and efficient adaptation of means to ends (formal rationalization). One may suspect, then, that historically there has been some kind of symbiotic relation between them. As Horkheimer put it, 'The facts of science and science itself are but segments of the life process of society, and in order to understand the significance . . . of science one must possess the key to the his-

torical situation, the right social theory.'[2] This sentence
neatly stands positivism on its head: far from natural science
providing the exemplar and model for social theory, it cannot itself be properly understood except in terms of a prior
social theory, that is, in terms of its 'social function', its role
in the 'social division of labour'.[3] This claim is not merely a
sociological one: it is also epistemological.

We are dealing with a Marxist, that is a materialist, theory of society and history; hence what is fundamental for it
is society's economic basis. Man's fundamental experience
according to Marx is in the world of work.[4] In work, men
struggle with nature and come to know it. The knowledge
acquired in this process is itself used in work, it becomes a
productive force. Capitalism is a particular social organization of work, compared with earlier systems a particularly
rational organization, in Weber's formal sense.[5] Correspondingly, the knowledge of nature of which it makes use is
more systematic and effective than the knowledge used in
earlier systems. This improved knowledge is natural
science.[6] In capitalist society, natural science is, in Horkheimer's words, a 'moment in the social process of production'.[7] The crucial point that is being made here is that
natural science, including 'theoretical' natural science,
while superior to pre-scientific knowledge of nature, is qualitatively similar in form, and that form is impressed on it by
its economic function, its role in social work.

That means that its form is fundamentally technical: natural science knowledge is 'technique'.[8] This shows itself in
the concepts and methods of natural science. Natural
science is empirical and nomological, that is, it states universal connections between empirical facts. This is precisely
the form that knowledge must take in order to be technically useful. If it is the case that 'Whenever A, then B,' and if
we want B to be the case, we can bring it about by bringing
about A. The laws of natural science permit conditional prediction and, thereby, control. The notion of a satisfactory
explanation in natural science (a 'theoretical' notion) is

based on the criterion of predictability (a potentially technical criterion): that is held to be explained which could have been predicted, had one had in advance knowledge of the facts which constitute the explanation (this point has been made by an American follower of the Frankfurt theorists, Brian Fay[9]). As Habermas puts it, natural science 'contains information about reality from the viewpoint of possible technical control'.[10] That is, natural scientific knowledge is not, as positivism naïvely assumes, a sort of carbon copy of a pre-existing reality; rather, in the concepts and laws of natural science reality is grasped from the point of view of a particular *knowledge-constitutive human interest*, the interest in technical control of nature. This interest shapes the language of science just as much as does the external world.[10] Thus, positivism is mistaken in supposing that natural science is value-free: on the contrary, it is the value attached to mastery of the environment that gives that science the form it has.[12] One might say that, in the Frankfurt interpretation, the usual view of the relation between science and technology is reversed: instead of technology being the application of science to practical affairs, science is the application of technology in the realm of theory.

We have seen that the Frankfurt theorists' interpretation of natural science is based on their reading of Marx, to the effect that man comes to a knowledge of nature through work. In addition, Habermas has extended this base through a consideration of the arguments of the pragmatist philosopher, C.S. Pierce.[13] According to Pierce, as Habermas reads him, science is a theoretical extrapolation of human learning processes, rooted, not specifically in work activity, but in 'instrumental' or 'purposive' activity generally — that is, any activity undertaken as a means to some end. And these learning-processes are themselves an extrapolation of (or a substitute for) instinctual responses of a kind selected by evolutionary pressures throughout the history of life on earth. Without appropriate responses to stimuli, no living creature could survive. If, as is the case with human beings, instinctive behaviour patterns are relatively lacking, they must be substituted by the learning of beliefs, based on experience as to what consequences are to be expected from a given sort of action. Patterns of behaviour based on these beliefs can then become habits (quasi-instincts); but they are also, as Habermas puts it, 'feedback-controlled',[14] that is, they are reinforced by continued experience of the expected consequences, but if these don't show up, the belief can be modified. 'The universal assumptions at the basis of purposive-rational action are subjected to permanent testing' (Habermas), with the aim of achieving the complete avoidance of surprise. The process here described only needs to be made more systematic and rigorous, to become an account of scientific method. Once again, science is seen as a grasping of reality from the viewpoint of the knowledge-constitutive interest in technical control. Habermas also stresses, in support of this interpretation, an argument of Pierce's to the effect that inductive reasoning, alleged to be basic to the scientific enterprise, has no logical justification, but derives its justification solely from its technical usefulness.[15]

Natural science, as we have seen, is, according to critical theory, not value-free knowledge, but knowledge structured in accordance with a prior evaluation (conscious or not) in favour of control or mastery over nature. As we shall see later, the critical theorists differ over whether knowledge of non-human nature can have only this orientation, and no other. But they agree that a social theory modelled on natural science incorporates a prior value-judgement which in this case is unacceptable, and that therefore such a social theory must be rejected. A social science modelled on natural science will, like natural science, give 'information about reality from the viewpoint of possible technical control': but in this case the objects of possible technical control are human beings. Such a science would thus be a set of formulae for the control, the manipulation, the domination, the oppression of men, of some men by others, that is, in a Marxist perspective, of the masses by a capitalist or other ruling class.[16]

Before exploring some of the ramifications of this idea in the writings of the critical theorists (above all Marcuse), I want to make two points. First, the argument of the critical theorists must be clearly distinguished from a quite different (though perhaps superficially similar) objection to a 'natural science of society', namely that human beings are inherently free, hence unpredictable, hence inherently unsuited to description in terms of universal deterministic laws. On the contrary, the critical theorists hold, not that such laws predicated of human beings must be untrue, but that they will be all too true, and thus afford to the powerful a weapon for oppressing the rest.

Secondly, I should like to point out the difference between the critical theorists and Max Weber on the relation between values and science. At the purely verbal level there is obviously a difference, in that Weber believed that both natural and social science could be and should be value-free. At a slightly deeper level it might seem that the disagreement vanishes, in that Weber held that social science must also be value-relevant, that is, its concepts must inevitably reflect the interests of social scientists. (This he held to be fully compatible with using only value-free concepts to make only value-free statements about social life.) Does the view of the critical theorists really differ from Weber's? Yes, it does. For Weber *contrasted* the selection of subject-matter from the standpoint of relevance to one's values (which he held to be inevitable in social science) with selection from the standpoint of interest in subsuming reality under universal laws, as in natural science. The scientific interest in laws of nature did not seem to him to reflect a value-judgement: non-human nature, he held, unlike social reality, is not interesting to us from an evaluative standpoint.[17]

It is now time to detail some of the evils of technical social science as seen by the Frankfurt theorists. First of all, advanced capitalism (as also Soviet society) is highly

bureaucratized: it is carried on by means of huge bureaucratic administrations, whether of the state or of 'private'
corporations.[18] These bureaucracies can be seen, on the one
hand, as themselves an application of a technical social
science, which shows the efficiency of such structures for
the organization of administration; and on the other hand, as
living tools or machines for the control by means of other
technical social sciences, of those at the bottom of them or
underneath them. Marcuse, indeed, believes that this control is so effective in advanced capitalist societies that they
can properly be described as totalitarian.[19] Among the technical social sciences used by bureaucratic capitalism to control its subject population are industrial sociology and
management science (used to keep the worker under control
at his place of work) and market and motivational research
(used to persuade consumers to buy the products of this capitalist machine, and electors to vote for capitalist political
parties); and, in general, technical, psychological science is
at the disposal of the powerful to enable them to condition
the people to acceptance of the system.[20] The logic of this
kind of social science, which treats men as mere objects of
manipulation, is seen by, for example, Habermas, to culmi-
nate in control by means of intervention at the biological
and genetic level.[21]

One of the most striking features of the Frankfurt theorists' vision of totalitarian manipulative capitalism is that
they can fit into it, without apparent difficulty, a number of
features which might be held to rank among the positive
achievements of capitalism or of liberal democracy. For one
way to reconcile people to the system is to give them at least
some of what they want. This, perhaps, could be considered
to be a piece of technical social science knowledge. Thus,
for Marcuse, the widespread consumer affluence achieved
in the 1950s and 1960s is one more technique of manipulation. For Habermas and his American follower Fay, and also
for another American, David Harvey, author of a recent,
highly praised book, *Social Justice and The City*, governmental

intervention in the economy guided by technical Keynesian economic science, which enables (enabled?) the suffering caused by severe unemployment to be avoided, is a method of stabilizing the capitalist system. (Harvey calls it a '*status quo* theory', i.e. a theory designed to preserve the *status quo*.) For Marcuse, Habermas and Fay, the welfare state itself, precisely insofar as it relieves or prevents suffering, serves the same function.[22]

Such are the crimes of which positivist social scientists are guilty, though they may not know it. Perhaps, though, they can take some comfort from the thought that their naïvety was shared, according to Habermas, by Karl Marx himself.[23] Not that Marx committed technical social science — on the contrary, he was the founder of critical social theory (a phenomenon which I must eventually consider in detail). But unfortunately he was unaware of the difference between the two, and therefore mistakenly assimilated his own social theory to natural science. The reason for this mistake Habermas traces to Marx's materialism. We noted above that for Marx it is in work that man knows nature; in addition, it is in work that man creates his *own* nature. Man, that is, creates himself in the realm of instrumental action; hence the science of man is seen by Marx as essentially similar to the science of instrumental (technical) action, natural science. Marx, says Habermas, has mistakenly reduced the whole of human experience to labour, whereas it is only his experience of inanimate nature that can properly be so understood.

It is interesting to compare Habermas's criticism of Marx's conception of social theory with that of Popper. They seem to be directly contradictory. While for Habermas Marx's conception of social theory is wrong because it is technical, for Popper it is wrong because it is not technical. Popper's complaint against Marx is, of course, that he offered a pseudo-science of holistic prophecy[24] instead of a genuine science that could be the basis of piecemeal social engineering (technique). As a description of Marxian social

science, Popper's characterization seems much more accurate than Habermas's (leaving aside the question of whether
Marx is properly to be criticised for it). For, insofar as Marx
interpreted his own theory deterministically, and, as he supposed, on the model of the natural sciences, he was concerned, first and foremost, with necessary laws of historical
development, which can be summarized as the inevitable
breakdown of capitalism through its internal contradictions, and its replacement by communism. Insofar as he was
concerned to elaborate 'synchronic' laws of social process
(e.g. that the state functions to maintain the power of the
class owning the means of production) these laws were seen
as ineluctable given a certain sort of social system (e.g. capitalism), but fated to disappear with that system. Neither the
historical nor the synchronic laws give any scope for purposive technical intervention.

2.   According to Habermas, Marx, although mistaken
about social theory, including his own, was right to see
man's knowledge of nature as necessarily technical in form,
hence having the form of natural science. No change in the
social system will alter this: natural science under socialism
must be similar in form to natural science as we know it.[25]
Natural science is a positive achievement of capitalism which
socialism will preserve. This also seems to be the view of
Horkheimer, at least when writing alone (as in 'Traditional
and Critical Theory'[26]) — when writing jointly with
Adorno as in their *Dialectic of Enlightenment*, he seems less
sure: (here we read that 'The totalitarian order . . . upholds
science as such'[27]). But some critical theorists definitely
assert that a non-repressive society will require a new, non-
technical natural science. Among them is Marcuse (though
he also, and in the same work — *One-Dimensional Man* —
asserts the contrary). Thus he writes that 'Qualitative
[social] change also involves a change in the technical basis
on which this society rests' (p. 31); that the technical utilization of man is not the contingent result of a particular appli-

cation of science but is inherent in pure science (p. 122); that
the abolition of hierarchical technical society would alter
the very structure of science ('It would arrive at essentially
different concepts of nature and establish essentially different facts (p. 136) . . . open a universe of qualitatively different relations between man and man, and man and nature.
Man's mastery of nature would be a liberating rather than a
repressive one' (p. 188)). Not only our present science is,
according to Marcuse, inherently repressive: so also is our
conventional formal logic; for this logic subjects objects to
general categories, and thus permits mastery over particular
cases through knowledge of universals; it is a stage in the
development of the instruments of universal control, including the control of man.[28]

These views may seem rather extreme, but the hostility
to natural science at least is shared by two Anglo-Saxon writers clearly influenced by Marcuse. According to David Harvey, theory acceptance in the natural sciences has been
controlled by the ruling class, their criterion for the accepta-
bility of a theory being its usefulness from the point of view
of manipulation and control. Harvey hopes this will change,
and that the new criterion will be 'realization of human
potential'.[29] Similarly Brian Easlea writes that capitalism
has alienated man from nature, and that the avoidance of
'total technocratic administration' requires the overthrow
of the 'technocratic image of *nature and man*' and its replacement by a new conception.[30]

This clarion call for a new natural science, it must be
admitted, turns out on inspection to be as vague as it is stri-
dent. How, *structurally*, would the new liberating natural
science differ from our present technical one? As one seeks
an answer to this question all that emerges clearly is that the
critical theorists, to their credit, are against cruelty to animals (cf. Marcuse, *One-Dimensional Man*, p. 187). Animals,
like men, should not be treated as mere things. Easlea has
constructed a remarkable fantasy to illustrate the point.[31] If
I wish to dry my clothes on a clothes-line, but the line has

unfortunately broken, I may be able to repair it by using a cat to tie together the broken ends (personally I doubt if I should have thought of this). The cat will then writhe in discomfort and pain, and these struggles will actually aid the drying of my clothes. The moral of this gruesome fable is that to treat instrumentally a nature which has its own purposes is to oppress it. However, I fail to see how this argument, undoubtedly valid in relation to cats, can be extended to nature in general. In regard to inanimate nature, talk of 'liberation' seems to be either mystical pantheism or a confused expression of the fashionable concern for the 'environment'.

Marcuse, it must be admitted, does make some suggestions as to what a liberating science or technology would do. It would, for example, show how to satisfy the vital needs of all members of society with minimum expenditure of labour, etc.[32] This science seems to me just as instrumental or technical as the one we have: only, it is instrumental to ends considered desirable by Marcuse and, indeed, many others. What is more, existing science is already used for these purposes, though not of course only for these. If it were used only for desirable purposes, this would be all to the good. But the good would be benefit to men (and perhaps other animals), not to inanimate nature.

Indeed, the notion that a technically oriented science, whether natural or social, must be manipulative, dominative, and therefore morally unacceptable seems to me quite false. In relation to social science the claim has a little more plausibility, because there are indeed certain possible techniques for controlling society which are unacceptable morally — for example, terror, and some forms of psychological manipulation. But not all such techniques are open to such objection: the couching of social knowledge in technically applicable lawlike form does not *ipso facto* make it immoral. Keynesian economics seems to me a good case in point. Keynesian techniques (if they work) amount to this: by running a budget deficit a government enables people to do what they would like to do, but would otherwise be unable to do, namely prosper. I see no trace of morally unacceptable manipulation here.

In fact, the moral status of means in relation to ends seems to me to be almost exactly the same whether the end in question be some desired state of society or of inanimate nature. Even if the end in question is desirable (as well as desired), not all means to that end are permissible, however efficient they may be. Examples of impermissible means to social ends have been mentioned; one can easily think of cases where application of a purely physical technology would be morally unacceptable, for example production of electricity by possibly dangerous methods such as nuclear fission. But if science — physical or social — is to be useful to mankind, it *must* be technical in form, that is, technically applicable. The absence of reliable social techniques seems to me, *pace* the Frankfurt theorists, both marked and regrettable.

In any case, are the Frankfurt theorists and their followers right in supposing that natural science embodies an inherently technical understanding of nature, that it grasps reality from a viewpoint of possible technical control? I believe not. As critics of the Frankfurt School such as Nicholas Lobkowicz have pointed out,[33] these theorists, ironically, have made the mistake of accepting too much of positivism. Their understanding of natural science is much too positivist. The technical applicability of that science is only one aspect of a more complex truth. It is only on the positivist model of science that explanation and prediction are held to be structurally identical, and that theoretical scientific laws are held to be merely instruments for conditional prediction (and hence, in some cases, control) of observable phenomena. But the positivist interpretation of natural science is wrong or at least incomplete. Physicists, in postulating such invisible entities as electrons or photons, are not seeking tools for prediction or manipulation but rather attempting to describe and understand reality (this philosophy of science is often called 'realism'). The value-judgement embodied in the activity of scientific theorizing is less the desirability of controlling the environment than that of understanding the universe. Habermas, somewhat surprisingly, would not, in fact, deny that this is the motive of much, perhaps most, work in theoretical physics. He even concedes that, historically, natural science and industrial technology had little or no organic connection until the late nineteenth century — the two modernizing developments went largely separate ways until then.[34] These facts would seem to cast some doubt on his thesis. But he remains unshaken. His argument seems to be expressible in the following three propositions:

(1) the human condition (perhaps, the animal condition) imposes the imperative of technical knowledge (this, he says is a 'transcendental necessity' imposed by the 'objective structure of human life'[35]);

(2) natural science provides technical knowledge; therefore

(3) natural science is essentially technical.

It is clear that the conclusion is not entailed by the two premises (both of which are perfectly true). The essence of natural science may be something more than or even other than technique. I should like to suggest that its essence is, in a broad sense, philosophical, even religious. The need to understand the universe seems to me to be as inescapable an aspect of the human (if not the animal) condition as the technical imperative, and one that can be called religious in a quite understandable sense.

It might be objected, on behalf of the Frankfurt theorists, that there are many possible approaches to an understanding of the universe, the natural scientific being only one.[36] Thus, the desire to understand the universe does not adequately explain the natural scientific enterprise. Why should one attach particular value to that particular approach? It was argued by Max Scheler[37] (to whom the Frankfurt critical theorists are certainly indebted) that, in the scientific revolution of the seventeenth century, what he called *Herrschaftswissen* (i.e. practical knowledge aimed at mastery of the environment) gained the upper hand over metaphysical and religious orientations to knowledge of the universe, to which it had previously been subordinate both intellectually and socially — in Frankfurt terms, the desire for knowledge came to subserve technical interests. I suggest that the truth is more complex. Theoretical natural science is rather the outcome of a remarkable and fruitful convergence between 'natural philosophy' and practical concerns, from which both gained. What was gained from the point of view of understanding the universe was the chance to *use* the technical interest, for the purpose of *testing* theoretical knowledge. As for the question, why *this* empirical form of test, rather than another, I suggest that the reason was primarily aesthetic or even moral. Satisfaction was to be derived from submitting to this form of discipline, perhaps to submit to it was even a duty, rather than indulging in flights of unrestrained and uncontrolled speculation. One might even dare to suggest some link here between the scientific revolution and the Reformation.

It is also worth mentioning that some difficulties for the technical interpretation of natural science are raised by Popper's philosophy of science, according to which scientific theories are hypotheses which are falsifiable and corroborable rather than verifiable, and which rest not at all on induction. For the technical application of science certainly does rest on induction. Habermas has indeed seen the problem that arises here, and his solution is to refuse to take seriously the hypothetical character of scientific laws that are continually applied and corroborated in industrial civilization.[38] But this technical applicability seems to me to underline rather than to obliterate the gap that Popper's philosophy opens up between natural science and technique — a gap which it must be admitted is very baffling, and raises problems for Popper as much as for Habermas.

3.   I now turn to the second half of the Frankfurt attack on
a social theory modelled on natural science, that it results in
hypostatization of the actual, of the *status quo*, and is thus a
conservative ideology. (Where the *status quo* is capitalist it is
presumably a bourgeois ideology.) First, some documenta-
tion of this accusation. Brian Easlea, in *Liberation and the Aims
of Science*, attacks the view that 'the only legitimate aim of
science is to understand what *is*, not what *could be* or *should
be*'.[39] According to Harvey, *'status quo'* theories 'characteristically reify (and thereby tacitly legitimize) an existing situation in concept form'.[40] Fay, too, writes that 'positivistic
social science necessarily reifies the basic social institutions
and customs of the society it is studying'[41] (I take it that by
'reify' Fay and Harvey mean that such a social science, by
confining itself to a description of what exists, implies that
what exists could not be otherwise than it is — whereas it
could and should). In *Dialectic of Englightenment*, Horkheimer
and Adorno write that in positivistic science 'the everlasting-
ness of the factual is confirmed', and that 'In the impartiality
of scientific language that which is powerless has wholly
lost any means of expression, and only the given finds its neutral sign'; again 'Under the title of brute facts, the social
injustice from which they proceed is [rendered] sacred.'[42]
The Frankfurt Institute textbook, *Aspects of Sociology*, pro-
claims the same message: positivistic sociology takes pride
in not transcending what is, hence merely duplicates reality
in thought, and because it does not criticise reality cannot
explain it.[43] Finally Marcuse expresses similar ideas through
the contrast between essence and appearance: positivist
social science merely describes appearance, entirely omitting the dimension of essence, which contradicts appearance
(what is) in the name of what ought to be.[44] (To illustrate the
shortcomings of positivism in this respect, Marcuse mentions in *One-Dimensional Man* the notorious definition of
'democracy' by positivist, political scientists, in terms of
something that actually exists in the U.S.A., imperfect
though that is, rather than what does not exist, but could

exist and should exist.)[45]

From all this a number of issues need to be disentangled. First, it is true that a social science which simply describes what exists will tell us nothing about what is possible. Second, reification of a *status quo* which could in fact be otherwise is certainly a mistake which social scientists have sometimes made. But what is extremely strange is that this charge should be made against positivist social science, which is at the same time accused of being technical. For the two charges seem mutually inconsistent. A technical social science is precisely one which shows how to bring into existence what does not yet exist, albeit in a manner to which the critical theorists object because it allegedly involves manipulation or control of human beings. But however objectionable this social science might be, it cannot be accused of reifying the *status quo* or merely duplicating existing reality. And how can the charge of 'merely duplicating reality' be reconciled with the assertion that positivist (technical) scientific concepts do *not* mirror a pre-existing reality, but structure it in accordance with the interest in technical control?

It seems apparent that the critical theorists have not made clear to themselves, much less consistent with one another, the two accusations they want to make against positivist social science, that of 'technicism' and that of 'hypostatization'. Once this is brought out, it casts some light on what would otherwise be a most puzzling feature of Habermas's social philosophy. Having characterized natural science as technical, and on that account rejected a social theory modelled on natural science, he goes on to make a partial retraction of this rejection. There is, after all, a legitimate place for *'systematic sciences of social action*, that is, economics, sociology and political science, [which] have the goal, as do the empirical-analytic [natural] sciences, of producing nomological knowledge' — knowledge of laws.[46] But if these laws are technical, hence manipulative, repressive etc., how can there be a legitimate place for them at all? However, it emerges that Habermas is not here thinking of the nomological knowledge produced by the systematic sciences of social action as technical. For these laws may represent either 'invariant regularities of social action as such', or regularities that can be transformed (abolished). The essential thing is to distinguish the two classes correctly, and not mistake the transformable for the invariant. To do that would be to 'hypostatize the actual'. In other words, the danger of positivism which Habermas is here concerned to guard against is that of hypostatization, not 'technicism'. It is this that enables him to make a concession to positivism which in view of his general position is puzzling. For on hypostatization Habermas has seen what is obviously true, namely, that to say that something is the case does not imply that it always must be.

We can now also clear up another puzzle. It will be recalled that critical theorists reject positivist social science as 'ideological', that is, as both false, and also immoral because supportive of an immoral system. It is easy enough to see how a technical social science, as conceived by the Frankfurt theorists and their followers, commits the second of these two sins, but it is not so easy to see in what sense it is false or as Habermas puts it 'illusory'[47] (if it were illusory, it would not provide effective means of manipulation and repression). However, if the concept of technical social science also includes, however inconsistently, the hypostatization of the actual, one may understand how Habermas has arrived at his position. For to assert the unchangeability of what can in fact be changed is indeed to assert what is false.

At this point it is worth looking more deeply into the notion of technique, for it is, I think, more complex than the critical theorists have realized, and a further analysis can point up the contrast between technicism and hypostatization. The standard formula for a scientific law is 'Whenever A, B' or 'All As are B'. Such a law is, however, not in itself technical — i.e. capable of technical application. Technical applicability requires that both A and not-A are possible, and that we have (or could have) control over whether A or not-A is the case. But more than this is required. There must also be some not-A, the existence of which we can ensure, which is universally conjoined with not-B. If we call this not-A, C, we require some law, 'Whenever C, not-B', such that we have control over whether C is the case. By manipulating these *two* laws, 'Whenever A, B', and 'Whenever C, not-B', we can control B. This seems to be essential to technical control in relation to B.

An important point is not all laws 'Whenever A, B' are such that the condition of technical control in relation to B can occur. A may be completely general, so that no case of not-A is possible. The law 'Whenever A, B' then reduces to 'B is always the case', or 'Not-B is impossible'. A law such as this can be called an absolute impossibility law (to be contrasted with laws of technical control).[48] Many of the most basic laws of theoretical physics are of this kind, for example the law of conservation of energy (non-conservation of energy is impossible) or the law that nothing travels faster than light. Here the A of 'Whenever A, B' covers all possible situations whatever. This further supports the contention that natural science is not simply technical in its essence.

Now if the A of the above formulation is not *completely* general, but is the existence of any *society* whatever, and B is some social phenomenon, the formula yields what may be called an absolute *social* impossibility law. The complaint of hypostatization levelled against positivist or scientistic social theory amounts in part to a charge that it leads to illegitimate assertion of social impossibility laws. Examples of such laws might be 'All societies are stratified' (= 'Social equality is impossible'); 'All societies are oligarchical' (hence, 'Democracy is impossible'). But even if such laws are not universally true, I do not think that they need be a hypostatization of the actual. For we have learnt from Popper to treat all scientific laws as hypotheses which we should make every effort to falsify. Impossibility laws need be no exception. Every attempt, therefore, to establish social equality or democracy (both vague concepts which would of course have to be more precisely formulated) is, on Popper's philosophy of science, a legitimate effort to falsify the corresponding impossibility law. Conversely, the fact that we continue to try to establish social equality or democracy or any other social form does not imply that we purge social theory of impossibility laws. Social impossibility laws, thus understood, would be clearly a part of social *theory* only: they would not determine social *practice* (engineering or technique) but would be tested by it.

4. We have still to consider an important element of the charge that positivist social science hypostatizes the actual, namely that it pays no attention to what ought to be the case. This of course is because it abstains from value-judgements, or more accurately because on this view of knowledge value-judgements cannot constitute part of a science (no matter how much, according to Weber's allegedly quasi-positivist position, they may guide the direction of enquiry and the conceptualization of social reality). Value-judgements themselves are, according to positivism and to Weber, irrational or at least non-rational, at any rate 'merely subjective' — they have no objective truth-value. According to the critical theorists this is not only an error but a dangerous error. For, in the first place, it makes the whole process of social decision-making fundamentally irrational, a matter of arbitrary decisions among equally irrational alternatives. Why, then, worry too much about social decision-making procedures? If there are elections, why should they not take the form of manipulation of electorates by 'charismatic' leaders served by technical social scientists — as indeed they do, according to Habermas and Marcuse, in advanced capitalist society?[49] And, if only technique is knowledge, should not political decisions be taken by technical experts, 'policy scientists' as Fay calls them, and removed from the area of public debate? — this too occurs in

advanced capitalist society, says Habermas.[50]

There are worse sins to be laid at the door of the positivist ideal of value-free social science. According to Marcuse, positivism so defines the nature of things 'as to justify repression and even suppression as perfectly rational'.[51] Horkheimer imagines a society in which men's 'intellectual development is retarded by . . . propaganda and they are driven out of their wits by horror and fear. . . Their country would resemble both an insane asylum and a prison'. Yet of such a society (clearly Horkheimer is describing Nazi Germany) positivist social scientists would agree that 'everything is in order'. Such a value-free social science will be welcome to 'powerful economic forces [which] expect the scientist to provide the technical means for perpetuating the established order'.[52] Marcuse holds, similarly, that Weber's value-freedom doctrine is in fact a deliberate attempt to set social science free to accept valuations imposed from outside, namely those of national power politics. This value-freedom is 'mere appearance', a sham.[53]

At this point one must protest, not only that Marcuse's account of Weber is a travesty, but also, more generally, that if, according to positivism, science can offer no objection to the various social forms, institutions and processes that the Frankfurt theorists dislike, neither can it in any way justify them. Perhaps, though, the doctrine that science can offer no objection to them is bad enough by itself. As Marcuse puts it, this unscientific character of values 'fatally weakens opposition to the established reality'. Positivism, even if its adherents wish to combat reactionary powers, 'succumbs to helpless relativism, thus promoting [these] very powers'.[54]

But even if this is so, it does not show that values are rationally knowable and therefore a part of science. How do the Frankfurt theorists come by their supposed knowledge of rational values (or of 'human essence', as Marcuse and Horkheimer might put it)? This question causes Marcuse a good deal of perplexity. Sometimes he takes the view that rational values must be known through historical trends: historical conditions 'determine the truth, the cognitive value of [metaphysical] propositions'. Furthermore, 'speculations about the Good Life, the Good Society . . . obtain an increasingly realistic content . . . the metaphysical tends to become physical'.[55] I take this to mean that the ideal tends to become real, which would be nice if it were true. But is it not a shade optimistic to assume so? In the end, Marcuse agrees: even in the absence of historical forces that can move society towards more freedom 'the critique of society would still be valid and rational [although] incapable of translating its rationality into terms of historical practice'.[56] Ultimately, Marcuse's knowledge of rational values comes not from history but from his own head.

What, anyway, *are* these rational values? Among those offered by Marcuse are freedom, beauty, peace, justice, satisfaction of human needs, and abolition of misery, violence, and cruelty.[57] An excellent, if platitudinous, list, but, as it stands, a little vague. What exactly are freedom, beauty, justice, human needs? I fear that politicians or citizens trying to use these values as their criteria in practical decision-taking would not find them sufficient. Do they, for example, imply that free abortion should be available on demand? That pornography should or should not be suppressed by law? That those who will not work should not eat? And so forth. It is when one gets down to details and to practical applications that the real problems arise, and that reasonable men may differ. Problems arise, in particular, because of conflicts between different values, and between the interests of different individuals — a fact which the Frankfurt theorists show no sign of appreciating.

Habermas has a different approach to the problem of rational values. For him the basic value is expressed in German as *Mündigkeit*, which can roughly be translated as 'individual autonomy' (with connotations of freedom and equality). How do we know that these are values? One answer that Habermas gives is that these values express one of humanity's 'knowledge-constitutive interests' from which 'with transcendental necessity' we apprehend reality — just like the technical interest, this 'emancipatory cognitive interest' corresponds to an inescapable human need, and provides a viewpoint from which our knowledge must be structured.[58] Yet the two cases do not seem to be parallel. Without technical knowledge, men could not live. Without *Mündigkeit*, they can and (as Habermas would agree) frequently, indeed usually, have done.

Habermas has another argument to show the objective *a priori* nature of the value of *Mündigkeit*, which has to do with the conditions for rational discussion and agreement in any sphere, including the technical/scientific. As Habermas puts it, the very structure of language, 'expresses unequivocally the intention of universal and unrestricted consensus' — a consensus possibly only in an emancipated society. That is, rational agreement presupposes discussion among free and equal persons, and therefore an emancipated society free from repression and domination.[59] But this argument is also unconvincing. That rational discussion is by definition free discussion does not imply that rational discussion is impossible unless everyone is free (whatever precisely, in a broader social context, that means). And the objective value-judgement that Habermas wants to establish is that everyone must be free.

5. It is now time to consider the kind of social theory favoured by the Frankfurt theorists and their followers, so-called critical theory or critique. One of the charges against positivist social theory that comes under the category of hypostatizing the actual is that a merely descriptive, non-critical sociology cannot explain the phenomena it discovers. Marcuse, as well as the authors of the Frankfurt textbook, makes this charge: a purely descriptive social science cannot 'comprehend', 'recognize the facts for what they are'. 'In social theory, recognition of facts is critique of facts'.[60] If one is puzzled as to why social facts cannot be

explained or comprehended unless they are criticized, the answer implicit in the Frankfurt position seems to be this: existing social reality is (almost always) bad, therefore a theory explaining that reality must be a theory which explains why it is bad, which discovers who or what (what underlying structure, for example) is to *blame* for the badness of social reality, and what therefore needs to be changed in order to improve it. Marxism, as understood by the critical theorists, is such a social theory.

Critical theory is not only a pinning of the blame, an identification of the structures that make social reality bad, it is also the critique of illusory beliefs about society, of ideology. Above all this takes the form of revealing the possibilities for changing existing society, possibilities that ideology conceals. This, in turn, is expected to free men's consciousness from 'dependence on hypostatized powers' (Habermas). For Habermas indeed, if this is achieved — if the oppressed freely accept the analysis of the critical theorist — then the critical theory is confirmed.[61] The theory does not 'prejudge the action of those concerned', it only enlightens them as to the past and present. But this scarcely seems sufficient. For if those concerned take no action to alter that *status quo* alleged by critical theory to be alterable, then its alterability is not confirmed, and therefore the critical theory is not confirmed. Other critical theorists have been more willing to accept the implications of this. Horkheimer admits that 'the proof of the pudding is in the eating', i.e. the future coming about of the change at which the critical theory aims.[62] For Brian Fay, also, critical theory includes predictions about 'the ways in which social conditions will change'.[63] Again, according to David Harvey, verification of theories is achieved through practice; what he calls 'revolutionary theory' has the function of stimulating revolutionary practice which, when it succeeds, verifies the theory; as he also puts it, revolutionary theory identifies choices that are immanent in existing reality, and the implementation of these choices validates the theory.[64]

To summarize. Critical theory starts from the perception that existing society is bad, explains why it is bad, shows how it can be made good, and predicts that it will be made good (or at least it seems logically committed to this prediction). If we accept the value-judgements involved here as legitimate, though not as 'scientific', only the last, predictive, element of this 'critique' differs from so-called technical social science. In the natural world, as well as the social we may find certain states of affairs unsatisfactory (e.g. infertility of the soil), seek an explanation of why they exist and, through technology, discover a remedy for them. What neither natural science not technology could justify is a prediction that the remedy will be applied. The predictive element in critical theory is prophecy, in Popper's sense.

Finally, one may ask how the critical theorists envisage that the changed society that they look for would come about. They are not, in fact, agreed on this. Habermas, for example, has advocated 'radical reformism',[65] whereas Marcuse is a leading contemporary exponent of revolution[66] — and here as elsewhere Harvey seems to be in agreement with him (and, indeed, with the original Marxist position of the Frankfurt School[67]). It is worth pondering the fact that critical theorists could endorse efforts to change society by revolutionary methods — that is, through large-scale conflict, widespread death and destruction, and so on. Is it not breath-taking that anyone who objects as passionately as do the critical theorists to technical social science, on the grounds that it involves manipulation of human beings, should have no scruples against the use of revolutionary means to bring about the society he desires? For that would be to use revolution as technique — a technique to bring about that desired society. That would indeed be technique with a vengeance.

Notes

1   Cf. T. W. Adorno, 'Introduction' to *The Positivist Dispute in German*

Sociology, Trans. G. Adey and D. Frisby (London, 1976): 'Positivism ... specifically lends itself ... to ideological abuse.' 'Positivism [is] a political fact. Its categories are latently the practical categories of the bourgeois class.' (pp. 30 and 57).

2   'The Latest Attack on Metaphysics' in M. Horkheimer, *Critical Theory* (New York, 1972), p. 159.

3   'Traditional and Critical Theory' in M. Horkheimer, *op. cit.*, pp. 196-7.

4   See, for example, J. Habermas, *Knowledge and Human Interests* (London, 1972), Ch. 2.

5   Cf. H. Marcuse, 'Industrialization and Capitalism in Max Weber' in *Negations* (London, 1972), pp. 203-5; also B. Fay, *Social Theory and Political Practice* (London, 1975), p. 44.

6   Cf. J. Habermas, *op.cit.*, p. 61 and *passim*.

7   See 3, above.

8   Cf. H. Marcuse, *One-Dimensional Man* (London, 1968), Ch. 6; J. Habermas, *op.cit.*, pp. 191 ff. (the German word *Technik* on p. 194 I have rendered as 'technique').

9   *Op.cit.*, pp. 31-43.

10 *Op.cit.*, p. 162.

11 *Op.cit.*, pp. 69, 135, 305, 307-9.

12 *Op.cit.*, p. 302-3, 308.

13 *Op.cit.*, ch. 6.

14 *Op.cit.*, pp. 120-4.

15 *Op.cit.*, pp. 116, 125, 128-9, 194.

16 Cf. H. Marcuse, *One-Dimensional Man*, Ch. 6; J. Habermas, *Toward a Rational Society* (London, 1971) pp. 106-7, 111-8, and *Knowledge and Human Interests*, p. 316; M. Horkheimer, *Critical Theory*, pp. 159-60, 193-6.

17 Cf. M. Weber, *Methodology of the Social Sciences* (Glencoe, 1949), pp. 21-2, 72-82.

18 Cf. H. Marcuse, *One-Dimensional Man*, pp. 38, 41; J. Habermas, *Toward a Rational Society*, pp. 62, 75.

19 *One-Dimensional Man*, pp. 13, 20.

20 *One-Dimensional Man*, pp. 25-6, 34, 66, 93.

21 *Toward a Rational Society*, p. 117.

22 Cf. H. Marcuse, *One-Dimensional Man*, pp. 26, 35, 52-4; J. Habermas, *Toward a Rational Society*, pp. 100-102; D. Harvey, *Social Justice and the City* (London, 1973), p. 148; B. Fay, *op.cit.*, p. 46.

23 Cf. *Knowledge and Human Interests*, pp. 42-63.

24 Cf. *The Poverty of Historicism* (London, 1961), pp. 45-52, 73.

25 *Toward a Rational Society*, pp. 85-8.

26 Cf. *Critical Theory*, pp. 205, 216, 240.

27 Quoted in G. Therborn, 'The Frankfurt School', *New Left Review*,

No. 63, Sep.-Oct., 1970, p. 83.

28 *One-Dimensional Man*, p. 114.

29 *Social Justice and the City*, pp. 126-7.

30 'Who Needs the Liberation of Nature?', *Science Studies*, Vol. 4, 1974, pp. 89-90.

31 *Op.cit.*, p. 88.

32 *One-Dimensional Man*, p. 183.

33 In 'Interest and objectivity', *Philosophy of the Social Sciences*, Vol. 2, 1972, p. 204.

34 *Toward a Rational Society*, p. 99.

35 *Knowledge and Human Interests*, pp. 195 and 313.

36 Cf. B. Fay, *op.cit.*, pp. 41-2.

37 Discussed in W. Leiss, *The Domination of Nature* (New York, 1972), pp. 105-11.

38 'Rationalism Divided in Two' in A. Giddens, *Positivism and Sociology* (London, 1974), p. 205.

39 *Liberation and the Aims of Science* (London, 1973), p. 167.

40 *Op.cit.*, p. 148.

41 *Op.cit.*, p. 58.

42 *Dialectic of Enlightenment* (London, 1973), pp. 23, 26, 28.

43 *Aspects of Sociology* (London, 1973), pp. 7, 11.

44 Cf. 'The Concept of Essence' in *Negations*, and *One-Dimensional Man*, pp. 86, 106 ff.

45 pp. 98-101.

46 *Knowledge and Human Interests*, pp. 308-10.

47 *Knowledge and Human Interests*, p. 316. See also *One-Dimensional Man*, p. 93, where positivist/technical social science is called 'ideological' and 'false'.

48 As Mr Hugh Mellor pointed out to me, all scientific laws are, in a sense, impossibility laws. A technical law 'Whenever A, B', states conditions under which not-B is impossible, and may be called a *conditional* impossibility law.

49 Cf. *Toward a Rational Society*, pp. 62-3, 67-8, 75, and 'Industrialization and Capitalism in Max Weber', *Negations*, pp. 217-19.

50 Fay, *op.cit.*, pp. 14, 26-8, 61; Habermas, *Toward a Rational Society*, pp. 103-5.

51 *One-Dimensional Man*, p. 122.

52 *Critical Theory*, pp. 160, 178.

53 'Industrialization and Capitalism in Max Weber', *Negations*, pp. 202-9, 215.

54 Marcuse, *One-Dimensional Man*, p. 123; *Negations*, p. 45.

55 *One-Dimensional Man*, p. 181.

56 *One-Dimensional Man*, p. 199.

57 *One-Dimensional Man*, pp. 170, 175, 181-3, 185-6.

58 *Knowledge and Human Interests*, pp. 191-8, 212, 308 ff.
59 *Knowledge and Human Interests*, pp. 314, 317.
60 *One-Dimensional Man*, p. 101.
61 Cf. Habermas, *Knowledge and Human Interests*, p. 310; and *Theory and Practice* (London, 1974), pp. 37-9.
62 *Critical Theory*, pp. 220-1.
63 *Op.cit.*, pp. 99-100.
64 *Op.cit.*, pp. 11-12, 125, 136 ff., 150.
65 *Toward a Rational Society*, p. 49.
66 Cf. Marcuse, 'Ethics and Revolution', in R.T. de George, *Ethics and Society* (New York, 1966); and *An Essay on Liberation* (London, 1972), p. 61. Mr Vinit Haksar kindly drew my attention to the former.
67 Cf. 'Traditional and Critical Theory' in *Critical Theory*, especially pp. 213-6, 219, 225-6.

5. Lessnoff's Critique of Critical Theory
by David Papineau

I am afraid that I find myself in the position all too familiarly bemoaned by commentators on conference papers. That is, I am in large measure of agreement with the original contributor. If you were to place me on the philosophical spectrum between critical rationalism and critical theory I would be closer to the former than the latter end. Though not, I think, quite as close as Lessnoff. It might seem, then, that it would have been a better arrangement for an accredited sympathiser of critical theory, to take initial issue with Lessnoff, and for me to have been cast in his role as a mediator.

But perhaps the arrangement is not all that bad. Part of what has prevented us, in the analytic tradition, from coming properly to grips with critical theory has simply been the immense distance separating our basic (and often unarticulated) philosophical presuppositions from their's. Debates between the committed and the sceptical on the merits of critical theory almost invariably collapse for lack of common ground. Maybe it will prove easier to span the gap if we proceed by stages. So what I shall do is to try to point out why, even from my standpoint, it seems that Lessnoff is too quick to dismiss the 'Frankfurt' critique of technique, and to explain what truth I find in this critique.

I shall consider three related questions. Firstly (and briefly, for here I disagree with Lessnoff not at all), does the practical application of nomological knowledge in the social realm necessarily involve political domination and manipulation? Second, should we deny a 'cognitive monopoly' to such 'technical' knowledge, modelled on the theories of the natural sciences? And finally, does an interest in

117

the emancipation and transformation of society (and man) require that we transcend the 'technical' approach?

1.   Lessnoff answers 'no' to the first question. His position is clear enough. Political decisions, like any others, are consequent on a certain range of *ends*, together with some (putative) *knowledge*, in the form of generalisations, about what *means* are, in the circumstances, most likely to achieve those ends. Values have to come in only at the level of political ends. Given the ends, the consequent choice of policies can be made quite impartially by reference to those social scientific theories that the factual evidence best supports. (And, indeed, for anybody who *does* want to achieve those ends, it would not serve him to make the choice in any other way.)

But is there not something a bit glib about this aseptic view of the influence of technical information on political choice? It is scarcely deniable that there is a marked 'decisionism' about many modern social choices. National policies everywhere are primarily directed towards economic growth. When attention is paid to such things as working conditions, the ecology, or even the actual distribution of GNP, it is, usually, merely insofar as they are instrumentally relevant to the primary aim of growth. Individual enterprises, public and private, also seem generally to aim at maximizing some simple quantity, be it profits, votes, viewers, or arrests, and to ignore such things as the quality of experience or the opportunities for self-determination given to the people involved in their running. And such 'optimizing' policies, based on quantified nomological theories, are often presented as being quite impartial, as based entirely on objective scientific considerations.

These observations lend considerable weight to the view that the use of technical social science implies an illegitimate restriction of the basis of political and social choice. And, in particular, that it leads to a situation where, under the guise of scientific objectivity, decisions are surreptitiously made in favour of the interests of the decision-making or ruling class, and against the real needs of the majority.

However, it is still by no means clear that the blame for this real and regrettable tendency in modern society is to be laid at the door of either the acceptance of technical theories, or the general strategy of choosing policies by reference to such theories. That the aims relevant to political choices are illegitimately restricted, and that this is defended in the name of 'objective science', is something to be condemned and altered. But this is a political point, not an epistemological one. The trouble still lies with the initial selection of ends, and the defence of that selection, not with what happens thereafter. And it is still true that if we do come to a time where we succeed in getting people's real needs onto the political agenda, it would be simply irresponsible to try to decide how best to satisfy them other than in the old way, by reference to the technical theories the factual evidence best supports.

2.   We turn now to the second question. No doubt some readers would object that it is only possible for Lessnoff and myself to consider technical social science as value-neutral in itself because we refuse to take seriously the possibility that there might be other modes of knowledge. For if such alternatives are possible, then perhaps what can be exposed as ideological is the general decision to accord a 'cognitive monopoly' to technical science, rather than any subsequent choices made with the help of such science. (This seems to be Habermas' position, in opposition to, say, Marcuse's.)

The critical theorists' view is that technical science is only one kind of knowledge, namely, that oriented towards the technical interest of control. To suppose that it is the only possibility is to make the positivist mistake of supposing that science is somehow 'given' as an unproblematic representation of reality.

Lessnoff's response (p. 101) is to suggest that the critical theorists find it possible so to devalue science only because they themselves take an overly 'positivistic' view of its nature. That is, he thinks they are mistaken to suppose that even natural science is merely a charting of regularities amongst observable phenomena; and he suggests that in actuality science is more concerned to 'understand reality' (including non-observable reality).

Lessnoff's initial point here is one with which I am in entire agreement. There is more to natural science than either positivism or the Frankfurt school makes of it. But I disagree with Lessnoff's further views on the issue at hand. For the deeper question raised by the Frankfurt school still remains, even after we have corrected their characterization of natural science. Namely, does natural science have exclusive access to reality?

Lessnoff mentions an 'aesthetic or even moral' impulse behind the natural sciences. Even if this explains the historical development of the natural sciences, it scarcely serves to *justify* their representation of reality over any alternatives. Nor does it do, in this context, to simply avow a 'realist' philosophy of science (p. 101). What is at issue is precisely the validity of such a philosophy of science.

We can imagine a spectrum of possible methodological attitudes towards systems of thought and their development: at one end we have the 'naïve falsificationist' who insists that we deal only with theory-neutral observable concepts and that we reject our hypotheses whenever we observe counter-examples; at the other end there is the pure metaphysician whose theories are couched in terms unconnected with observable reality, or in terms so heavily theory-dependent that apparent counter-examples can always be explained away by re-interpreting the observations.

What recent writers in the analytic tradition (like Hanson, Kuhn, Feyerabend and Lakatos) have shown, is that, *contra* the logical positivists and the Frankfurt school, natural science is by no means unequivocally at the former end of the spectrum. Rather it falls somewhere in between the two poles — the natural scientist is characteristically committed to some account of non-observable reality which then plays an essential role in his interpretation of observations, though at the same time he does not go so far as to seal his hypotheses off from the empirical data altogether.

To digress briefly, it is significant that this theoretical impregnation of all natural scientific concepts narrows the gap between natural science as it is actually practised and the critical theorists' conception of other forms of knowledge. In particular the 'circle' which is said to characterize hermeneutic understanding (that interpretation of actions requires prior knowledge of culturally specific meanings, which knowledge can only be derived from interpretations of actions) is mirrored in natural scientific investigation (the description of natural phenomena presupposes scientific theory, which can only be derived from descriptions of natural phenomena). This blurring of the gap between 'empirical-analytic' and 'hermeneutic' understanding calls in question a number of further strands in critical theory. In particular, it goes some way towards defending natural scientific methods from the accusation that they preclude a grasp of intentions, desires and meanings and the consequent notion of human need.

But let us stick to the immediate point. Once we allow that there is a range of possible methodological attitudes to systems of thought then we cannot avoid the question: what decides which methodological attitude is adopted; and, in particular, what makes it appropriate to adopt the natural scientific attitude, which combines an interest in unobservable reality with a definite concern to make current hypotheses responsive to new empirical data? We cannot in this context just *presuppose* that the standards of natural science are a uniquely priviledged specification of what counts as an accurate representation of empirical reality. To simply take a 'realist' philosophy of science for granted is to succumb to the 'objectivist illusion' that the Frankfurt school detects in positivism.

Consider the case of a theory whose basic hypotheses are completely immunized from revision under empirical pressure. An example might be a traditional African theory of witchcraft. The central tenets of such a belief system are notoriously protected from revision by a barrage of devices for explaining away unexpected results. As such it is not a satisfactory scientific theory. But the objection cannot be that it is straightforwardly contradicted by the empirical data. The 'second-guessing' devices are built into the theory precisely to avoid any such straightforward contradictions. If we are to object, we cannot simply appeal to the empirically given, but must rather point to the empirical degeneracy of the theory, to the lack of even the most minimal level of experimental testability of basic assumptions, etc. In doing so we are invoking standards which transcend any general and unelaborated appeal to 'reality' or 'truth'. So we are stuck with the problem: what does justify those standards?

As pointed out above, Lessnoff's 'aesthetico-moral' impulse, at best, only serves to give a historical explanation of the adoption of natural scientific standards. Once we allow ourselves to ask about the *justification* of the techniques of natural science it is difficult to avoid the diagnosis of critical theory. If our primary concern is the contrast between natural science and 'unrestrained and uncontrolled speculation' (p. 103), then surely the justification for choosing the former has to be that it serves the technical interest better; that is, that it better allows prediction and control. For what distinguishes natural science is that it adds to a general metaphysical concern the desire to have theories which account for and tally with the empirical data in the most precise and informative way possible.

What then of the application of the natural scientific attitude to the social realm?

Here there seems to me to be an even closer link between the rules of science and the technical interest. I have argued that in the natural realm the technical interest justifies the scientific attitude, even if it does not explain its historical emergence. In the social realm, by contrast, it seems to me to do both.

What I have in mind here is the phenomenon, first pointed to by Weber, that with the increasing complexity and bureaucracy of modern industrial society there is an increasing need to anticipate and control social activities. The behaviour of such things as costs, demand, discontent, output, etc. are all crucial to the running of complex enterprises. Without the ability to 'calculate' such relevant factors it would be impossible for the large-scale organizations characteristic of modern society to function at all. I would argue (though this is scarcely the place) that in consequence there is a close historical link between the emergence of modern industrial society and attempts to develop precise, empirical theories in the social sciences.

The significance of this for our present subject is this. Those forms of social organization that call forth a technical social science are just those which institute a split between those that administrate and those that are administered, between the controllers and the controlled. It is here that we find the real explanation of the characteristic tendency, mentioned earlier, for social choices in modern society to be oriented to a systematically restricted range of ends. Insofar as the choices concerned are entirely in the hands of a particular section of society, those choices are likely to be directed towards the interests of that section rather than those of the general population. The possibility of them presenting those choices as being based purely on objective and scientific considerations naturally serves to accentuate this tendency.

It is no repudiation of this point to draw attention (as Lessnoff does) to those special cases, such as the expansion of public expenditure to reduce unemployment, where the result aimed at is unequivocally in the general interest. It is scarcely convincing to maintain that such instances are in the majority; and in any case it will often be possible to account for such satisfactions of the public good as incidental or instrumental to the achievement of some other end.

Still, even given all this, it would be a mistake to concur with the Frankfurt school's blanket condemnation of social scientific knowledge oriented towards the technical interest. For we have still not shown that 'technique' is, in any serious sense, evaluatively supportive of systems of domination and oppression. We can allow that just those social formations that call into being technical social science simultaneously hand over the resulting power to sectional interests, and that as a matter of historical fact it is therefore more likely to be used for bad than general good. But this does not establish any intrinsic link between its epistemological status and its social effects. For nothing said so far rules out the logical possibility of a situation where technical social science would be used for the good. And in such a situation good would still better be served the more technical was that science.

To sum up: even if we allow, with critical theory, that technical methods are to be justified, if at all, by reference to the technical interest, and even if we recognize also that, historically, when technical methods are applied to the social realm they are likely to be used for domination, it still does not follow that technical social sciences are *necessarily* on the side of oppression. (Of course, to point to an abstract possibility is not to solve any practical problems. But it would take me too far afield to pursue the political questions here.)

3. I shall use the remaining space to make a few brief comments on the third question raised by Lessnoff's paper: whether technical social science necessarily 'hypostatizes the actual'. Again, I agree with Lessnoff's general stance, but have some reservations about the arguments.

Lessnoff finds an inconsistency in the Frankfurt school's adding this new charge to the original complaint of 'technism'. His reason is that a social scientific theory cannot simultaneously add to the ruling class's power to *control* society *and* present social *change* as impossible.

While this is true enough of a *particular* social scientific generalization, it is surely quite possible for different theories, or even different bits of the same theory, to do both jobs at once. That is, one can have certain beliefs about how certain small social changes can be effected, yet have other beliefs implying that large social changes are impossible. Indeed Lessnoff's Popperian preference for piecemeal social innovations over holistic ones seems to embody a generalized version of just such a position. Incidentally, another strand in his Popperism leads Lessnoff to deny that the acceptance of 'social impossibility laws' should preclude attempts to change society, on the grounds that we should try our hardest to falsify what we hypothesize. As far as I can see, he seems to end up in the rather uncomfortable position that we are not justified in attempting to instigate large-scale social change unless we think it won't work.

However, I am with Lessnoff in not seeing any reason why technical social science should necessarily be guilty of 'hypostatizing the actual'. Of course the dominant social theory in a given society will frequently be such that it presents existing social arrangements as superior in various respects to possible alternatives, when in fact the evidence does not bear out that claim. But such a tendency, perhaps resulting from systematic institutional pressures, is objectionable precisely because it *fails* to conform to the standards of technical science. (If the evidence actually *did* show alternative societies to be inferior to the *status quo*, then we should do well to believe it).

Perhaps there is another thought at the basis of critical theory's objection. Rather than the possibility of such superficial distortion, it is technique's supposed refusal to treat of desires, intentions and needs, and its consequent inability to expose the contradictions in society that critical theorists see as forcing it to ignore what *should* be for what *is*.

If technical methodology did indeed preclude any grasp of the mental realm then I think this latter argument would be incontrovertible. Even if a clear split between fact and value is insisted on, it still remains true that a practically oriented science ought at least to be 'value-relevant', in the sense of indicating how the (independently adopted) values can be achieved. A technical social science which disavowed any competence to treat of the mental would indeed imply that we were powerless to do anything about just those things most central to our values.

This is a line of thought that might well appeal to those in the Anglo-American tradition who refuse to identify reasons with causes. One would expect analytic philosophers who see the mental as intractable to scientific analysis to be sympathetic to the view that nomological science cannot help to uncover and remedy the wrongs in existing societies.

Be that as it may, once it is recognized, as I suggested earlier, that there is no essential incompatibility between the methods of the natural sciences and the investigation of the mental realm, the objection to technique collapses. If the difference between theories in the natural sciences and our general framework of thinking about human action and thought is, as I believe, merely a quantitative matter of difference in empirical rigour, then there is no bar to technical social science uncovering the real ailments of society and showing what is to be done about them.

6. Towards a Reconstruction of Critical Theory
by Karl-Otto Apel

On reading Lessnoff's paper, I realized with some surprise to what extent my own approach is still associated with the *genius loci* of Frankfurt University, such that I feel addressed, and even challenged, as regards almost all my own tenets, by Lessnoff's critique of the so-called 'Frankfurt School'. Before trying to make some comments on that critique, though, I must remark that I feel neither obliged nor entitled to defend specific neomarxist positions as held by the classical Frankfurt School, say by Horkheimer and Adorno, or by Herbert Marcuse. I would, however, like to defend, largely with Habermas and against Lessnoff, the epistemological (transcendental-pragmatic) conception of three fundamental cognitive interests as the basis for a differentiated philosophy of scientific methods and their different possible relations to human praxis.

With regard to the specific positions of the so-called 'Frankfurt School', I would characterize my own position rather as one of participation (perhaps as an outsider) in the critical reconstruction of the philsophical foundations of 'Critical Theory'. By the label 'Transcendental Pragmatics' (which largely corresponds to what Habermas calls 'Universal Pragmatics', as may be seen from our discussion-volume *Sprachpragmatik und Philosophie* (Frankfurt: Suhrkamp, 1976), I would stress, in this context, the fundamental philosophical character of my own possible contribution to that critical reconstruction. This means, in my opinion, that a certain dissociation (or disentanglement) of epistemological, and, for that matter, also of ethical, problems and tenets from all, too-special sociological, political and historical doctrines of

Marxist provenance has to be carried out before the way to specific Marxist consequences, or alternative ones, may be traced afresh within the context of the refounded programme of critical reconstructive social science.

Thus, for example, I would not agree with the position of Horkheimer, apostrophized by Lessnoff, that understanding the significance of natural science is fundamentally, and hence primarily, a matter of a social history of modern capitalism, so that, instead of philosophical epistemology, social history could adequately account for the cognitive validity of science by reducing it to being just a moment in the rationalized social process of production that belongs to the economic system of capitalism. I think one may fully recognize that modern capitalism was a crucial empirical condition, i.e. *external* causal stimulation, for the rise of a technologically relevant, natural science, and yet, nonetheless, reject Horkheimer's position as a sociologistic-historistic overstatement, which jeopardizes the universal truth-claim of science and hence also of Marxist social history as a science.

This much criticism of the older position of the Frankfurt School is, in my opinion, a consequence of the position of Habermas and myself, according to which the universal truth-claim of scientific knowledge, which can be implemented only within the framework of an argumentative discourse that is unburdened from practical interests, constitutes the point of unity of all types of science. This position, however, does not prevent us from simultaneously insisting on the thesis that a methodologically relevant differentiation between types of science (and, I think, even between types of social science) is grounded in the fact that different types of 'objects' of possible scientific experience are constituted by different cognitive-interests. Through their different relations to life-praxis, the knowledge-constitutive interests, in my opinion, comprise an antipole, as it were, to the praxis-unburdened reflection on all types of truth-claims within the framework of argumentative discourse.

The whole structure of a bi-polarized tension and inter-dependence between praxis-engaged meaning- or object-constitution and praxis-unburdened reflection upon validity has to provide a concretized substitute for the unity of object consciousness and self-consciousness which, according to Kant, is involved in the transcendental unity of apperception. In this way we would overcome the theoretician's illusion about traditional epistemology that we could simply set out from the pure cognition of what there is, i.e. of the objective phenomena that are, as it were, 'over there'.

(Kant's and even Husserl's transcentental idealism of a categorial or noetic-noematic apparatus of pure consciousness would be supplemented in two respects: with regard to the problem of meaning- or object-constitution, it would be supplemented and differentiated by the organon of interpretative language-games, functioning according to different cognitive interests as modes of practical world-engagement of consciousness; with regard to the problem of reflection upon validity, it would be integrated into, and concretized through the language-game of argumentative discourse of an indefinite communication-community.)

From this dipolarized (transcendental-pragmatic) foundation of epistemology it follows, in my opinion, that the technical interest that underlies experimental natural science is not only an external empirical interest in application and hence a motive for the rise and development of modern science within the framework of modern capitalism, but, in contradistinction to all socio-economic factors, it is an internal condition for the possibility of experimental physics. And this may be stated, I think, without reducing the truth-claim of theoretical physics to being *nothing but* an ideological veiling of its instrumental value for the domination of nature; although — or better, since — the need for the technical domination of nature or, in other words, the control of the environment *must* provide the view-point from which the physicalist type of true information about nature (or, to speak along with the Popperians, 'deep understanding' of nature) is alone possible. So it seems to me that the well-understood thesis of the technical interest as condition of the possibility of natural science (more precisely, of physics and quasi-physicalistic types of biological and social science) may be defended as a contention that is relevant not only for the so-called 'context of discovery' but also for the 'context of justification' of science. Further, this contention may be maintained without recourse to instrumentalist reductionism, as adopted by W. James, H. Bergson, Nietzsche, M. Scheler and maybe, in some earlier versions of Critical Theory, but not by C. S. Peirce. (I have tried to interpret the position of Peirce as that of 'Sense-critical realism' and the prefiguration of a Transcendental Pragmatics in my book *Der Denkweg von C. S. Peirce*, Frankfurt: Suhrkamp 1975.)

So far as I can see, it is the last-sketched conception of the technical interest as a special knowledge-constitutive interest among three different knowledge-constitutive interests which makes up the fundamental difference between Lessnoff's and my own approach. And since the latter is, after all, very close to Habermas', I will try to show in what follows that many of Lessnoff's points of criticism — even in respect of the older Frankfurt School — are based on misunderstandings that might be dissolved in the light of a deeper reflection upon our different ultimate presuppositions.

1. First I should make clear, that it is not the indeed fallacious conclusion from the human need for technical knowledge and natural science's provision of technical knowledge that provides the crucial argument for the thesis that natural science is information about the world from a technical point of view. Rather, this is provided by the contention that technique, as a type of interest and as a type of praxis, is a necessary condition of the possibility of natural science as experimentally testable knowledge about nature.

Lessnoff comes close to the point, I think, when he remarks that the 'essential' condition for technical control in relation to some state of affairs B is made up by our capability of 'manipulating *two* laws', viz. '"Whenever A, B" and "Whenever C, not-B"'. For this very capability, taken as a conceptual or categorial presupposition of thought, is, in my opinion, the condition for the possibility not only of technique but of experiments and thereby of the theoretical conception of causal laws. Whereas Hume already showed that a relation of causal necessity between two events cannot be detected by passive observation, and whereas Kant rightly postulated that natural scientists must take the initiative by compelling nature, through experiments in the light of categorial view-points, to answer their questions about such things as causal laws, it has been shown in our day (e.g. by G. H. von Wright in his book *Explanation and Understanding*, 1971, ch. II) that the very idea of a causal law, i.e. the concept of a relation of causal necessity between two events A and B, is dependent on our thinking of A and B as belonging to a closed system or world-fragment that can be put in motion by our experimentally producing A. This, in turn, presupposes, in principle, that A and its effect B would not come about but instead of it some other sequence, say 'ω,C', if we did not intervene in nature.

This interventionalist or experimentalist conception of causality may be considered as one paradigmatic hint at the intrinsic connection between technique and experimental, i.e. experimentally testable, theoretical physics. For, again, with regard to astro-physical systems, it is, of course, not possible to theoretically conceive of genuine causal relations without presupposing, in a thought-experiment, that we *could* put them in motion by producing their initial state. Other paradigmatical hints at the *a priori* interdependence of technique and physics have been given in Lorenzen's conception of 'protophysics' as the methodology of the praxis of measurement, and in Bridgman's 'Operationalism', notwithstanding the fact that 'Operationalism', as a reductionist theory of meaning, has to be restricted by the reference-semantical dimension of 'theoretical concepts' and hence of so-called 'deep theories'. The point of a transcendental-pragmatic statement of the technical viewpoint of physical knowledge is not, in my opinion, that the meaning of physical concepts, or even of entire theories, could be reduced to factual technical operations. Rather, it may be expressed by the thesis that the possible meaning of causally (and also statistically) explanatory theories, the more so the greater their onto-semantic depth or truth-content, is *a priori* predetermined by those categories of questions that can be translated into nature's own language through experimental interventions in order to elicit possible answers from nature.

In order to contrast this type of technically prejudiced, natural science against the background of other possible types of knowledge, it is not possible, in my opinion, to conceive of another type of physics. (There may be a rational core to Marcuse's demand for 'another natural science' that might be realized by biological, especially ecological, systems-theory as a non-physicalist type of natural science which conceives of nature not as closed systems to be manipulated by us according to causal laws, but rather as something — e.g. biotop or ecosphere — to which we humans belong by way of sharing in the objective teleology of functional systems.) But the epistemologically crucial alternatives to technically prejudiced natural science (and quasi-physicalistic types of biological and social science) are clearly provided by those sciences (in a broader sense of the term 'science') that spring from the interest in improving communicative understanding between men as subjects of science and from the interest in critically reconstructing the history of human society as an always-counterfactually-anticipated, but never realized, communication-community.

The first of these types, pure hermeneutic science, is clearly distinguished from the language-game of experimental intervention in nature (or human behavioural quasi-nature) by the fact that it asks not for causes, but for reasons or meaning-intentions. Further, it does not presuppose a language-game separating subject and object, but the possibility of a common language between co-subjects. The second type presupposes *both* the subject-co-subject-relation of communicative understanding to be improved by hermeneutic methods *and* the subject-object-relation of causal explanation; but it makes use of the latter presupposition not in terms of a thorough connection of genuine causal laws but rather in terms of a presupposition of regularities based on historically determined human habits of a frozen, quasi- or pseudo-nature, so to speak; and it uses the results of its causal explanations not in the service of social technology, as is done by quasi-physicalistic social science, but in order to provoke the critical-historical self-reflection of the human society, i.e. its reflection upon the hermeneutically opaque parts of its history, in order to make possible thereby a deeper self-understanding of the communication-community.

2.   This re-formulation of the functions of and basic differences between cognitive interests and corresponding types of science leads me to a further point in my argument with Lessnoff. I would like to make an attempt at clarifying the question of *valuing* or *value-freedom* as it is raised by Lessnoff through a comparison between Critical Theory and Max Weber. I think one should, in any case, make a distinction between two levels of the problem which Max Weber, following the neoKantians (Windelband and Rickert), separated out by his terminological distinction between 'valuing' (*'Werten'*) and 'value-relation' (*'Wert-Beziehung'*). Only the latter term, which at least for the neoKantians designates a transcendental problem of object-constitution, marks a problem-level that may be compared with the transcendental-pragmatic problematic of knowledge-constitutive interests. (In fact Windelband already speaks of different *'Erkenntnisinteressen'* in connection with his distinction between the 'idiographic' method of historical understanding and the 'nomothetic' method of natural science.) The

transcendental pragmatics of knowledge-constitutive interests in fact takes the place of the neoKantian combination of a transcendental logic of concept-formation (and methodological classification) and philosophy of (eternally valid) *values*. In fact, it restores the transcendental-epistemological status to the problem of meaning — or object-constitution — as against its psychological-pragmatic reduction to a question of the merely empirically-genetically relevant 'context of discovery' — as it leads from Max Weber's position to that of the analytical logic of science, including Popperian 'logic of scientific discovery'. The difference between, on the one hand, Lessnoff's and, on the other, Habermas' and my own stand with respect to the problem of value-freedom, hangs together, I presume, with the empirical- or transcendental-pragmatic assessment of the epistemological function of meaning-constitution, through cognitive interests.

According to the distinction introduced between problem-levels, I would not claim that the transcendental-pragmatic (i.e. meaning-constitutive) function of cognitive interests shows that all types of science, and hence also of physics as *a priori* technologically relevant science, must be 'valuing', because their objects can indeed only be constituted on the basis of an evaluative human interest or engagement with respect to the world of possible experience. I would claim, rather, that the restitution of the transcendental-epistemological function of '*Wert-Beziehung*' in terms of a transcendental pragmatics of cognitive interests results in the fact that the methodological problem of valuing or, respectively, value-freedom calls for *different* answers for different types of science (and even social science) that correspond to different meaning-constitutive cognitive-interests. Thus, in the case of physics, because the technical cognitive-interest is the precondition for its object-constitution, it follows that, at the methodological level, it must in fact be *value-free*, in Max Weber's sense. Otherwise we would never obtain the information about nature which is useful for its technological control. I think that Bacon expressed the point of this *a priori* relationship of cunning renunciation and recompense very well by his dictum *natura non nisi parendo vincitur*. The same intrinsic relationship between the transcendental-epistemological and the methodological levels holds good in the case of technologically relevant (quasi-physicalistic) social science. On the other hand, in the case of critical-reconstructive (emancipatory) social science our object-constitutive cognitive interest does not allow us to be satisfied by value-neutral descriptions or quasi-nomological explanations of human behaviour in terms of those contingent regularities (e.g. habits) that make up the historically determined, contingent quasi-nature or pseudo-nature of human beings. We are now *a priori* obliged to reconstruct their actions, habits and institutions in an empirically and normatively relevant sense, i.e. to measure their contingent factual behaviour up against not only pertinent, contingent, conventional norms (which are already presupposed by every hermeneutic-descriptive understanding of human actions) but also against universal normative ideals of human competence. With Kant or Peirce, these may be considered as ideal laws of a still to-be-realized human second nature — laws that cannot be falsified because, even in the case of deviant factual behaviour or deviant habits of institutions, they preserve their validity as rational standards of hermeneutical understanding and of possible critique of the contingent, behavioural and institutional facts of human quasi-nature as pseudonature).

Max Weber believed that social scientists should be entitled to reconstruct human behaviour (and even historical progress) by measuring it against ideal standards in only one respect, namely, in respect of means-end-rationality which he considered a matter of intersubjective validity; whereas any further claim to ground the choice of one's ultimate goals by so called 'value-rationality' (which was still maintained by the neoKantians at the level of philosophy) had to be given up as a metaphysical illusion that unmasked and dissolved itself in the same measure as means-ends-rationality was carried through in all sectors of western civilization. (Weber's assessment, incidentally, is one of the great signals for the establishment of the Western, ideological complementarity-system between public scientism-technicism and private existentialism-decisionism.)

It is interesting, in the present context, to note that there is *one* area where Max Weber (implicitly) and K. Popper (explicitly) transgress this border-line between the rational and the irrational or between value-free science and normatively engaged value-judgements. It is not by accident that this area is represented by science and its history. Since the striving for truth as unlimited intersubjective validity is itself the ultimate reason for drawing the border-line between value-free, (i.e. possibly intersubjectively valid), and non-value-free, (i.e. allegedly necessarily subjective), judgements, the history of scientific progress towards unlimited intersubjective validity, i.e. truth, must be excepted from the dichotomy between value-free rationality and non-value-free irrationality. It must be considered as an area of empirical *and* normative, or, from another perspective, of 'external' and 'internal', reconstruction of the realization and prevented realization of a human competence. If one now reflects upon the fact that the historical realization of scientific truth as a norm or ultimate value presupposes, at least as a regulative principle, that some ethical norms or ultimate values must also be realized in the 'community of investigators' (Peirce), one might then come to question Weber's axiom and the Western complementarity-system, according to which ultimate norms or values must be subjective and irrational and hence a rational foundation of ethics and of non-value-free (critical-reconstructive) social science must be impossible.

It can easily be seen that different attitudes with regard to Max Weber's idea of value-free rationality make up the deepest cleavage between, on the one hand, the founders and critical re-constructionists of Critical Theory, and Lessnoff and the predominant philosophy of science, on the other. And it may be shown, in particular, that the distinction made earlier between the ideal norms or laws of a non-realized, human, second nature and the contingent facts (including regularities) of human quasi-nature as pseudo-nature points to the reason why Lessnoff finds difficulties or even paradoxes in the most characteristic themes of the Frankfurt School's criticism of current empirical-analytic, i.e. technologically relevant, methods of social or behavioural science.

3.   Let us consider his puzzlement about the alleged inconsistency between the two accusations of the Frankfurt School against positivist social science, viz. that of 'technicism' and that of 'reification' or 'hypostatization' or, in another version, that of being false or illusory and that of being immoral or supportive of an immoral system. It seems clear to me that the reason for this charge of inconsistency is Lessnoff's presupposition, taken as a matter of common sense, that truth and falsehood in the social scientist's knowledge are unambiguous matters of value-free empirical descriptions or explanations, as is, in fact, the case with regard to the truth and falsehood of natural science. Within the framework of presupposition, Lessnoff obviously cannot imagine that quasi-physicalistic social-science, in contradistinction to physics itself, may lead to true results (in a restricted sense of the term 'true') and nevertheless comprise a moral danger for the true understanding of human potentiality and hence for the realization of that potentiality. Hence he cannot understand either that one may and must hold that 'hypostatization' or 'reification' of human nature are necessary preconditions of manipulative social engineering and hence by no means, as he seems to assume, automatically prevented by social-technical changes in existing states of affairs.

If, however, one takes into account the possibility that

there might be a *difference* between contingent regularities of the historically conditioned quasi- or even pseudo-nature of human beings and their always, still to-be-realized, ideal, second nature (the 'realm of freedom' in terms of Hegel and Marx), then it is not difficult to understand that the descriptive, explanatory and predictive results of technologically relevant empirical-analytic social science may be *true* and *useful* (I would even say *necessary*) within the bounds of their questions. On the other hand, the presuppositions concerning the nature of man implied in those questions might nevertheless be *untrue* and *illusory* and hence lead to the support of immoral, i.e. not legitimizable, social systems, if those questions and their corresponding methods are not compensated for, as it were, or counter-balanced, by other questions and methods of the hermeneutical and critical-reconstructive social sciences.

In my paper on 'Types of Social Science . . .', I have tried to illustrate this point and the related danger of social technological reification, which Lessnoff considers paradoxical, by the problematics of self-fulfilling and self-destroying prophecies. If one sought to avoid these difficulties, for example, by preventing the flow of information between social scientists and their human objects (i.e. 'subject-objects' in terms of a dialectical social philosophy), then one would indeed come close to the situation of subject-object-relation in natural science. In so doing, one would at the same time, tend to support the 'reification' of social relations and institutions *and* facilitate experimental social science and its application in social engineering — *quod erat demonstrandum*, in order to solve Lessnoff's paradox.

Habermas, who, as Lessnoff knows, has advocated 'radical reformism' — more exactly, for all those situations where revolution is not the result of an irresistible movement of the repressed masses — obviously shares Lessnoff's insight that revolution involves a special danger of manipulation of human beings by a revolutionary elite of social engineers (one may think of Lenin, who, presumably, had no other choice!). So Popper, Lessnoff, Habermas and I seem to agree about this point and hence about a policy of reformism. But what still remains 'breath-taking', to use Lessnoff's words, is the curious fact that Popper and Lessnoff still seem to connect the possibility of a reformist policy — I may perhaps be more precise, of a policy toward the realization of the 'open society' with which I would also agree — exclusively with that one type of social (behavioural) science that in a post-industrial society is indeed indispensable as a basis for social engineering but which, after all, involves the constant danger of a technocratic perversion of democracy into technocracy. This point was always puzzling for me and I could only explain it to myself by the conjecture that, due to a certain programme of unified methodology, the Popperians simply could not conceive of another type of social science besides that which I have tried to characterize as a quasi-physicalistic limiting case of social science. Hence, I would assign it a place within the spectrum of possible types of social science.

7. Reply to Papineau and Apel
by Michael Lessnoff

I shall reply to the criticisms of Papineau and Apel under four heads (three are borrowed from Papineau with slight changes). They are:

(1) What is the relation between the 'technical interest' and natural science?
(2) Should we deny a 'cognitive monopoly' to knowledge modelled on natural science?
(3) Does an interest in the transformation of society require that we transcend the technical approach?
(4) Does the technical application of nomological knowledge in the social realm necessarily involve political domination and manipulation?

(1) What is the relation between the 'technical interest' and natural science?

'The technical interest' writes Apel 'is an internal condition of the possibility of experimental physics'. He expands the point as follows: 'technique, as a type of interest and as a type of praxis, is a necessary condition of the possibility of natural science as experimentally testable knowledge about nature.'[1] There is, I believe, a sense in which this is true, but it does not warrant the conclusion that natural science or experimental physics simply *is* knowledge of nature from the viewpoint of mankind's interest in technical control.

Apel rests his argument on the essential role of experimental intervention in the validation of natural scientific knowledge. But let us be clear about this. Scientific experiment is, of course, purposive alteration of the empirically obser-

140

vable world, but it is not thereby *in itself* an application or expression of the interest in technical control (nor do I think that Apel argues that it is). It is not an expression of the interest in technical control, if one manipulates the factor A, in order to test the hypothetical law that 'Whenever A, B,' and for no other purpose; the technical interest is directly in play only if there is also the ulterior purpose to use the knowledge in future to bring about B.

Apel's argument is that, while the technical interest may not directly manifest itself in scientific experimentation, it is a necessary condition thereof. In what sense, if any, is this true? Clearly *not* in the sense of logical necessity. It is clearly not logically necessary that if a person wishes to test the truth of 'Whenever A, B,' he or anyone else wishes to use the knowledge thus gained to bring about B. Nor (and this brings us closer perhaps to the ideas central to Apel's argument) is it logically necessary that, if a community of people ('scientists') wish to test hypothetical knowledge of the form 'Whenever A, B,' anyone wishes to apply, or does apply, or has applied knowledge of this form for purposes of technical control. Thus much for the logical relation. But Apel is not wrong to suggest a structural similarity between experiment and technique — this after all is the condition for the *possibility* of technical application of nomological scientific knowledge, which nobody denies. But the point can be pressed further. We know in fact not only that many people do wish to apply theoretical scientific knowledge technically, but that mankind necessarily and continually manipulates the natural world through nomological knowledge, and did so long before the rise of modern science. It is therefore very likely that, as a matter of the historical evolution of the human intellect, mankind owes its habit of thinking nomologically about the natural world to its interest in technical mastery over it, and that the nomological structure of scientific knowledge is in turn dependent on that habit. In this quasi-causal sense, it may be said that the technical interest is a necessary condition of experimental natural science.

This is a plausible story, and I have no wish to deny it. I have argued only that, as an account of natural science, even of physics, it is not the whole story, it 'is only one aspect of a more complex truth'.[2] The technical interest may be a necessary condition of experimental physics, but it is not a sufficient condition, and therefore not a sufficient account of it. In my paper I briefly indicated other 'human interests' — which might be called cosmological, philosophical or even religious — which are also necessary conditions of natural science, just as much as the technical interest. Neither the structural resemblance between science and technique, nor its consequence, the technical applicability of science, warrants the conclusion that scientific knowledge just *is* knowledge from the viewpoint of the technical interest.

I turn now to Papineau's suggestion that it is our interest in technical control that *justifies* the characteristically scientific approach to knowledge.[3] I would not for a moment dispute that this is a possible justification of science, even a sufficient justification (given that the realization of human purposes is on the whole desirable). But to justify science in this way is not to justify it as *knowledge*; and it is indeed justified as knowledge — knowledge of the empirical world. Even if science led to no increase in technical control of the world, it would be sufficiently justified in this way. More precisely, science is so justified if the following three statements are true: (1) there is an empirical world;[4] (2) knowledge of the empirical world is worth having, for its own sake; (3) the scientific method is well adapted to produce knowledge of the empirical world. I believe that all three statements are true, though (3) requires some further elaboration. The knowledge that science seeks is of an ordered kind, and the order in question is nomological — no doubt for reasons that, as explained above, have some connection with the 'technical interest', even if nomological knowledge is sought for its own sake. Nor is scientific method perfectly adapted to discovering such knowledge, otherwise science would not be a continuing enterprise, and one whose status and presuppositions need constant criticism from philosophers of science. But the fact that fundamental philosophical criticism is part and parcel of the whole scientific enterprise simply underlines the point I wish to make, namely that there is no superior or even alternative route to knowledge of the empirical world — science simply is the rational pursuit of such knowledge. Integral to this rationality is the *critical* attitude of science to its own statements, the habit of taking seriously the possibility that they may be false, and the systematic attempt to test them by comparing them with observation. No other attitude to statements about the empirical world is rational, from the point of view of assessing their truth (that is, their status as knowledge). It is for this reason that science is to be preferred to theories 'whose basic hypotheses are completely immunized from revision under empirical pressure'[5] — not just because of its greater technical efficacy.

(2) Should we deny a cognitive monopoly to knowledge modelled on natural science?

Nothing I have said implies that knowledge modelled on natural science should enjoy cognitive monopoly. Science is the rational method for discovering the nomological ordering of the empirical world, if such a world and such an ordering exist. But even if there is a nomologically ordered empirical world, it is not necessarily the only reality, nor knowledge of it the only knowledge. This is a question I did not address in my paper, and Apel has, I fear, imputed to me views I do *not* hold. I do not hold that no other social science is possible besides that which Apel describes as 'behavioural', 'quasi-physicalistic' and usable 'as a basis for social engineering'.[6] On the contrary, I believe that no understanding of the social is possible without a grasping of its mental dimension, and this I take to be precisely what Apel calls 'hermeneutic science', characterized by the search for reasons and meanings.[7] It is a further question whether social reality, thus grasped, is capable of description in nomological terms. The problem of free will is of course at issue here, about which I can say nothing useful now. Nevertheless, I am considerably more sceptical than either of my critics as to the possibility of nomological social science, at any rate prior to the total physicalistic reduction of the social — a reduction that is not currently in sight, to put it mildly.[8] Apel and the critical theorists must necessarily accept the feasibility of nomological social science, otherwise it could not be the menace they hold it must be. I, on the contrary, believe that if such a science, and corresponding social technology, are possible, they are not intrinsically undesirable. But it does not follow that I must therefore think it undesirable (or impossible) to use social scientific knowledge to provoke critical 'self-reflection' on the part of human societies.[9]

The natural scientific and hermeneutic methods of understanding, while different, have elements in common — both issue in statements in the indicative or subjunctive mood, to which the concept of evidence (for or against) seems clearly relevant, this evidence consisting, ideally, of publicly repeatable experience. More problematic is another putative field of cognition, that of values. Here again Apel attributes to me views I do not hold. It is *not* my opinion that values are (unlike the facts described by natural science) 'subjective and irrational'.[10] My view here is not Humean (or Weberian), but perhaps more nearly Kantian. Moral judgements, certainly, such as 'X is good', 'Y is wrong', are statements, objectively true or false — they are not mere expressions of feelings. However, moral statements and natural scientific statements are radically different from one another. Natural science methods are ultimately irrelevant to the validity of moral judgements — it's not clear that the concept of evidence has any relevance to the latter, or indeed what has. It is in this sense that science (whether physical or hermeneutic) is value-free, while in no sense superior to morality, or a replacement for it. Both science and moral judgement are necessarily involved in any technical application of science, natural or social. But that is not to say that moral judgements can be part of (indeed the basic part of) a special kind of social science, called 'emancipatory'. Moral judgements, though objectively true or false, remain nonetheless inherently controversial — a point I documented, if briefly, in my paper.[11]

(3) Does an interest in the transformation of society require that we transcend the technical approach?

It seems to me clear that there is nothing in the technical approach to social science to hinder the transformation of society — the changes envisaged to be brought about by technique may be on as large a scale as you like, in principle. Apel implicitly admits this when he describes Lenin as a revolutionary social engineer.[12] (Contrary to what Papineau suggests,[13] I did not state any preference for *piecemeal* engineering in my paper.) Nonetheless, both my critics object to my contention that it is inconsistent in the critical theorists to accuse 'positivist social science' of being both technical and a hypostatization of the actual. Papineau points out[14] that it is possible for a body of scientific theory to assert (perhaps truly) that certain small-scale changes can be achieved by certain techniques, and at the same time to assert (perhaps falsely) that large-scale changes are impossible. This is true. But my point is that the latter assertions are not of a technical character, but rather of an anti-technical character (that is, they deny the possibility of bringing about certain changes), and it is their anti-technical character that is, or should be, objectionable from the viewpoint of critical theorists. It seems to me that they have not seen this, and that this is why they think (wrongly) that the kind of social science needed to affect a transformation of society is other than technical.

Social techniques, no doubt, can be used to prevent change, just as much as to bring it about. But one should not confuse the statement 'Change can be prevented in such-and-such a way' (a technical law) with the statement 'Change is impossible' (hypostatization of the actual). I believe Apel does just this in his example about self-fulfilling and self-destroying prophecies.[15] To restrict the flow of information between social scientists and their human objects (potential subject-objects) in order to prevent this information from changing the situation it describes through self-reflection of the subject-objects, is precisely the manipulation of two technical laws to prevent change — the two laws being as follows: 'If certain beliefs are made public, they will provoke change;' and 'If certain beliefs are kept secret, change will be prevented.' Neither of these laws involves hypostatization of the actual; they can be manipulated in a way hostile to change, or favourable to it. Indeed, their manipulation in a way favourable to change seems very similar to the role Apel envisages for critical theory.[16]

(4) Does the technical application of nomological knowledge in the social realm necessarily involve political domination and manipulation?

I suspect that Apel would object to the concluding sentence of the foregoing section, that change resulting from critical self-reflection on existing social structures is an altogether different matter from change brought about by technical manipulation. The former, he might suggest, is a case of free and 'democratic' choice by those affected, while the latter is a case of 'technocratic' control from above.[17] In my opinion, however, there is nothing intrinsically undemocratic or hostile to freedom or 'manipulative', in a sinister sense, in the technical application of nomological social knowledge. 'Technocratic perversion', to use Apel's expression, will arise only if the goals to be achieved, and/or means to be adopted in order to achieve them, are decided by technocrats. This of course is always a danger, but not a danger that arises from the use of social techniques. Even if social goals are determined in a perfectly democratic fashion, there still arises the question of how to achieve them. This decision too could no doubt be taken democratically, but only in the sense of choosing among those means which are likely to achieve the desired result — in other words, choosing which piece of technical social knowledge to apply. For example, the community might decide democratically to try to eliminate unemployment by the use of Keynesian techniques. In sum, the most 'emancipated' society imaginable would still have a use for technical social knowledge. Apel, perhaps, would not deny this, but it appears that some of his fellow critical theorists would.

Notes

1   See above, p. 130.
2   See above, p. 101.
3   See above, p. 122.
4   That is, a world accessible, directly or indirectly, to our senses.
5   See above, p. 121f.
6   See above, p. 139.
7   See above, p. 132
8   My scepticism about nomological social science may mitigate Papineau's surprise that I countenance trying to bring about social changes which, according to someone's hypothesis, are impossible. I do not see that such an hypothesis, even if well-corroborated (which it could scarcely be if no such attempts were made) constitutes a good reason to believe that such an attempt must fail.
9   See above, p. 133.
10   See above, p. 136.
11   See above, p. 110.
12   See above, p. 138.
13   See above, p. 125.
14   See above, p. 125.
15   See above, p. 138.
16   See above, p. 133 and pp. 134-5. N.B. the reference to '*critical -reconstructive* social science'. See also, above, pp. 25-6.
17   See above, p. 139.

PART THREE

RELATIVISM IN SOCIAL ANTHROPOLOGY

8. Pangolin Power
by John Skorupski

1. With magisterial severity, Mary Douglas reproves Durkheim, and the philosophers, for not taking his own insight into (in his words) 'the part of society in the genesis of logical thought' to its conclusion: (IM, pp xi–xii, xvii–xviii)[1]

> Around the beginning of this century Durkheim demonstrated the social factors controlling thought. He demonstrated it for one portion of humanity only, those tribes whose members were united by mechanical solidarity. Somehow he managed to be satisfied that his critique did not apply to modern industrial man or to the findings of science... If Durkheim did not push his thoughts on the social determination of knowledge to their full and radical conclusion, the barrier that inhibited him may well have been the same that has stopped others from carrying his programme through ... [primitives'] knowledge of the world could readily be understood as unanchored to any fixed material points, and secured only by the stability of the social relations which generated it and which it legitimised. For them he evolved a brilliant epistemology which set no limits to the organising power of mind. He could not say the same for ourselves. His other assumption allowed him to reserve part of our knowledge from his own sociological theory. This was his belief in objective scientific truth, itself the product of our own kind of society, with its scope for individual diversity of thought... With one arm he was brandishing the sabre of sociological determinism, and with the other he was protecting from any such criticism the

151

intellectual achievements of his own culture. He
believed in things, in 'the world as it is', in an unvarying reality and truth. The social construction of reality
applied fully to them, the primitives, and only partially
to us. And so, for this contradiction, his central thesis
deserved to remain obscure and his programme unrealized ... then follow his thought through to the bitter
end: we seem to have a thoroughly relativized theory
of knowledge. The boundaries which philosophers
rally instinctively to protect from the threat of relativism would seem to hedge something very sacred. The
volumes which are written to defend that thing testify
to its obscurity and difficulty of access. Relativity
would seem to sum up all the threats to our cognitive
security. Were truth and reality to be made context-
dependent and culture-dependent by relativizing philosophy, then the truth status of that philosophy is itself
automatically destroyed. Therefore, anyone who
would follow Durkheim must give up the comfort of
stable anchorage for his cognitive efforts. His only security lies in the evolution of the cognitive scheme,
unashamedly and openly culture-bound, and accepting
all the challenges of that culture. . . It is part of our culture to be forced to take aboard the idea that other cultures are rational in the same way as ours. Their
organisation of experience is different, their objectives
different, their successes and weak points different
too. . .

Relativism is the common enemy of philosophers
who are otherwise very much at odds with one
another. To avoid its threat of cognitive precariousness, they shore up their theory of knowledge by invest-
ing some part of it with certain authority. For some
there is fundamental reality in the propositions of logic
or in mathematics. For others, the physical world is
real and thought is a process of coming to know that
real external reality — as if there could be any way of

talking about it without preconceiving its constitutive boundaries. . . The disestablishing anthropologist finds in W.V.O. Quine a sympathetic philosopher. Quine's whole 'ontic commitment' is to the evolving cognitive scheme itself. This implies a theory of knowledge in which the mind is admitted to be actively creating its universe. An active theory of knowledge fits the needs of a radicalised Durkheimian theory.

2.   In these striking passages, some points are particularly striking. One is struck, to begin with, by the transition from the 'social determination of knowledge' through the 'social construction of reality' to a 'thoroughly relativised theory of knowledge'. This transition will provide me with my main theme. But first I need to make some initial remarks about relativism; the following sentence from the quoted passage will serve as a starting point: 'Were truth and reality to be made context-dependent and culture-dependent by relativising philosophy then the truth status of that philosophy is itself automatically destroyed'.

Leaving aside for a moment the question whether relativism is to apply to philosophy and thus to itself as a philosophical doctrine, what I find open to objection here is the apparent thought that to relativize the truth values of a corpus of statements is to destroy their truth values altogether. The relativist should certainly deny this, on pain of falling into the absurd consequence that nothing is true or false. This is more than a trivial reminder: any serious account of relativism needs to keep it firmly in view. Relativism is not a view that denies that statements have truth value. It is the view that their truth value is relative: relativized to an overall theoretical framework, a set of core statements, or whatever it may be. The relativist does not deny that the earth is round. Nor does he need to deny — and I think he is well-advised not to deny — that it's true that the earth is round, that in reality it is the case that the earth is round, and so on. So far, then, he is neither to be condemned nor admired for denying that there is such a thing as 'an unvarying reality and truth', or failing to believe in 'the world as it is'. It's just that each of these assertions, that the earth is round, that it's true that the earth is round, that in reality the earth is round, is itself true, relative to whatever it is to which the truth value of all our assertions is relative.

This line of thought can be followed through in such a way that it ends by making relativism a transcendental doctrine, in the sense of being strictly unsayable. Let us consider whether the relativist must apply his thesis to philosophy. If philosophy is narrowly conceived, as a second-order study of our first-order beliefs about the world, then it's not obvious that he must. Why shouldn't relativism be a second-order assertion about the truth-status of first-order assertions? Let us however suppose that philosophy is itself subject to the relativist doctrine: *everything* we say is relativized, including what we say about what we say. What is it relativized to? The core or framework of our thought, to which the content of our thought is relativized, will not itself be something which it makes proper sense to characterize as true or false. It will, rather, provide a set of parameters relative to which the truth value of all assertions within the parameters is, in conjunction with experience, determined. Call this set 'W'; then for any assertion to be true or false is for it to be true or false relative to W. Now what of this last assertion — it is true relative to W? Relativism becomes a transcendental doctrine if one says that the parameters of, or limits on, our thought or language are not something we can think or express *within* the limits of our thought or language: in short, not something we can think or express. For then we can make no sense of a relativized truth predicate, 'true relative to W', which contains a purported reference to them, and so our purported assertion of relativism, which contains this senseless predicate, will itself be senseless, and the question of the assertion's truth value will not arise, no assertion having been made. This kind of relativism is of a piece with the transcendental idealism Bernard Williams has in mind, if I understand him correctly, in his paper on 'Wittgenstein and Idealism' (*Royal Institute of Philosophy Lectures Vol. 7, Understanding Wittgenstein*, London, 1975). It can be said of it, as Wittgenstein said of solipsism, that 'when its implications are followed out strictly, [it] coincides with pure realism' (TLP5.64). But as with the idealism Williams claims to diagnose in the later Wittgenstein, the 'I' of solipsism is, in the form of relativism in question, replaced by 'we'. However the 'we' is, again, transcendental: since the parameters on 'our' thought, to which thought is relativized, are not stateable at all, they cannot be empirically identifiable and therefore stateable features of the thought system of one culture as against another. So we cannot get from this to a relativism according to which 'our', i.e. moderns', thought is relativized to the modern world view and 'their', i.e. primitives', thought is relativized to their world view. For the transcendental thesis asserts or means to assert a relativising limit on *all* thought, i.e. (for someone who holds that thesis) on anything recognizable to us as thought. By the same token, it is not even *prima facie* plausible to suppose that any line of argument leads from the social determination of knowledge as premise to this transcendental form of relativism as conclusion. We have isolated it only to set it aside.

Let us go back again, then, to the relativist thesis: for a statement to be true is for it to be true relative to W. We've considered two kinds of relativist who — for very different reasons — would not apply this statement to itself. The transcendental relativist wouldn't because he thinks there is no genuine statement here at all: nothing to apply to anything. The thesis that one tries to express in this way is 'quite correct, only it cannot be *said*' (Wittgenstein, TLP5.62). The other kind of relativist wouldn't because for him the thesis is a meta-thesis about first-order statements about the world. But we should take into account the relativist who, in a sense, lies between these two: who wants to apply his relativism to itself without taking it to vanishing point.

It is sometimes thought[2] that there is an obvious and unacceptable pragmatic paradox in this position. This is not so: a relativism which includes itself in its scope is not self-defeating in the way that, e.g. the assertion 'We know nothing' is self-defeating when it includes itself in its scope — if there are difficulties (as I think there are) they do not lie on the surface. It is worth developing the position a little further.

It needn't claim that 'true' *means* 'true relative to W', any more than 'I' *means* 'John Skorupski'. The claim is that truth *is* truth relative to W; and this — when asserted by us — is true, i.e. true relative to W. If someone speaks within a culture whose assertions are relativized to some other set of cognitive parameters, say W_0, then he can say, using the word 'truth' in just the sense we do, 'truth is truth relative to W_0', and what he says will be true relative to W_0.

To provide a further point of contrast, consider how our three relativists cope with the statement '"The earth is round" is true if, and only if, the earth is round'. The transcendental relativist says about it just what a straightforward realist would say. The 'self-referential' relativist considers it true relative to W. Replacing 'true' in it by 'true relative to W' produces a statement with a different sense but the same (relativized) truth value. A self-referential relativist speaking from within a culture whose cognitive parameters were W_0 would attach the same sense to the statement, but for him it would be true relative to W_0. In a similar way the 'first-order' relativist can distinguish the *meaning* of 'true' and 'true relative to W' (where 'W' denotes his set of parameters). He then considers the statement absolutely true. Replacing 'true' in it by 'true relative to W' produces a statement with a different sense but the same absolute truth-value.

3.   My object is to find a relativist conclusion for which one can sketch an argument starting from Mary Douglas' Durkheimian premise. With this in view 'transcendental relativism' has already been ruled out as irrelevant. I want to

rule out 'self-referential relativism' as well: I see no likely route from the social determination of knowledge — the thesis that our beliefs about the world are socially determined — to the relativity of our reflections about, among other things, the relation of these beliefs to the world. I leave this for the moment as mere assertion; some reasons for it will I think emerge indirectly later.

So without further ado, let us exempt philosophy, logic and mathematics from the relativist's remit, and in the same sweep, help ourselves to the assumption that a distinction exists between these domains on the one hand and the domain of empirical truth on the other.

Our target thesis, then, is that the truth of an empirical statement, a statement about the world, is relative. Let us call the totality of empirical statements held true by an individual or accepted in a culture his or its 'world view'. (This stipulation of course implies a multitude of simplifications and idealizations, but let it stand for the moment.) Now, what is a statement within a world view relative to? I shall suppose that our relativist's line is that every world view contains a core of statements which are, in Wittgenstein's phrase, 'propositions which have the form of empirical propositions' (OC 401). They are not genuinely empirical because they are not put to the question by experience; rather they provide the context or channel (OC 96-8) within which empirical statements arrive at an experiential reckoning. They are not properly speaking true or false: genuinely empirical statements have a truth value which is relativized to these core statements. An example of a core statement from the world view of the Lele, of Central Africa, might be that if someone who does not belong to the cult-group of Begetters — a group open to men who have fathered a child in wedlock — eats the chest of a game animal he is likely to die of pulmonary disease (IM Ch. 1). A structurally deeper-lying example might be that there are spirits; non-human intelligent agencies with cosmological powers, and responsive to human events. An example of a

core statement from our own world view might be the statement that the solar system is heliocentric.

Of course a relativist could reject these particular examples of core statements. He could also reject the division of a
world view into core statements and statements whose truth
value is relativized to the core statements, while still thinking of truth as relative to a world view: though perhaps only
at the cost of making it impossible to change one's opinion
without changing one's world view. But I shall assume that
our relativist accepts the division. In terms of my examples,
he will say that 'There are spirits' is core-true in the Lele
world view, but certainly not core-true, and perhaps false,
relative to our world view. Let us now add that a 'world
view' is to be individuated by its core statements: so that W
and W_O are the same world view if, and only if, they contain
the same core statements. There can be many versions of a
world view. This, to some degree, mitigates the unrealism
inherent in the way I first introduced the term.

We can now sum up the relativist's position in two theses.
(a) A given statement may be true relative to one world
view, false relative to another, and part of the core in a
third.
(b) The core statements of a world view are not properly
speaking true or false at all.

Should Durkheim have come to this conclusion?

4.   It's at least not obvious that he should. Durkeim's conviction was that the beliefs about the world received in a
society — its collective representations — could, at least in
part, be causally explained in terms of the social relations
which prevailed or had prevailed in that society. But it is at
once clear that no thesis of this general shape, to the effect
that a given belief can be explained in terms of such and such
antecedents, can, in and of itself, have any implication as to
the relativity or otherwise of that belief's truth value. The
relativist's claim is a metaphysical claim about the nature of
reality and its relation to the knowing subject. No causal

story about how a belief or world view comes to be held is, by itself, going to establish this claim. What is needed is a philosophical argument, and one which contains some extra and unobvious premisses.

Mary Douglas does not provide it. She provides instead a rhetorical shift, in which the mediating term is that ambiguously fertile phrase 'the social construction of reality'. Durkheim, we are told, believed that 'the social construction of reality applied to them, the primitives, and only partially to us.' Now if the 'social construction of reality' here means nothing other than 'the social determination of beliefs about reality', then Durkheim's views have been correctly reported. But thus understood, he can be convicted of no contradiction. Indeed there is nothing obviously implausible in his view. Consider the ever-growing, and now massive, proliferation, specialization, and differentiation of scientific élites in advanced industrial societies, and the relative efficiency and openness of the channels by which the ideas they produce are disseminated. Note the, in comparison, low, though of course not non-existent, degree of cognitive specialization in a traditional society like that of the Lele, and the degree to which cosmological lore is esoteric. Add to this the differences between a literate and a non-literate culture, note further the prevailing 'rational-critical' ideology of scientific élites, and compare it with the broadly 'traditional' ideology of primitive societies, which authorizes the legitimation of belief in terms of what (in Weber's words) 'actually, allegedly, or presumably has always existed'. With these points in mind one might find it extraordinary if the superstructure of cosmological ideas in our society did *not* possess a considerably greater degree of relative autonomy from its social base than did the superstructure of cosmological ideas in a traditional society.

On the other hand if Durkheim were understood as claiming that primitive world views are relativized, whereas ours is absolute, the position would be quite different. It is difficult to see how, if some beliefs about the world are absolutely true or false, there could be any beliefs with the same domain of reference which are relativistically true or false. Durkheim however did not hold this view. His way of saving primitive religious cosmologies was not to argue that, taken literally as cosmologies, they were true relative to their own cognitive parameters. It was to argue that they could be understood hermeneutically not as cosmologies at all, but as an accurate symbolic representation of the social order in which they existed. This is probably the most famous thread in the complicated tangle of ideas presented in the *Elementary Forms of Religious Life.* I've argued elsewhere[3] that it can't be reconciled with Durkheim's views on the social origin of cosmological thought, according to which the theoretical concepts of primitive cosmologies are modelled on, rather than symbolic of, patterns and relations in the social order. However if one simply removes the symbolist thread, one is left with, in effect, a Durkheimian intellectualism which contains neither contradiction nor special pleading in its account of the relation between primitive and modern thought systems.

5. But let Durkheim rest. Our question is whether an argument can be supplied which will take one from the social determination to the relativity of knowledge.

Although in most cases one cannot deduce the truth value of a belief from knowledge of its causal antecedents, the causal antecedents of a belief are not irrelevant to its status as knowledge. There are reasons for thinking that knowledge is a causal concept. (Here again, as with the relativist thesis we are to consider, I am restricting myself to empirical, or *a posteriori*, knowledge.) Let me very briefly review these reasons. The classical conception of knowledge as justified, true belief appears to be undermined by Gettier counter-examples.[4] The stage is set for these by the following facts. (a) One can be epistemically justified in holding a belief which is in fact false. (b) A belief deduced from a justified belief is justified. (c) A true belief may be deduced from a false belief. The upshot is that I can hold a true belief which is justified inasmuch as I infer it from a belief which I am justified in holding although it is false. This is the kind of case we feel reluctant to describe as knowledge: it seems an accident that I have hit on something true. Consider an example.[5]

I am sitting in a room and in front of me is a large mirror positioned in such a way that I can't see my own reflection. Behind me is a three-legged table which I can see reflected in the mirror. I am unaware of these facts. In front of me, and behind the mirror, is an identical three-legged table, positioned at just the depth and angle suggested by the mirror image as seen from where I am sitting. Unaware that I am looking into a mirror, I falsely — but given what I seem to see — justifiably believe that I see a three-legged table in front of me. From this I infer that there is a three-legged table in front of me. So I have a true belief, and one that I am justified in holding. But in these circumstances most people would agree that I cannot be said to *know* that there is a three-legged table in front of me. The point is that my belief is causally insulated from the table behind the mirror. Its causal antecedents involve the mirror in front of me and the table behind me. Because the fact that there is a table in front of me plays no causal role in the formation of my belief that there is a table in front of me, that belief cannot be said to constitute knowledge.

Let us now return to the social determination of knowledge. One is uneasy with the claim that a social group's beliefs about the natural world are determined by its social relations. The uneasiness results, at least in part, I think, from the feeling that if this is so then the knowledge status of these beliefs is impugned: and for reasons having nothing to do with the question whether the beliefs are true or false. Thus consider the belief held in many societies, Lele society among them, that there are spirits. Let us suppose this belief can be explained purely sociologically. It is a belief which is not derived from experience of the natural world, although, once acquired, it is used in ordering and explaining that experience.

Naturally, if there are no spirits the Lele cannot be said to know that there are spirits. But even if there *are* spirits, if the Lele belief in spirits simply reflects the social relations of Lele society, then surely they cannot be said to *know* that there are spirits. They do not stand in the required causal relation to the spirits, and the truth of their beliefs is an accident. The knower, his knowledge, and its object — here I include theoretically postulated objects — constitute a causal system. If the object drops out of this causal transaction we no longer have knowledge, but only a belief which happens to be true.

Of course it does not follow just from the fact that there can be a sociology or social psychology of cosmological ideas that the status of these ideas as knowledge must be impugned. 'Collective representations' of the natural world, both in primitive and in modern societies, may have social determinants and yet, at the same time, they may have determinants in collective experience of the natural world: determinants which suffice to put these ideas into the kind of causal relation to their object which is required for the ideas to count as knowledge. What is ruled out is that these ideas should have no causal relation to their object at all — it is not ruled out that social factors are causally relevant.

However I think we can see here a stepping stone that our relativist is likely to use. He will say that every world view contains some statements, 'which have the form of empirical' statements about the world, but the acceptance of which is in fact determined *purely* by social factors. Of the belief expressible in such a statement he will say, with Mary Douglas, that it is to be 'understood as unanchored to any fixed material points, and secured only by the stability of the social relations which generated it and which it legitimized'. Since it is not anchored to natural reality by any causal line, it cannot properly be said to constitute knowledge of that reality at all. Such a statement, according to the relativist, will be what, in my account of his position, I called a 'core statement'. But this has still to be argued for: that is, it still has to be shown that even given that every world view contains beliefs which are 'secured only by the stability of the social relations which generated' them, such beliefs have the further characteristics of being, properly speaking, neither true nor false and of setting the cognitive parameters relative to which other beliefs in the world view are true or false. At the moment we have shown no more than that these beliefs will not themselves constitute knowledge.

6. There is another stepping stone to which the relativist can move. It is the thesis that any world view is underdetermined by the data of experience: that is, first, that no rationally incorrigible, immediate, experiential judgements are forced on us by experience, and second, that there is no rationally inescapable, inferential path from such judgements to a single world view. The relativist is likely to require only the second of these points, but he need not look a gift horse in the mouth by turning down the first. The underdetermination thesis has nothing to do with the problem of induction: it asserts that with some or *all* the experience there is to be had taken into account, and with all *a priori* canons of good scientific method applied, an indefinite number of world views may still tie for first place as the best explanatory story about that experience.

Now the underdetermination by experience of beliefs about the world is an epistemic underdetermination, whereas the social determination, in a given society, of some among these beliefs is a causal determination. However, grant that reasoning and inference are, as I believe them to be, causal processes: if, *per impossibile*, rational inference from a body of experience lead determinately to one best story *about* that experience, then nothing *other* than that story could constitute empirical knowledge of the world, resting on that experience. And so on the face of it, no-one could be said to have such knowledge if he did not accept the story, and accept it in virtue of deriving it from the given body of experience by the inferential path in question. In short, where there was knowledge of the world based on a given range of experience, that knowledge would be causally determined by the experience on which it was based.

Given the underdetermination thesis, however, this conclusion cannot be established in this way. Of course it might nevertheless be true and capable of being established in some other way. My knowledge that putting my fingers in the fire is painful may be causally determined by experiences of putting my fingers in the fire, even if it is in some sense epistemically underdetermined by these experiences. There may be an argument to show that even though empirical knowledge is epistemically underdetermined, it must nevertheless be fully determined causally by experience. But still, given the thesis that if there is empirical knowledge of the world at all, it is epistemically underdetermined, we can perhaps add, as an at least plausible accompanying point, that such empirical knowledge, where it exists, is causally underdetermined by experience of the world.

At this point I should acknowledge that the concepts of belief as 'completely causally determined' by 'social factors' or by 'experience of the non-social world' are extremely unclear. I am using them in order to mark out roughly a line of thought: a critique of that line of thought might, precisely, pick out and take apart these concepts. I should add that in fixing on a particular line, in order to keep the discussion reasonably uncluttered, I am choosing at a number of points among options which are on the face of it open to someone following through a relativist argument.

To return to the theme. We may suppose our relativist to argue thus: any world-view is underdetermined by the data of experience, but in any socially accepted world view certain beliefs are socially determined. If the corpus of socially determined beliefs is sufficiently rich, then, when the truth value of the statements expressing these beliefs is set parametrically at 'true', the number of variables is reduced in such a way that experiential inquiry allows a determinate solution regarding the truth-value of other statements in the world-view. In these circumstances, where the truth-value of a statement becomes determinable by experiential inquiry, the statement has that truth-value relative to the parameters. The relativist whose particular line of thought we are following would endorse the following remarks from Wittgenstein's *On Certainty*:

> 410. I want to say: propositions of the form of empirical propositions, and not only propositions of logic, form the foundation of all operating with thoughts (with language). . .

Wittgenstein goes on to say:

> 402. In this remark the expression 'propositions having the form of empirical propositions' is itself thoroughly bad; the statements in question are statements about material objects. And they do not serve as foundations in the same way as hypotheses which, if they turn out to be false, are replaced by others. . .

The implication of these remarks, as understood by the relativist, and perhaps correctly understood, is radical. To see this, consider the obvious philosophical objection to the picture he is proposing. 'It may be true', the objection will run,

> 'that if the truth of certain statements about the world is taken for granted, it becomes possible to determine, on that assumption, and in the light of experience, the truth value of certain other statements about the world. But this establishes no more than the conditional that, if the assumptions are correct, then certain other statements have a certain truth value; it certainly does not show that those statements have that truth value *relative* to the assumptions, where this is taken to

mean something different to the innocuous conditional proposition which has been established. Moreover if you are right in thinking that acceptance of certain statements about the world which we take for granted is determined purely by the social relations existing in our society, and this means what it seems to mean, then we cannot be said to *know* the truth of these statements and consequently cannot be said to know the truth of any other statements whose truth is established conditionally on the truth of these statements.'

7.   The only way in which the relativist can overcome this objection is by taking the further step of abandoning altogether something which it is very difficult to abandon, namely, a realist conception of meaning and truth. By this I mean the idea that a statement has meaning if, and only if, it has truth conditions, where 'truth conditions' are understood in accordance with a correspondence conception of truth. The sense of a statement lies in its use to assert that a state of affairs obtains, and it is true or false according as to whether that state of affairs does or does not obtain.[6] This is an explicit and too brief formulation of a philosophical idea which I think lies deep in the thinking of just about everyone.

Now suppose we combine this realist approach to meaning and truth with another sort of realism, scientific realism, according to which theoretical science, or indeed, religious cosmology in a primitive society, is neither reducible to statements about observable goings-on, nor to be treated as a heuristic instrument, but is to be understood as offering an account of the unobservable constitution of reality. From the resulting philosophical standpoint, which I will henceforth refer to simply as 'realism', the relativist's two doctrines are unintelligible. It will make no sense, to begin with, to talk of a statement's truth value being relative to the acceptance of or the truth of some other statements. 'The earth is round' is true if the state of affairs which constitutes its truth condition, viz. the earth's being round, obtains: and whether or not this state of affairs obtains is something quite independent of what we or anyone else believes, and in general quite independent of whether the truth condition of any other statement, which has no entailment relation to 'The earth is round', obtains. Furthermore, if the relativist's core statements are, in Wittgenstein's words, 'statements about material objects' — or come to that, if they are statements about non-material constituents of reality, then this is a fact about their meaning which implies that they have truth conditions, relating to the possession by the objects that the statements are about, of the properties ascribed to those objects by the statements. If these truth conditions obtain, the statements will be true in a perfectly normal sense, and whether or not they obtain is an empirical matter.

It is evidence of how deep realist assumptions about meaning and truth lie in our thinking that the relativist position is often expressed in language which, if taken literally, seems to assert a kind of empirical idealism. If one tries to think relativism through within these assumptions one is forced to conclude that the truth value of a set of beliefs about reality can be relative to the mind or society which holds them only if reality is constructed by that mind or society: since a belief is true or false according to whether or not it corresponds to reality, the only sense one can give to its truth value being relative to society or mind is by supposing that which is real and what is not real depends on society and mind. That gives rise to much solemn talk of 'multiple realities' and the like; the point to note for the purpose of this paper however is that the resulting position is not, in the strict sense, a form of relativism at all. Realism and relativism just don't mix.

What account, then must our relativist give of meaning and truth? He must replace the ontological notion of a truth condition by the epistemological notion of an assertibility condition: an assertibility condition for a statement will be an observable state of affairs which gives one non-indictive epistemic justification for asserting that statement. Now as to truth, either it becomes assertibility or it becomes redundant. The relativist can choose either option, and is I think well-advised to choose the second: that is, he should accept a redundancy theory of truth. The reasons for this, however, have to do with general considerations — concerning the desirability, for an anti-realist, of avoiding reductionism, and the relation between anti-realism and intuitionistic logic — which are irrelevant for present purposes; the conclusion arrived at, though less clear-cut than if the first option is adopted, is still I think recognizably 'relativist'. Since the discussion is more complicated on the second option than on the first, and the conclusion less clear cut, I shall take it that the relativist line we are following treats truth as assertibility. A statement is true, then, if, and only if, assertibility conditions obtain warranting its assertion. Next, as to meaning, a statement has meaning if and only if it has assertibility conditions. In short what the relativist does is to substitute a verificationist conception of truth and meaning for a realist one.[7]

For a statement to be true is for there to be a humanly followable procedure which would produce, if followed, experiential evidence justifying assertion of that statement. (The procedure must be one for ascertaining, and not altering, what is the case.) But if belief is epistemically underdetermined by experience, how can any experiential evidence justify the assertion of any statement? How can there *be* such a thing as truth? The relativist's answer is that belief is underdetermined only so long as the truth-values of the core statements of a world view are taken as variables and not as parameters. But if their truth value is simply *taken as, ruled to be*, given, then other statements have a truth value: that is to say it becomes possible that experiential evidence should justify their assertion or denial. Now of course this is as much as to say that the core statements of a world view do not genuinely have a truth-value, for truth has been explicated as experientially grounded assertibility, and the core statements are simply taken as true quite independently of experience.

Wittgenstein's *On Certainty* again provides texts for the relativist.

> 87.   Can't an assertoric sentence, which was capable of functioning as an hypothesis, also be used as a foundation for research and action? I.e. can't it simply be isolated from doubt, though not according to any explicit rule? It simply gets assumed as a truism, never called in question, perhaps not even formulated.
>
> 98.   . . . the same proposition may get treated at one time as something to test by experience, at another as a rule of testing.
>
> 205.   If the true is what is grounded, then the ground is not *true*, nor yet false.
>
> 253.   At the foundation of well-founded belief lies belief that is not founded.
>
> 308.   . . . about certain propositions no doubt can exist if making judgements is to be possible at all. Or again: I am inclined to belief that not everything that has the form of an empirical proposition *is* one.

Many similar passages may be found.

Now the relativist moves from his first doctrine, about core statements, to his vital, second doctrine about the other ones. We considered an obvious philosophical objection to his view, which suggested that he had, at best, only shown that if certain empirical statements are assumed we can, in the light of experience, infer the truth-value of others. But the relativist replies that this presupposes the realist conception of truth and meaning which he rejects. The point for him is not that no statements can be known to be true if none are 'assumed', where an assumption is something that can be incorrect; it is that no statements could *be* true or false unless the 'truth' of some is given. And 'if the true is what is grounded then the ground is not *true*, nor yet false'. Add, finally, that when the choice of core statements varies, the truth value of other statements varies, and you arrive at a genuine relativity of truth value.

Our relativist is in no way committed to empirical idealism. He doesn't think for a moment that what we think makes a difference to what is the case. He simply thinks that what is the case can be equally well described in terms of an indefinite number of world views centring on different cores. There is, for example, our way and the Lele way. Perhaps neither we nor the Lele have found the best story within our current world view. Perhaps we never will, because, owing to exogeneous social factors, our core of statements will have changed before we get there. But as between the best version of our world view and the best version of the Lele world view there is no choosing. Each is true relative to its own core. And each is a true story about the only world there is.

To the realist, the relativist speaks thus.

> You reject relativism on the ground that a statement is true if and only if its truth condition obtains, and whether its truth conditions obtains is independent of what we believe. If you are making the empirical claim that, e.g. whether or not the earth is round is causally independent of what we believe about the earth or about anything else, then I entirely agree: what you say is true — relative to my world view. But if you are making a metaphysical claim then I'm not clear what it is.

8.   This completes my sketch of the route from the 'social determination of knowledge' to a 'thoroughly relativized theory of knowledge'. It's a route which keeps well clear of 'the social construction of reality' — a by-road of deserved ill repute among philosophers. But what I have said falls very far short of showing relativism to be a finally defensible position, and I do not think that it is.

Though a great deal could be said about issues like the 'underdetermination thesis', the key issues, I believe, are whether the verificationist conception of meaning and truth is to be preferred to the realist one, and whether, if it is accepted, it provides a framework within which relativism can be made coherent. I am inclined to believe that the issues are related in this way: given the underdetermination thesis, verificationist semantics leads to a relativism of something like the kind I have been discussing;[8] this relativism, however, cannot in the end be made coherent.

I do not have the space here to set out my reasons for thinking this,[9] so I shall give a brief outline. The relativist's position begins to crumble when we turn from considering what he has to say about truth to what he has to say about meaning. The essence of relativism is that the truth values of a set of statements can be varied while their experiential base and their meaning are both held constant. For there is nothing in the least surprising in the fact that truth values would be different if experience were different from what it actually is, or if the meaning of the statements in question (assertoric sentences) were to change. The reason for thinking that truth values could change while experience and meaning were held constant was that, in virtue of the variation in core statements from one world view to another, the same range of experience might justify assertion of a statement in one world view and not in the other. But the reason, in turn, for this, would be that the assertibility conditions of the statement were different as between the one world view and the other. And this seems to imply that the meaning of the statement changes from one world view to the other. I think that this in effect forces on the relativist a kind of semantic holism. He will have to say that the primary units of meaning, the primary bearers of assertibility conditions, are whole versions of world views. The meaning of a statement will be the contribution it makes to the assertibility conditions of the versions of world views in which it appears. If this line of thought made sense it would secure an invariant meaning across world views for any statement, while allowing its truth value to vary. But I don't think it does make sense — how, for example, could one learn a language on this model? — and if it doesn't, then I think the relativist has run out of answers.

9. Let's now leave the rarified territory of realist versus verificationist theories of meaning and truth, and return finally to Mary Douglas's criticisms of Durkheim's philosophical anthropology. By a philosophical anthropology I mean an attempt to form a conception of man and man's powers which is rooted in ethnological inquiry but reaches up to the purest philosopher's questions about 'Mind and Society' and 'Mind and Its Place in Nature'. Although books with that kind of title are not pouring from the presses at the moment, it remains true that the grand tradition of philosophical anthropology, to which belongs Durkheim's project of showing, as against Kant, that the categories of thought are socially determined categories and vary and develop with social variation and development — this grand tradition is not dead in social anthropology. Mary Douglas is, of course, one of those who keep it alive. Like Durkheim and like the 'English intellectualists' Tylor and Frazer, she sees primitive modes of thought as cosmologies which emerge from men's need to categorize, to explain, to control their natural environment. Like Lévy-Bruhl, she criticises 'Tylor and Frazer, who tried to explain primitive belief in terms of individual psychology' and follows 'Durkheim in seeing collective representations as social phenomena, as common patterns of thought which are related to social institutions'. (PD p.93) Like Durkheim, she thinks modern and primitive modes of thought should be compared and that the categories of modern thought also have their genesis in society. Beyond these Durkheimian themes she follows Quine, or the Evans-Pritchard of *Witchcraft, Oracles and Magic among the Azande,* or the Wittgenstein of *On Certainty,* in the thesis that belief is underdetermined by experience, and finally, I believe that she rightly thinks herself to

be following Wittgenstein, or at least the direction in which *On Certainty* points, in her relativism, and in basing it on the claim that the limits of empiricism are shared ways of acting.

It's obvious that there is room for a position distinguished from Mary Douglas's philosophical anthropology not in its Durkheimian intellectualist elements — though of course the appropriateness of these elements in understanding the thought of a primitive society is also in dispute — but in being realist rather than relativist. Here one thinks naturally of Robin Horton's writings on science and traditional African thought. If Mary Douglas is Wittgensteinian in the anti-realist picture she offers of social world views whose boundaries are constituted, so to speak 'from the inside', by conventional limits on what one questions and how one 'goes on', Robin Horton is Popperian in his implicit realism about meaning and truth, in his explicit scientific realism — where this again encompasses the theoretical terms of primitive religious cosmologies as well as those of scientific theories — and in his account of the relation between primitive and modern modes of thought in terms of a contrast between closed and open predicaments.

I shall end by briefly considering the implications of the two theses about the determination of belief that we have touched on for this kind of realist philosophical anthropology. One of the theses states that belief fits loosely on even the most comprehensive body of experience. This must lead the realist, who rejects all truth by convention, to an uncomfortably fallibilist epistemology. It is therefore he, and not the relativist, who can lay claim to Mary Douglas's bold rhetoric, in the passages I quoted at the beginning, about facing up to challenges, accepting the cognitive precariousness which results from realizing that no belief (not even the belief that I have two hands) can be invested with certain authority, and so on. In fact the realist's problem is that of warding off scepticism, whereas the relativist, as Ernest Gellner has remarked, can sit back and take things easy.

Faced with competing world views the realist puzzles over how to establish which, if any, is correct; for the relativist, all of them are, in their own terms. There's no need for the realist's critical look and furrowed brow — my neighbour's world view is potentially at least as good as my own, and both are potentially as good as can be.

As to the other thesis, relating to the social determination of knowledge, the realist cannot accept this in its strongest form. He can accept that a belief may be determined by purely social factors, but, if what has been said about the causal character of knowledge is right, then he cannot accept that knowledge of non-social reality can be determined by purely social factors. But this is quite compatible with the view, e.g. that acquiring such knowledge is a matter of fitting theoretical models to experience, and that the elaboration of these models is influenced or determined by social conditions in the society which produces the models. So the limits placed by realism on the sociology of knowledge are hardly opressive.

To relate ideas convincingly to their social context is a task much more difficult than the triteness of the programme would suggest. Few, however, would deny that when the programme produces results they can be very illuminating. Mary Douglas has a theory of pollution which, if it is correct, is a case in point. It begins with the idea that every society imposes a more or less elaborate system of classification on the world, in terms of which the world can be thought about. It can happen that an object fails to fit the classificatory system. Objects of this kind, which constitute classificatory anomalies, tend to be venerated or abominated, treated as holy or unclean. Thus the pangolin, a scaly anteater which climbs trees, is like a fish and unlike an animal or bird in having scales, is like an animal in that it lives out of water and has four legs, and yet, like a creature of the air, it avoids the earth and frequents trees. Moreover, unlike other animals it does not run away from men, but instead curls up into an armoured ball, and, so the Lele believe, it gives birth to one child at a time, like humans but unlike other animals. This taxonomical wonder is, for the Lele, a sacred creature, surrounded by rules which set it apart and which it is dangerous to break; it is the object of a cult and plays an important role in a number of cosmological rites. But why is it holy rather than unclean? Here Mary Douglas has a further theory. Social attitudes towards classificatory anomalies will be determined by a society's experience of strangers, who mediate in exchanges between society and the outside world. 'A people who have nothing to lose by exchange and everything to gain will be predisposed towards the hybrid being, wearing the conflicting signs, man/god or man/beast. A people whose experience of foreigners is disastrous will cherish perfect categories, reject exchange and refuse mediation.' (IM p.307). The former will venerate anomalies, the latter will reject them: a new version of the open and closed society.

From these ideas, it may be, a full theory of the purely social determination of pollution beliefs will emerge. If so, then the realist will refuse to accept that pollution beliefs, such as the Lele belief that eating a pangolin can help with the hunt, can constitute knowledge. But I see no reason why the truth of this theory about pollution beliefs should prevent him from agreeing with Durkheim about the relative autonomy, from their social base, of modern scientific cosmologies, or why it should make him agree, with Mary Douglas, that 'it is an anachronism to believe that our world is more securely founded in knowledge than one that is driven by pangolin power'. (IM p.xxi).

Notes

1 Abbreviations used in citation:
  IM : Mary Douglas, *Implicit Meanings*, London, 1975.
  PD : Mary Douglas, *Purity and Danger*, Harmondsworth, 1970.
  OC : L. Wittgenstein, *On Certainty*, (repr. with corrections) Oxford 1974
  TLP : L. Wittgenstein, *Tractatus Logico-Philosophicus* transl. Pears and McGuinness, London, 1961.

2 Cp. e.g. A. Giddens, *New Rules of Sociological Method*, London, 1976 pp. 144-5.

3 J. Skorupski, *Symbol and Theory*, Cambridge, 1976, Chs. 2-3, 11.

4 See E. Gettier 'Is Justified True Belief Knowledge?' *Analysis* 23, 1963. For a recent discussion cp. C. McGinn, '*A Priori* and *A Posteriori* Knowledge' *Proceedings of the Aristotelian Society*, LXXVI, 1975-6.

5 This is an example slightly changed, from G. Harman, *Thought*, Princeton, 1973 See pp. 22-3.

6 In the sense of correspondence required here, Tarskian truth theory is not in itself a correspondence theory, although it may be incorporated in a realist conception of meaning and truth. It can equally, however, be incorporated in an anti-realist conception, with an intuitionistic meta-logic. (On these matters, and others touched on later in section VII, I hardly need say that much more could be said.)

7 He *must* introduce a verificationist ('pragmatist', 'contructivist') conception of meaning, he *can* — and as just noted, we're assuming that he does — introduce a verificationist (etc.) conception of truth.

8 More exactly: either to a relativism of this kind, or to the view that the meaning of a sentence in a given language is incommensurable across world-views expressed in that language. The existence of the option is implied by what I say in the last paragraph of this section. If one works 'forwards', so to speak, from verificationism, rather than 'backwards' from relativism, the latter view is in many ways more attractive. But the relativist needs something which can non-trivially be said to be true in one world-view and false in another.

9 I say a little more in *Symbol and Theory*, appendix.

9. World View and the Core
by Mary Douglas

It is always a great help to have attention from another discipline focussed upon one's work and I am therefore grateful for the essay on 'Pangolin Power'. However our philosopher uses several assumptions which present difficulties for this anthropologist. Obviously it would be rash to engage formally with a trained philosopher about them, but here they are. First is the concept of world-view, second the concept of core statements, third the causal analysis of beliefs. World-view is a vague expression, over-reified as soon as uttered. Anthropologists are usually very conscious of its possible misleading meanings and use it apologetically for a short hand summary of a heterogeneous collection of values and beliefs, more or less coherent, held by the majority of a given population at a given time. Sometimes the word culture does service instead. Our philosopher is bolder. He uses it more confidently in a tidier, more rigid and holistic way than we would care to try. He writes, for example, of 'the cost of making it impossible to change one's opinion without changing one's world view'. What cost? For the term world-view to be used flexibly enough to have application to real life, it should include the idea of fluidity and continual change.

When it comes to a set of core statements to which the truth-value of statements in the world-view are relativized, our philosopher is surely right in describing it as an overall, theoretical framework, which it will never make sense to characterize as true or false; it merely provides the set of parameters relative to which the truth-values of assertion are determined. Unfortunately, the examples of core statements he offers lie below the required level of theoretical abstraction.

> An example of a core statement from the world view of the Lele of Central Africa might be that if someone who does not belong to the cult group of Begetters . . . eats the chest of a game animal he is likely to die of pulmonary disease. A structurally deeper-lying example might be that there are spirits; non-human intelligent agencies with cosmological powers, and responsive to human events. An example of a core statement from our own world view might be the statement that the solar system is heliocentric.

These examples cannot be seriously accepted as core statements in the full sense. The Lele examples are touch-and-test ideas developed out of the Lele experience of morality, health and disease; they can be characterized as true or false within the normal Lele discourse and indeed are challengable. 'The solar system is heliocentric' (if it is not actually tautological) is likewise an idea about the physical connections within the experienced world, and not an example of a theoretical framework within which the particular elements of a given world view get their plausibility. An anthropologist's idea of core statements will be discussed later as this is the part of the philosophical essay of greatest relevance and interest.

Some slackness in thinking about core statements, is matched in our philosopher's discussion of knowledge as a causal process. Knowledge need not be and better not be a causal concept, unless (or even if) the philosopher focusses only upon inferential processes. The causal approach to knowledge which he advocates leaves to the knowing subject only a passive role as receiving information from the real world, and correcting earlier ideas by incorporating information from counter-examples. This approach plays down the importance of metaphorical learning as a source of knowledge. It also fails to give credit to the active, organizing energies of the knower, or to recognize the subjective input into cognition. It seems, on this anthropologist's reading, to be barely on the fringe of twentieth-century thought about the learning process, recognition, memory, how knowledge is constituted. It seems strange to pay so little attention to a well-known, feedback process between the construction of a particular conceptual boundary, and the rest of the thinking and acting that flows from that construction. Our philosopher is wrong in supposing that our relativist 'doesn't for a moment think that what we think makes a difference to what is the case'. It makes a lot of difference, because of multiple complex feedbacks between thought and action which reorganize the possibilities of perception. This implies a sense in which I could agree to a kind of semantic holism which I am expected to deny — only if the core statement is abstract enough, only if it is a general bias with respect to the possible classifications in the world view, then — as a primary bearer of assertibility conditions, it would be a whole version, a summarizing, guiding principle of the world view.

Before I raise the other difficulties, let me first admit that I find the philosophical discussion quite dizzying, like a Victorian parlour game devised by Lewis Carroll. Better admit my difficulties and better not try to enter a discussion with the philosophers who work within that world view and are aware of its core statements: instead, having named the difficulties, try to expound more clearly what our philosopher has misunderstood of the anthropological world-view that he has sought to rearrange.

It is generally a major failure of judgement to brush aside the whole of the argument which one claims to be considering. Our philosopher has made just such a mistake when he makes it a point of pride to have written a long paper, ostensibly about a particular anthropologist's advocacy of relativism, keeping 'well clear of the social construction of reality, a by-road of deserved ill-repute among philosophers'. But it is not enough to fix a label of ill-repute. There is a responsibility to try to grasp the rejected argument. The quotations and remarks about Durkheim reveal a central misunderstanding of that thinker. Less important, there is a parallel misunderstanding of my own writing, insofar as that is modelled on Durkheim's thought. Neither misunderstanding is surprising since a proper grasp of the social construction of reality is the first step in the programme which I advocated in an appeal for a thorough relativizing of the sociology of knowledge. Here is one more philosopher, like a bull, charging in such a headlong gallop at the red rag (relativism) that he misses the target. At least he gives me credit for not denying the achievements of science, and offers me a realist label for doing what I want to do. But he is mistaken in attributing to me the idea that there is no way of choosing between world views. First, I would not at all agree that 'as between the best version of our world view and the best version of the Lele world view there is no choosing'. All I have ventured to say is that the way that humans construct their world views and the grounds for believing in them are the same. I am interested in what can be understood about the grounds for believing and about core statements. There certainly can be judgement from one core as to the value of the other world views, so long as the objectives to which the choice is angled are made explicit. There are plenty of ways of specifying a particular level of technological control and comparing world views on their success in achieving it. Or they could be compared according to the scope for emotional maturity, or for developing the memory or the sense of smell or for other strengths. Comparison between world-views poses no specially thorny problems for an anthropologist who is not interested in maintaining that one is as good as another. Rather the contrary if anything: I am interested in finding criteria for agreeing, within our world view, that among other core structures some are not as good as others. So the misunderstanding is total.

Our philosopher writes about meaning and truth in the same breath, treating them as synonyms within the same analytical field. But there are differences. To use the word 'meaning' does not automatically raise the problems of knowledge, truth and reality. Since the problems of truth and reality are not directly relevant to the anthropolgist's discussion, it would be better to separate truth and meaning for the moment, treating truth as belonging to the special province of philosophical discourse. Meaning indicates an area of speculation about transmission between thinkers, about translation, possible misinterpretation, enlargement or constriction of the scope of concepts. Meanings change easily, even while their verbal or nonverbal vehicles may remain apparently the same. Knowledge is related to meaning at the level of analysis at which particular meanings connect with one another, to make a coherent interdependent set, each part guaranteeing the place of the others. The testing by experience of each part of a set provides some of the grounds of its claim to be entered as belief and knowledge in a world view, and its coherent relation with the rest of the set probably provides the rest.

Durkheim's main focus of interest was upon how beliefs are generated, that is upon belief and meaning rather than upon truth and knowledge. Our philosopher has carefully read 'the complicated tangle of ideas presented in the *Elementary Forms of Religious Life*', and he claims to be able to disengage three threads from it: one, the modelling thread, Durkheim's view that the theoretical concepts of primitive cosmologies are modelled on the social order; two, the symbolist thread, that they are symbolic of the social order; and three, an intellectualist thread, that they arise out of the primitive society's need to find intellectually satisfying explanations for the phenomena encountered. He claims that the first two are mutually inconsistent and that 'if one simply removes the symbolist thread, one is left with, in effect, a Durkheimian intellectualism which contains neither contradiction nor special pleading in its account of the relation between primitive and modern thought systems'. By intellectualism an earlier passage suggests that he means that primitives (like us) have a need to explain and he also refers to Robin Horton's work on available choice of theoretical models.

It is a sad travesty to reduce Durkheim's distinctions between mechanical (primitive) and organic (industrial) modes of solidarity and between sacred and profane situations to purely intellectual needs for acceptable theoretical construction. As our philosopher said, Durkheim argued explicitly that primitive cosmologies 'could be understood hermeneutically, not as cosmologies at all, but as an accurate symbolic representation of the social order in which they existed'. Stephen Lukes, one of his biographers, has indeed dismissed the sacred/profane distinction as a minor and barely relevant source of confusion in the great man's thought, but our philosopher is ready to throw away much more. 'Let Durkheim rest', he said. But he can certainly not be left to rest, stripped of his important message.

Durkheim unfortunately is often misunderstood in this way, usually by readers who have been content only to read *The Elementary Forms of Religious Life*. The missing theme in this book, the part of his theory which twists the modelling thread and the symbolist thread into a single rope is the implied transactionalism between individuals. How does Durkheim argue that people arrive at their idea of the sacred? He could perhaps imply that it just happens, that there is an innate tendency to internalize the classifications of society. But no — certain considerations impel us to credit him with intending a transactionalist process. The sacred, he expounds in the *Division of Labor*, arises as a powerful idea when individuals see a need to protect the social order from deviant individuals' attack. He recognizes that it does not always or automatically arise, hence the contrast between mechanical and organic forms of solidarity. If we put the *Division of Labor*, which is mainly about the judicial process, together with the *Elementary Forms of Religious Life*, we get the argument, from Durkheim himself, about political and semi-contractual conditions which lead individuals in primitive society to internalize the social order. The weight of his analysis in *Suicide*, makes clear his concern to understand the nature of individual commitment to society and dependence upon it. His argument about cosmology is not intellectualist, but sociological. There is no way of understanding Durkheim's meaning in the *Elementary Forms* taking it in isolation. It has to be related to his other work, also to his joint work with Marcel Mauss and to that of other close colleagues in regular communication with him. His idea that experience of social models is the source for logical types, the modelling thread, and his idea of social processes being symbolized in cosmology, the symbolizing thread, come together as a single description of the social construction of knowledge: the symbolizing is possible because of the modelling, how else? Both processes construct the collective consciousness. For example, *Primitive Classification* shows how the very points of the compass are established and known operatively by people living in camps that can be regularly distinguished with reference to the sun's position, and so associated with north, south etc. Calendrical and geographical knowledge depends on use. Hertz's essay (difficult and intriguing) on *The Preeminence of the Right Hand* argues that the consistent loading of concepts of authority and subordination on to the right and left of the human body and the frequent association of these with east and west and male and female should not be attributed to the physiology of right and left in the brain, or to natural right-handedness, but to a process by which individuals come to select rightness to represent the sacred power of society. Halbwachs' essay on the collective consciousness of musicians shows how much that group of sociologists took it for granted that shared knowledge which could have any title to constituting part of a world view is achieved by social interaction. Apart from the testimony of his contemporary colleagues towards this interpretation, there is the further tradition among social anthropologists that all classifications are potentially points of contention, somehow to be transacted if there is to be agreement. This is the tradition in which I am writing and which our philosopher misinterprets. My plea for a more complete acceptance of the bargaining, negotiating process for reaching consensus about the very boundaries of conceptual categories absolutely requires science, philosophy, logic and maths to be not excluded.

The view of science which our philosopher presents has a strong smell of the 1950's about it. He writes unselfconsciously about 'All the *a priori* canons of good scientific method'; he appeals to the 'ever-growing and now massive proliferation, specialization and differentiation of scientific élites in advanced industrial societies, and the relative efficiency and openness of the channels by which the ideas they produce are diseminated'. Not only has Robert Merton written in vain, Kuhn also and even Marx. Our philosopher really thinks that 'the superstructure of cosmological ideas in our society' possesses a 'degree of relative autonomy from its social base'. The only relevant social base must be the loose association of scientists and the more tightly related groups among them. Our philosopher is unaware of the deep conflicts and grave doubts not only between the major branches of science, but within them, and not on matters of detail, but on absolutely fundamental principles. Up till the 1950's the industrial world did indeed seem to be represented by a solitary scientific community with commonly agreed canons. But if Durkheim were writing now, he would be less tempted than at any time since the start of the century to exempt the scientific community from his analysis. Durkheim claimed that the primitive world views are relativized to their social structure: he believed that this was not the case with modern society where, thanks to the methods of science, our world views are relativized to its findings, to agreement about the heliocentricity of the solar system, to the roundness of the earth. Our cosmology, he thought, is constructed with entirely intellectualist intentions, their's is constructed as part of the construction of society, with social intentions. Their theories are better appreciated not as theories but as media of social relations: the sacred/profane divide is not properly understood as a theory about how nature works, but as a live dialogue about boundaries between spheres of action.

Since our philosopher has missed out on the line of thought which assumes a transactional basis for the congruence between symbolic behaviour, modelling of social forms and satisfying of intellectual curiosity, it is probably not worthwhile to spell out his misinterpretations of my own earlier work. Instead, I will concentrate on the concept of core statements. This idea may be useful for opening the door of understanding to philosophers. 'Any serious account of relativism' needs to keep in view that the truth-value of statements is 'relativized to an overall theoretical framework, a set of core statements, or whatever it may be'. Our philosopher evinced some difficulty in imagining examples of core statements. In the last chapter of the book which gave him the starting point and initial quotation for his essay I came as close as I can, without more help from philosophers, to suggesting what the cores of world-views might be like. Because I was stuck there, I wrote the provocative call to develop the thoroughgoing relativizing from which Durkheim had stayed his hand. The chapter, entitled 'Self Evidence' starts with the old problem of how causal relations are found in nature and come to be credited with unchallengeable, 'self-evident' inherent connectedness. Using the background of work stemming from Durkheim, I concentrated on three examples of tribal classifications of nature. Each of these three examples had been studied from the same theoretical perspective that I have outlined. Each showed how the classifications of society were projected upon the universe so richly and consistently that it would be difficult to justify the distinction between social and non-social objects. Every kind of living thing and every inch of space is incorporated into the set of social classifications which correspond to rules of human behaviour. They were world-views of the Durkheimian kind. The truth of their statements, if they are relativized to any core, are relativized to the structure of social relations. Core statements, then, would have to be statements about society. They would also be statements of great generality: I would argue that a set of core-statements ought to be no more than very abstract valuations of classificatory possibilities. In Head's theory of learning, items of information acquired are assimilable by virtue of their relation to the individual learner's general schemata of ideas. Bartlett used 'schemata' and also mental 'set' for the same structural principle organizing sensory input. As information stands to mental set, so should item of culture or of world view stand to core. Core statements are not like the many branched hatrack or tree trunk on which complete hats or leaves are suspended. The core is a set of abstract organizing principles which affects the very shape of experience. Following Durkheim (and pressing further the implications of his approach), I believe that the core is first and always a set of principles about social relations. The three tribal examples suggest that their world view can be distinguished by a bias running straight through all the classificatory systems employed, and that the bias derives from social attitudes to inclusion, exclusion and hierarchy. Our scientific communities, villages, middle class housing areas, big corporations and so on, all develop attitudes to inclusion, exclusion and hierarchy. For us too I would claim that the core of a world-view will be abstractable from social attitudes and that it sets the parameters of credibility for particular statements by its influence on the whole structure of classification. I would argue that this is as true of our modern communities as of primitives. (There is a technical problem in identifying the relevant community to which a particular world-view may be attributed.) The programme for which I am requesting support is to investigate how world-views are relativized to core statements which abstractly summarize states of society. My own procedures for investigating this idea call for a relevant categorizing of social experience. This is why most of my research is devoted to grid/group analysis, a scheme devised to uncover the mental set, cultural bias, cosmology or core statements which sustain particular interpretations of social experience.

Bibliography

1 Bartlett, F.C., *Remembering: A Study in Experimental and Social Psychology*, 1932.
2 Durkheim, Emile, *Suicide: A Study in Sociology*, translated by George Simpson, Routledge & Kegan Paul, 1952 from *le Suicide*, 1897.
3 ———, *The Elementary Forms of Religious Life*, trans J. W. Swain, Collier Books, 1961, pp. 240-242. Originally *Les Formes Elementaires de le vie Religieuse: le système totémique en Australia* (Paris, Alcan) 1912.
4 ———, *The Division of Labor in Society*, trans. George Simpson, 1933. Originally *De la division du travail social*, 1893.
5 ——— and Mauss, Marcel, *Primitive Classification*, translated by Rodney Needham, Cohen & West, 1963. Originally 'De quelques formes primitives de classification', *Année Sociologique*, 1901-02, Paris, 1903, pp. 1-72
6 Halbwachs, M., 'la Mémoire Collective chez les Musiciens', *Revue Philosophique*, 1939, No. 3-4.
7 Hertz, Robert, 'The Pre-eminence of the Right Hand; A Study in Religious Polarity', pp. 89-160 in *Death and the Right Hand*, R. Hertz, translated by Rodney and Claudia Needham, Cohen & West, 1960. Originally 'La Prééminence de la main droite: étude sur la polarité religieuse', *Revue Philosophique*, Vol. LXVIII, 1909, pp. 553-580.
8 Lukes, Steven, *Emile Durkheim His Life and Work: A Historical and Critical Study*, Allen Lane, The Penguin Press, 1973, pp. 26-28.

10. OurPhilosopher Replies
by John Skorupski

1. Professor Douglas has had difficulty identifying who's who in my paper. Let me try to make things clearer. My purpose, as I said, was to find that form of relativism for which one could construct the most plausible line of argument, starting from the premise that beliefs about the world are in some non-trivial sense 'socially determined'. I concluded that a line of argument no less plausible than any other (there may be equally plausible variants) included as further premisses: the 'causal theory of knowledge', the thesis that belief is underdetermined by experience, and most important, an anti-realist conception of meaning and truth. It also involved use of the concept of a 'world-view': where a world-view was to be thought of as implicitly articulated into a core of 'statements' not revisable within the world-view, and having no truth-value, this core lying in a cocoon or network of statements all of which have a truth-value and are revisable without changing world-views. It is, of course, one question whether this is the most plausible line of argument that can be given — another question, whether it *is* ultimately plausible. I touched on the latter question all too briefly in section 8 of my paper.

The person who adopts the line of argument I suggest, from the 'social determination of knowledge' to a 'thoroughly relativized theory of knowledge', I call — if I may be allowed the phrase — 'our relativist'. Professor Douglas thinks, sometimes at least, that she is our relativist, or that I think she is. Either view is quite wrong. As the long quotation with which I started my paper shows, and as I explicitly noted, Douglas's route to a 'thoroughly relativized theory of knowledge' goes via 'the social construction of reality'. I also mentioned that the move from causal determination to relativity of belief required a philosophical argument, and that Douglas fails to provide it — providing instead no more than an underlying equivocation on the phrase 'social construction of reality' (p.159). It's the argument Professor Douglas fails to provide that our relativist tries to supply. This argument steers clear of 'empirical idealism' (pp. 165, 168); whereas the equivocal view that reality is socially constructed, which Douglas adheres to, is, on one reading, a form of empirical idealism. (See section 4 below).

2. So our relativist's argument seeks to fill a gap which Douglas leaves unfilled — except by a form of empirical idealism which our relativist seeks to avoid. Since our relativist is not, and is not meant to be, Mary Douglas, it makes no sense to say 'Our philosopher is wrong in supposing that our relativist "doesn't for a moment think that what we think makes a difference to what is the case"' (above p. 179). Our relativist is simply defined as a person who, unlike Mary Douglas, doesn't think that. Again, when on p.170 I say that (according to our relativist) 'as between the best version of our world view and the best version of the Lele world-view there is no choosing', it is not to Mary Douglas that I am attributing 'the idea that there is no way of choosing between world-views' (above, p.180). However, on this point, it should also be noted that the force of my remark, in its context, is that our relativist thinks there is no choosing in respect of *degree of truth* between best versions of world-views. This does not rule out other forms of comparison, such as those whose possibility Douglas accepts on p. 180 above. On the other hand, if one thinks (i) that competing world views can in some way be arranged in order of verisimilitude, or (ii) that even if it cannot be determined which of two world views is potentially 'more true' (a better overall representation of reality) it is nevertheless possible that one of them is — then one isn't a relativist as I understand the term.

3. Mary Douglas is not our relativist; but nor am I. So my commitment to his premises and concepts is no stronger than the one I have already stated: that a version of relativism as plausible as any other would contain them. Consequently to criticize the concept of a 'world-view', used in the semi-technical way I used it in expounding our relativist's position, is not to criticize a concept I endorse. It would be more apt to criticize it on the ground that it isn't a concept which the best version of relativism would endorse either. As regards this latter criticism, it should be clear that in my paper I used an idealized model of 'world-view and core' in order to simplify discussion of the relativist position. In this respect both our relativist and I could accept that the model of a world-view in my paper is 'tidier, more rigid' than world-views actually are. On the other hand, the 'holistic' (above, p. 177) way in which our relativist conceives of world views *is* an essential part of his argument, and one I would fasten on in criticizing it.

Incidentally, Professor Douglas has quite misunderstood what 'the cost of making it impossible to change one's opinion without changing one's world view' is supposed to be. The cost is, precisely, the fact that when world-views are conceived in such a way that that *is* impossible, the concept of a world-view becomes so 'inflexible', so unable to accommodate any degree of 'fluidity' (above, p. 177) as to be implausible right from the start.

4. As Professor Douglas says — in a double-edged remark — 'it is generally a major failure of judgement to brush aside the whole of the argument which one claims to be considering' (above, p. 179). I don't, as I hope I've made clear, claim to consider her argument for relativism: my only claim on that score is that she doesn't give one. If I am right about that, I can hardly make amends by considering it. But I can at least briefly consider the only argument for relativism I can imagine that *would* go via the 'social construction of reality'. It is this. The world-view an individual or group holds

determines the nature of the reality inhabited by the individual or group, which the world-view purports to represent. That is, the relation between world-view and reality is not that of correspondence to something independently given; rather the world-view in some way constitutively fixes the reality to which it is supposed to correspond. But since world-views are socially constructed, so are the worlds they represent. Hence a given statement may differ in truth-value as between the world-views of two different societies, corresponding to the reality constructed by one, failing to correspond to the reality constructed by the other.

The crucial leap in this argument, from the claim that mind or society constructs its world-view, to the claim that it constructs the reality the world-view is *about*, is an idealist one. (World and world-view are either identical or distinct. If identical, no leap is required, but the position is already an idealist one. If distinct — at least at one level — then some sort of idealist account is needed to explain how world-view determines world.) What results is an 'empirical idealism' inasmuch as it implies an empirical plurality of worlds, given the empirical plurality of world-views.

Douglas gives no argument to justify the crucial leap. The argument must be a philosophical one. (I *don't* of course mean that it is in some way the exclusive preserve of 'philosophers': nor, however, is it to be fenced off by notices marked 'Anthropologists only'.) It would also need to be a very good one, in view of the apparent absurdity of its consequence: a literal multiplicity of worlds. ('The world is everything that is the case'. So there is something over and above everything that is the case?)

5. In her reply to my paper Douglas still gives no such argument. She mentions the importance of 'a proper grasp of the social construction of reality' (above, p. 180). But in the rest of her reply there is talk only of the thesis that classifications of, and beliefs about, the natural environment are the products of society. I am far from denying such truisms (they

are pregnant ones) as that the 'collective consciousness' is socially constructed, or that 'shared knowledge which could have any title to constitute part of a world-view is achieved by social interaction' (above, p. 183). But these truisms only take one to the point from which a relativist argument might start: they don't constitute the argument.

Given the absence in her previous work, and in her reply to my paper, of any such argument — and also of any sense that some such argument is needed — I am now not at all sure that Douglas's views are relativist, properly speaking, at all. Even where she hints that she does believe that 'what we think makes a difference to what is the case' (above, p. 179), the reason she gives could show only that what we think makes a difference to what we perceive as being the case. Perhaps there is to be found here, not radical relativism, but only radical-sounding metaphor.

This brings me to a claim in my paper that I would now like to withdraw. There is indeed a danger in starting with some passages from a 'particular anthropologist' (above, p. 179), developing an abstract argument not attributed or attributable to that anthropologist, and finally returning to the views of the anthropologist in question. Inevitably the relativist argument I developed in my paper influenced my description, in section 9, of what I took to be Professor Douglas's 'philosophical anthropology'. I read the conclusion of that argument into her writings on a 'relativized theory of knowledge' with a degree of firmness which isn't justified by the shifting ambiguities of the writings themselves. In part, I was lured on by Douglas's references to Durkheim, Wittgenstein and Quine — a pattern of sources of inspiration which 'our relativist' would also acknowledge. In part, it was the attraction of a contrast — altogether too neat of course — between the position represented by Horton on the one hand, and the position I was attributing to Douglas on the other. This latter position is particularly intriguing to anyone interested in the philosophy of mind and society, because of the chance it seems to offer of carrying out Durkheim's modified Kantian project, in a deeper way than Durkheim, because of his realism, was able to do. I accept, however, that I was wrong in suggesting that Professor Douglas's work represents something like the ethnographic embodiment of that abstract philosophical position.

World-wearily, Professor Douglas sees in me 'one more philosopher like a bull charging in such a headlong gallop at the red rag 'relativism' that he misses the target.' (above, p. 180) I find this curious, given the space I devote to developing the relativist case on the one hand and criticizing it on the other. These proportions reflect my view — that relativism is a greatly underestimated doctrine. Like many doctrines, though, it can come in 'vulgar' or 'naive' versions which give it a bad name. That is another reason why I was hoping to find an anthropologist to pin the true doctrine's colours on — an anthropologist, because much of the drive to explore such philosophical doctrines must come from outside philosophy: in this case from anthropology or the history of ideas.

6. There are a number of errors and misunderstandings in Professor Douglas's comments. (Some of them are due to over-hasty or allusive formulations in my paper.) Lacking the space for a proper discussion, I can only mention some of them.

(i) The thesis that knowledge is a causal concept states it to be a semantic feature of 'know' and its cognates that the fact that p must be among the causal antecedents of any state that can be correctly described as *knowledge* that p. (There are provisos about *a priori* knowledge and variants to the particular formulation given here.) The thesis does not leave 'to the knowing subject only a passive role' (above, p. 178), nor does it have the other implications Douglas believes it to have. On the other hand, if I have understood correctly the tone of 'Our philosopher really thinks that "the superstructure of cosmological ideas in our society" posesses a "degree of relative autonomy from its social base" ' (above, p. 184), Professor Douglas thinks the superstructure possesses no autonomy at all. Such a view might indeed be thought to leave the knowing subject only a passive role.

(ii) I am at a loss to know on what basis Douglas thinks me 'unaware of the deep conflicts and grave doubts' (above, p. 184) in contemporary science, unless she takes that to be an implication of my point about the proliferation of scientific élites, and the relative (in comparison with primitive societies) efficiency of the channels for transmitting their ideas. There is, of course, no such implication. On the contrary, relative openness in the dissemination and exchange of ideas may increase conflicts and doubts.

(iii) I do not mention Durkeim's distinctions between 'organic' and 'mechanical', and 'sacred' and 'profane', and certainly would not want to 'reduce' them to 'purely intellectual needs for acceptable theoretical construction' (above, p. 182). I don't even know what that would involve. I don't deny that Durkheim held religious ideas to be symbolic representations of the social order; only that he was right. Since Douglas does not disagree on the presence of a 'modelling' and a 'symbolist' thread in Durkheim's writings, I fail to see what my misunderstanding is supposed to be. Whether the threads, which we agree are there, are compatible with each other is another question.

PART FOUR

TOWARDS A NON-RELATIVIST
SOCIOLOGY OF THOUGHT

11. Material-object Language and Theoretical Language: Towards a Strawsonian Sociology of Thought
by Robin Horton

TRADITIONALLY, much Anglo-American work on the sociology of thought has been directly dependent on continental European inspiration. One might, indeed, say that it has been a poor relative of continental 'sociology of knowledge'. My own feeling is that we have more or less exhausted the potential of this poor-relation status. In particular, anglophone works in the German 'sociology of knowledge' tradition seem to heave every year more mountainously for the production of smaller and smaller mice.

Recently, however, there have been signs of the development of a more vigorous and independent English line in this area. And it is this line whose potential I wish to explore in the present paper.

To be fair, of course, we shall have to start by acknowledging the ultimate continental paternity of these ideas. For if they have any one father, it is clearly Wittgenstein. And although his influence on Anglo-American philosophy has been so great that many people have come to think of him as an English figure, he, in fact, brought with him to the English scene a preoccupation with the structure and limits of reason which was clearly in the great German tradition.[1] Nonetheless, the English intellectual milieu in which he spent so many fruitful years of his life did, in turn, put its mark upon him. As a result, he left us with a body of work in which the rich but often misty depths of continental rationalism were tempered, to a remarkable degree, with the sturdy, no-nonsense character of the English empiricism of his time.

For the sociologist of thought, the inevitable starting-point is the later Wittgenstein's insistence on placing the use of language in its full context of ongoing social life. Some of his disciples, alas, succeeded in trivializing this theme, reducing it to a pedantic investigation of the minutiae of English usage. They bear much of the responsibility for the generally negative, lay image of recent Anglo-American philosophy. Fortunately, however, there were others who realized that Wittgenstein's later work was a treasure-trove of profound, if often elliptical, suggestions as to the nature of the circular dependency linking thought/language and society, a potential source of inspiration for a whole new tradition in the sociology of thought.

The results so far are not enormous; but they are the more exciting in that they seem to be taking the form of a debate rather than of an orthodoxy. I think we can best understand this debate if we take as its pioneering protagonists the philosophers Winch and Strawson,[2] and if we view the difference between them as stemming from a difference with respect to the question of which part of the circle of dependency deserves the greatest emphasis. Winch's attitude is aptly summarized by his slogan: 'Logical relations between propositions depend on social relations between men'.[3] And I think we might summarize Strawson's attitude, without too much injustice, by putting into his mouth the opposing slogan; 'Social relations between men depend on logical relations between propositions.'

I shall elaborate a little on what lies behind these slogans. Winch starts with social relations as his independent variable. Given his acquaintance with the findings of modern social anthropology, it is natural for him to conceive of such relations as almost infinitely plastic. And since he sees patterns of thought as dependent on them, he is drawn inexorably into seeing the latter as having an equal plasticity. What emerges is a vision, not just of a myriad alternative world-views, but of a myriad alternative logics, basic category-systems, truth-criteria, and so on. This, of course, is a travesty of Winch's extremely subtle line of overt argumentation; but I suspect that it is a good approximation to the underlying vectors of his thought. In the event, despite several attempts to draw back from extremity, he gives us the preliminary sketch for a sociology of thought which combines a thoroughgoing sociological determinism with an equally thoroughgoing relativism in the realm of criteria of truth, agreement with reality, causality, and so on. How such a sociology of thought might develop is hinted at in a most exhilarating manner in some of Mary Douglas' recent essays.[4]

Strawson, by contrast, starts with patterns of thought as his independent variable. More specifically, he starts with the old Kantian problem of how it is that we feel ourselves 'stuck' with certain categories of thought, processes of influence, etc. He follows Kant to the point of agreeing with him that such categories and processes are the inescapable basis of all our more particular chains of thought. However, in answering the question: 'Why this basis rather than another?', he is not content with Kant's answer that this is simply our innate human heritage. Instead, he gives a decidedly sociological answer. He says, in effect, that language is the indispensable instrument of the kind of social co-ordination that is distinctive of the human species. Further, if it is to be effective as such an instrument, it must include the following: something like our everyday Western conception of material objects which exist and persist independently of ourselves; something like our everyday spatial and temporal concepts; something like our everyday differentiation between persons and non-persons; something like our everyday notion of causality; something like our everyday idea of and attitude to contradiction; something like our everyday concepts of truth, falsity and agreement with reality. There is neither the time nor the space here for Strawson's detailed arguments for the indispensability of each of these items. Suffice it to say that he considers them, jointly, to be the vital prerequisite to the persistence of human social co-ordination. And it is this status, in turn, that keeps them entrenched at the basis of everyday thought/language in all human cultures. Here, once again, we have the preliminary sketch for a whole programme in the sociology of thought; but it is a sketch very different from the one offered by Winch. Although there is the same thoroughgoing sociological determinism,[5] there is a strong stress on cross-cultural invariants underlying the apparent diversity of human thought. In particular, there is an emphasis on invariant criteria in realms such as causality, truth, and agreement with reality. How *this* sociology of thought might develop in detail has been outlined in a number of well-known papers by Steven Lukes.[6]

Amongst sociologists of thought generally, the Winchian programme seems so far to have enjoyed a greater vogue than the Strawsonian. To this particular sociologist of thought, however, the Strawsonian programme seems vastly more attractive. And in the present paper, I shall try to add what I can to Lukes' valiant efforts at redressing the balance.

In this matter, I must confess at the outset to being subject to strong situational pressures. As Mary Douglas points out, the kind of relativism inherent in the Winchian position is a threat to our cognitive security; and it therefore requires a certain amount of daring to uphold.[7] What Douglas neglects to mention, however, is that the intensity of the threat and the amount of daring necessary to defy it vary enormously with circumstances.

For the sociologist who has never been exposed to life in a radically alien culture, or for the social anthropologist who has long since retired from 'the field', neither the threat nor the daring required to defy it are very great. It is easy to preach relativism from the confines of a particular world-view, secure in the knowledge that problems involving choice *between* world-views are never, or never again, going to arise in the course of one's own personal life. It is far less easy to accept relativism if (like me) one is an expatriate Englishman living in a country racked by cognitive transition — a country where most of those around one constantly face problems involving choice *between* world-views, and where indeed such problems intrude quite often into one's own personal life. In short, given my own situation, I find the threat too great and the daring required too much to allow me to opt for Winch as against Strawson. I don't think there is much to be ashamed of in this. After all, front line prudence is neither more nor less honourable than rear echelon bravado! Further, I think that, in this setting, a Winchian stand could be held to be a sign of incipient psychosis and a Strawsonian stand a sign of sanity. Having said all this, however, I must admit that it still does not amount to rationally adequate grounds for preferring Strawson to Winch. It is such grounds that I shall try to supply in what follows.

However great one's admiration for Strawson, one must recognize, at the outset, that both his basic premisses about the nature of human social life and the part played in the latter by language, and his deductions from these premisses, emanate from an Oxford armchair. If he wishes, as he clearly does, to have his thesis accepted as valid for mankind at all times and places, then he has got to agree to its treatment as a theory which can be confirmed or falsified by the findings of historians, social anthropologists, ethno-scientists and cross-cultural psychologists.

What I find surprising is that so many reputable commentators on Strawson's thesis seem convinced, more or less in advance of any massive body of relevant work, that such a cross-cultural check will inevitably invalidate it.[8] For it seems to me that such evidence as has come in so far is by no means unambiguously negative.

In this connection, I should like to start by drawing your attention to two pieces of evidence which, for all their homeliness, seem to me to provide considerable positive support for the Strawson line. The first is the confidence with which linguists, a breed whom one would expect to be more-than-averagely cautious about such things, make use, for the purpose of their cross-cultural comparisons, of standard English word-lists which draw heavily on items derived from the realm of everyday material-object discourse. (The relevance of this, of course, being that such confidence rests on the conviction that in all other languages it is possible to find direct, word-for-word translations of the items on these lists.) The second is the near-unanimity with which anthropologists who have followed the British tradition of long periods of participant observation have testified to the effect that, through much of their daily lives in various alien cultures, they have felt themselves to be living in a world whose conceptual organization is basically the same as that of their familiar everyday world. It was this conviction, indeed, which led to the massive outcry by field anthropologists against Levy-Bruhl's early thesis of the radical 'otherness' of the thought-patterns of prescientific cultures.[9] And it was the cogency of the anthropologists' arguments that forced Levy-Bruhl to modify this thesis quite considerably in his later writings. Thus he swept away his earlier picture of primitive man as entirely 'mystical' and radically puzzling to the anthropologist. Instead, he introduced a picture in which primitive man lived out most of his life at the commonsense, everyday level where the anthropologist could meet him with the greatest of ease. If the primitive jumped periodically to the 'mystical' level, thereby leaving the earthbound anthropologist with a puzzled frown on his face, these jumps were fairly transient abandonments of the world of everyday.[10] As a general picture of the situation of the anthropologist in a radically alien culture, this has remained broadly acceptable in the profession till quite recent times. If some no longer accept it, I suggest that this is because, in their intoxication with Winchian doctrines, they have forgotten the human realities of their fieldwork experience.[11]

In both of these cases, it is the experience of learning various languages, patterns of thought and ways of life from scratch in the field (i.e. without the aid of written dictionaries, grammars and ethnographies) that we take as ground for our conviction as to the universality of a basic material-object discourse. Such experience seems as good a ground as any for confidence in the thesis under discussion. It must be admitted, however, that there are two influential lines of criticism of this position. So far as I know, neither of them has been taken up by Winch himself. But there are signs that both are attractive to sociologists of a Winchian pursuasion; and we must give them very serious consideration before returning even a provisional verdict in favour of Strawson.

The first line of criticism is a philosophical one. It comes from Quine and those of his disciples who suggest that the thesis of a universal, everyday material-object framework is simply the artefact of concealed *a priori* postulates. According to the Quineans, the field linguist/anthropologist, for all his faith in the objective basis of his translations of words, phrases and sentences, has in fact no basis for these operations other than a set of arbitrarily-established equivalences which beg the very questions of translational correctness that are at issue. Worse still, he *can* have no other basis for such operations.[12]

Clearly, this line of argument strikes at the very foundations of the anthropologist's fieldwork *credo*. It threatens to degrade the entire soul-rending struggle for translational correctness to the status of a delusion. At the same time, I think every anthropologist confronted with it will feel that there is something missing: that, by omitting some element of his procedure of whose importance he is dimly aware but which he can't quite specify, the clever philosophers have made him seem more deluded than he really is. He will feel like an honest but somewhat slow-witted man about to be deprived of his birthright in a civil court by a super-smart opposing counsel. Fortunately, however, excellent defending counsel have now appeared to articulate his case. Here, I refer to a number of other philosophers of language who, in reply to the Quineans, have pointed out that the anthropologist's translational hunches depend to an important extent on non-linguistic behavioural criteria, and hence cannot just be dismissed as begging the questions they seek to answer.[13]

The second line of criticism comes from the ethno-scientists and the cross-cultural psychologists. These are people who rely for the most part on carefully controlled tests and questionnaires, rather than upon the long periods of participant observation beloved of the anthropologist. Predictably, they criticize the anthropologist's assertions about the universality of the everyday material-object framework on the ground that they rest, not on carefully controlled, exactly specified and readily repeatable operations, but rather on largely intuitive assessments.[14]

In reply, I would make two points. First: for all their controlled, scientific character, the tests and questionnaires of the cross-cultural psychologists remain to some extent vulnerable to the old question so often asked of IQ tests: 'Just what do they tell us about the thought/language of their subjects outside the immediate context of the test situation?'[15] Second: that the assessments of the anthropologist are none the worse for being largely intuitive. For 'intuitive', here, refers to a long and intricate process of translational trial-and-error; a process in which each step is controlled by feedback from members of the community in which the anthropologist is trying to settle. The anthropologist, desperately concerned as he is with the task of trying to 'fit in', has neither the time nor the disposition to stand back and watch himself at it, so, naturally enough, he can report little or nothing about the detail of the process. However, if all goes well, he eventually reaches a kind of plateau of acculturation. Once here, he finds himself able to anticipate the broad outlines of people's reactions to most everyday situations, and able to comprehend in retrospect where he cannot actually anticipate. In its own particular way, the achievement of such a plateau is surely an impressive guarantee of the objectivity of the complex process of on-the-job experiment which led up to it.

So much for the general criticism from ethno-science and cross-cultural psychology. We must also, however, give serious consideration to two more specific attempts to refute the Strawsonian thesis with the aid of data drawn from these disciplines. Here, I am thinking of the chapter on 'The Apparent Invariants of Thought and Language' in Toulmin's *Human Understanding*, and the more recent article by Hallpike entitled 'Is There a Primitive Mind?'[16] Both of these pieces adduce a wealth of evidence from cross-cultural experiments on colour-classification, Piagetian conservation, perception of visual illusions and so on. And both purport to show that such evidence rules out the possibility of a universal, everyday material-object framework.

To my mind, both of these pieces fail in their aim. At the very most, what the evidence they adduce shows is: (a) that certain non-Western cultures exploit the potentialities of everyday, material-object thought/language less efficiently in the area of non-human entities and processes than in the area of human relationships; and (b) that the converse is true for modern Western culture. The evidence also shows that such differences manifest themselves in individual members of the cultures concerned at a very early age. What it certainly does not show is that the non-Western cultures examined *lack* the kind of material-object concept which is the basis of everyday life in the modern West, or that they possess entirely different concepts of causality, truth, and agreement with reality. It is with these key features *of* the everyday framework that Strawson is concerned; not with differences of elaboration, emphasis and development *within* the framework. Such differences obviously constitute a problem from the Strawsonian; but, as I hope to show later, the problem is far from insuperable.

To sum up, then, the evidence available to date is by no means unfavourable to Strawson. In particular, the Strawsonian hunches of an earlier generation of social anthropologists emerge remarkably well from the assaults upon them by younger scholars hailing both from within social anthropology and from a variety of neighbouring disciplines.

Having cleared the ground for a more receptive attitude to the thesis of a universal, everday material-object language, I should like to show, with reference to some work of my own, that this thesis can be a powerful source of positive understanding in a cross-cultural sociology of thought.

Over the past few years, I have been concerned with a somewhat ambitious comparative study of patterns of thought in Africa and the West. I have been trying, first, to map similarities and differences between the two sets of patterns, and second, to work toward an ultimate sociological explanation of both the similarities and the differences. In the course of this work, I have found myself relying increasingly on an extended version of the Strawsonian thesis: a version which sees the everyday, material-object framework as operating at all times and places in conjunction with one or more theoretical frameworks, but which stresses the multifarious dependence of the latter upon the former.

In good Strawsonian fashion, I start with the suggestion that traditional African and modern Western cultures share the same basic, everyday framework.

The ease of direct, word-for-word translation of so much of the everyday sector of European languages into the various African tongues makes it clear that the cultures associated with these tongues share a great many material-object concepts with the modern West. Further, in both African and Western cultures, material-objects are defined and differentiated to an important extent in terms of their dispositional/causal properties, and particularly in terms of those of such properties as make them directly or indirectly instrumental to the achievement of common human goals.

The foregoing remarks suggest a shared, everyday concept of causality. And Western anthropologists whose fieldwork has included participation in such everyday activities as farming, fishing, and house-building will readily fall in with this suggestion. In both sets of cultures, the idea of causation seems to draw its inspiration from the realm of human action upon the non-human environment. In both, however, the idea is made applicable beyond this realm by abstracting certain features which are typical of cases within it, but which are also discoverable in the wider world beyond it. There has been considerable debate as to what should be included in the inventory of such abstracted features. Everyone, however, seems to agree on the importance in this context of the contiguity of the events concerned in space and time.[17]

Wherever the observer perceives such features as instantiated in his environment, he makes an immediate judgement of causal connection. And, for the normal run of everyday events, this immediacy of judgement makes possible a great rapidity of practical decision. It must be admitted, however, that the verdict of such judgement is not always unambiguous. For there are times when, in the light of the standard everyday criteria, several events stand out as possible causes of a particular effect. In such situations, an informal version of Mill's Canons is brought into play, in order to eliminate all but one of the proposed alternatives. Now the possibility of using such a process of elimination depends upon one's ability to supply a limited list of eligible causes — an ability which cannot be taken for granted.[18] At the level which we are currently discussing, however, there is no problem. For the everyday criteria of assessment (in particular the criterion of spatio-temporal contiguity) ensure that the list of eligible causes is strictly limited. Even where the verdict of everyday causal judgement is ambiguous, then, a rapid resolution of the ambiguity is usually possible.

Both sets of cultures also share the same everyday concepts of truth and falsity: concepts closely associated with criteria of confirmation and falsification by inter-subjectively repeatable experience. As Lukes has pointed out,[19] such cases of deviant truth-concepts as have been reported from African cultures by anthropologists turn out to be parasitic on the more usual concepts. They assume the ultimate validity of the latter, and are only brought into play where the requisite confirming or falsifying experience is unavailable.

Finally, both sets of cultures share the same everyday abhorrence of contradiction: an abhorrence manifested in the correction and/or ridicule of those who either knowingly or inadvertently contradict themselves. So much for the everyday framework. Let us now turn to theory.

In both sets of cultures, it is where everyday language reaches the limits of its competence that theoretical language comes into play. The most important of such limits is that associated with causal judgement. The mechanism of immediate causal perception, though it contributes so much to the smooth running of everyday social life, works, nonetheless, only under fairly specific circumstances, and is of little use where these do not obtain. Notably, it is of no further use in cases where eliminative induction has failed to reveal any causal correlates amongst events standing in immediate spatio-temporal contiguity to some puzzling phenomenon. Theory can be understood, first and foremost, in terms of the pressing need to supply the missing causal context in such recalcitrant cases.[20]

At this point, we are faced with an intriguing paradox. It is that, although theoretical language is brought into play to make up for the deficiencies of everyday language, its structure and content are nonetheless almost wholly derived from the latter. Theory performs its functions, not by introducing entirely new linguistic and conceptual resources, but by extending and indeed 'stretching' the resources of everyday discourse.

One aspect of this 'stretching' process which has been widely recognized already is the use of analogies drawn from everyday experience in the building up of theoretical schemata. The crucial role played by analogies drawn from the realm of human social relations in building up the spiritual cosmologies of African cultures has long been recognized by social anthropologists. The equally crucial role played by analogies drawn from the non-personal realm of everyday experience in building up the various theories of modern Western science has now been given a belated but nonetheless clear recognition by philosophers such as Harré and Hesse.[21]

What is less widely recognized is that the 'stretching' of everyday conceptual resources is crucial, not just to the building of particular theoretical schemes, but to the development of the most basic concepts of theoretical thought generally.

Here, the most striking instance is provided by the concept of causality. In both African and Western cultures, as we have seen, the criterion of spatio-temporal contiguity is crucial to everyday causal judgements. But it also turns up as a guiding notion, both in the personal theories of Africa, and in the impersonal theories of the West.

In the personal theories, it is manifested in the idea of spiritual omnipresence. Though at first glance this seems to be the most un-everyday idea of them all, a more searching look at the particular contexts in which it occurs soon dispels this impression. Thus the contexts in which the idea is most clearly exhibited are the innumerable situations where ideas about spiritual beings serve to link a great array of events to causal antecedents that, because they are not contiguous in space and time, cannot be picked out by the everyday eye. Now, in such situations, there seems to be a compulsion to conceive of the beings involved as present, both wherever the events they are invoked to explain take place, wherever the causal antecedents of these events occurred, and at all points in between. Whence this compulsion? The only plausible explanation would seem to be that it is our old friend the principle of spatio-temporal contiguity at work, requiring the assertion that, although at the everyday level there is a gap between effect and cause, at the level of unobservables there is contiguity.[22]

In modern Western science, there is a parallel tendency to accept only those theoretical models in which all postulated causal connections assert spatio-temporal contiguity between the events and entities involved. In this context, the prominence given to Newtonian dynamics in discussions of scientific method is misleading. For not only did Newton's contemporaries regard his idea of action at a distance as scandalous: he himself had misgivings about it.[23] Again, as a modern leader in the field has said, the whole of post-Newtonian physics can be regarded as an attempt to restore spatio-temporal contiguity as a guiding principle in the formulation of ideas about causal connections between the events and entities postulated by theory.[24]

Another clear instance of the 'stretching' of everyday conceptual resources is in the realm of concepts of truth and reality.

One of the notable things about African theoretical thinking is the frequency with which ideas about the nature and behaviour of the wind are used to explicate ideas about the nature and behaviour of spiritual beings. There is no particular mystery about this, however. For although the tangibility of the wind places it in the everyday world, its invisibility gives it a kinship with the entities of the theoretical world. Having, so to speak, a foot in both worlds, it is an ideal vehicle for the transfer of concepts from the one to the other. And one of its commonest uses is to show how everyday concepts of truth and reality can be given a 'stretched' application to the realm of theoretical entities. In this context, a typical explicatory statement is that made by the Tonga: 'We know what the spirits are by what they do; just as we do not see the wind but know that it is present by what it does'.[25] Such statements are symptomatic of a very widespread tendency to justify ideas about spiritual action in terms of the same criteria of empirical confirmation/falsification as reign in the everyday world. This tendency has received its clearest articulation in recent years, when indigenous thinkers have been faced with the somewhat obscure truth-criteria for statements about spiritual forces offered by the Christian missionary churches. Indeed, one of the more characteristically African features of the hundreds of 'spiritual' churches which have been breaking away from the missionary foundations all over the continent is their highly explicit insistence on the here-and-now, empirical cash-value of all statements about spiritual beings.[26]

In the sciences, the situation is a little more complex. For in the Instrumentalists, we have a body of thinkers who assert that theoretical statements make no factual claims, but are merely tools for prediction. Nonetheless, I think it is reasonable to say that the mainstream of theoretical thinking in the sciences has been realistically inclined.[27] And in trying to suggest what criteria of truth and agreement with reality are appropriate to scientific theory, realist writers have by and large relied on extensions of everyday criteria of empirical confirmation/falsification.[28]

Yet another instance of 'stretching' is to be found in the language used to conceptualize the relation *between* the world portrayed by everyday discourse and the world portrayed by theoretical discourse.

Whether in Africa or in the West, we find that much of the terminology used in this context is the same. Thus, on some occasions, the events of everyday life are talked of as perceptually given, whilst the events referred to by theory are talked of as 'hidden', 'underlying', 'inner'. On other occasions, the events of everyday life are seen as effects, and the events referred to by theory as causes. And on yet other occasions, the events of everyday are *identified* with events referred to by theory. Characteristically, none of these different ways of conceptualizing the relation between the two realms is felt to be entirely adequate in itself: hence a tendency to oscillate amongst them. What is striking is that all three ways of talking about the relation between the realms are entirely dependent on concepts taken from everyday discourse.[29]

Finally in this discussion of the 'stretching' process, I

should like to mention briefly a phenomenon which is more accurately described as a symptom than an instance.

In both African and Western cultures, as we have seen, contradiction is both avoided and condemned at the everyday level. Yet at the level of theory, and in the attempt to define the relation of the world of everyday to the world of theory, contradictions are rather frequent. Indeed, their abundance in these areas is one of the things that helps to keep philosophers in business. Puzzling as this phenomenon has been, both to philosophers and to anthropologists, its explanation follows clearly enough from what I have been saying about the 'stretching' process, and indeed is implicit in the very metaphor of 'stretching'. It is an inevitable consequence of the deployment of the resources of everyday material-object language in contexts entirely different from those for which they were primarily designed. Over-stretching leads to breakage. And contradiction, here, is the symptom of breakage.[30]

It should now be evident that, both in African and in Western cultures, the most ambitious flights of the theoretical imagination are constrained by limits which, in the last analysis, are the limits imposed by the everyday material-object language. And at this point, we must ask ourselves why the material-object framework has had such an all-pervasive, inescapable influence on human thought generally.

In attempting an answer, let us return to our source of inspiration. Strawson, you will recall, makes the persistence of the distinctively human type of social co-ordination dependent on the presence of the various salient features of the everyday material-object framework. And he makes the latter's entrenched position at the heart of culture, dependent, in turn, on its status as a prerequisite for the survival of human society.

This explanation, as I hope to show presently, may take us very near the heart of the matter. As it stands, however, it wears an air of vague teleological circularity which does less than justice to its potential. In what follows, I shall suggest how we may increase its bite by giving it some more definite, causal teeth.

As a start, let us look back past Strawson to Kant, and seriously reconsider the possibility that we are dealing here with an area in which innate predisposition plays an important part. Nobody, I think, will jib at the proposition that both the human eye and the human hand are organs specialized to cope with the perception and manipulation of middle-sized persisting objects at medium distances from the body, and that such specialization is part of our inate biological inheritance. In principle, then, it should be no harder to accept that the brain, as the organ which co-ordinates the two, is similarly specialized, and that such specialization is similarly innate.

Recent studies of cognitive development in very young children would seem to have given renewed popularity to the thesis of innate predispositions in this area. Thus it is suggested that the new-born infant is somehow 'set' to perceive, pick up causal connections among and manipulate enduring physical objects of medium size, and to differentiate between non-human objects and persons. Although this cluster of aptitudes needs learning and practice for its full development, much of the groundwork has been laid by the time language learning begins.[31] As regards language itself, many psychologists and linguists, even though they will not go all the way with the Chomskian thesis of an innate 'grammatical faculty', accept nonetheless that linguistic learning and development are subject to certain innate constraints. A typical suggestion is that: (a) the correspondence between the structure of everyday material-object language and the structure of the cognitive schemata already formed in the infant mind is what makes possible the great rapidity of infant language learning; and (b) language could not be learned at all if it did not include a key element whose structure corresponded with and latched on to these pre-established schemata.[32]

For suggestions as to how man might have come to

acquire such innate predispositions, we must turn to the work of those biologists who have interested themselves in specifically human evolution. The biologists see everyday material-object language and its associated cognitive aptitudes as crucial to the manual technology, social co-operation and transmission of acquired knowledge which distinguished early man from the beasts. They suggest, moreover, that it was these linguistic, cognitive and behavioural characteristics which enabled early man to carve out an ecological niche for himself and survive in coexistence with non-human primates and other large predatory mammals. From this suggestion about biological survival value, an interesting thesis follows. It is that material-object language and its associated cognitive aptitudes did not just *result* accidentally from certain evolutionary developments in the structure of eye, brain and hand. Once present in their rudimentary forms, they actually *caused* additional evolutionary developments in these areas, of a kind conducive to their own further elaboration. For their survival value encouraged the persistence and spread of all genetic mutations giving rise to ocular, cerebral and manual characteristics which particularly favoured them. As a result, innate predisposition to the cognitive aptitudes associated with material-object language may well have been stamped into man's genetic heritage well before natural selection ceased to be a force in human development.[33]

Obviously we have to proceed with caution in an area like this, where current consensus can change overnight with the impact of new findings, and where there is, in any case, considerable debate over the interpretation of existing findings. Nonetheless, it seems that we have here at least a prospect of accounting for the universal and deeply-entrenched character of the material-object framework, and for its controlling influence, even on the theoretical thought, whose central role is that of making up for its deficiencies. These proposals, if correct, are a further vindication of Strawson; for although they substitute a causal for a teleological account, they retain the circular relationship between organized society and the material-object framework which is essential to his interpretation.

So far in this exposition, I have concentrated on showing that, underlying the apparently large differences between African and Western thought-patterns, there is a shared (and probably universal) cognitive framework. As yet, however, I have done nothing to show just how these differences arose and why they persist. In what follows, I shall try to show that a Strawsonian approach is adequate to this second task also.

One could of course spend years arguing over the composition of a list of differences between African and Western cultures. Here, I shall restrict myself to three points upon which some kind of consensus seems to obtain.

(1) African cultures exploit the potentialities of everyday thought/language more efficiently in the area of human personal relationships than in the area of non-human entities and processes. Western cultures, by contrast, exploit the potentialities of everyday thought/language more efficiently in the non-human area than in the human, personal area.

(2) African cultures have by and large opted for a personal idiom in their theoretical constructions, building up cosmologies which are essentially spiritualistic in character. Western cultures have, by contrast, opted more and more for an impersonal idiom of theory.

(3) African cultures have not gone very far in developing that complex of attitudes toward theory which we call scientific. In Western cultures, by contrast, scientific attitudes have come to cast their shadow over the whole of human life.

(1) We start here with the question of why sub-saharan Africa 'refused' mechanical technology whilst the mediaeval West embraced it. As Antony Hopkins shows with great

brilliance, this is a question to which we can give at least a plausible answer without any assumption of deep-seated prior differences in modes of thought.[34] Hopkins points out that the sub-saharan peoples were early acquainted with a number of basic mechanical devices such as the wheel. Given the nature of the early economies of the area, however, such devices were not particularly attractive in cost-benefit terms; and they were therefore rejected. In mediaeval Europe, by contrast, the character of the economy not only made the same basic devices attractive in cost-benefit terms: it also made the role of mechanical inventor economically and socially attractive.

Once this initial divergence of response had taken place, a lot of things followed. In Africa, exploration of the realm of non-human and especially of non-living things lagged behind exploration of the realm of human social relations. In the West, exploration of the realm of the non-living shot ahead of exploration of the human social realm. Indeed, as the latter became progressively destabilized by the rapid growth of technology, it became more and more difficult to explore.

Such differences, once established at the adult level, would not have been confined in their effects to that level. Sooner or later, they would have been felt at the earliest stages of socialization. And this, I think, is the point at which we may be able to integrate some of the findings of the cross-cultural developmental psychologist's. As I said earlier, it is by no means easy to know what broader implications to draw from many of their tests and experiments. One piece of research stands out, however, because it is based on close observation of children in family settings during their first few years of life. This is Rabain-Zempleni's work on Wolof children.[35] Rabain-Zempleni's main finding is that Wolof children, from their very earliest months, develop in an environment in which fellow human beings enjoy a vastly greater prominence than non-living objects, and in which their responses to fellow human beings are much more actively encouraged and evaluated than their responses to non-living objects. She suggests that Western infants, by contrast, develop in an environment in which the non-living sector is a good deal more prominent, and in which their responses to this sector receive considerably greater encouragement and evaluation. To my (not perhaps up-to-date?) knowledge, this is still an isolated piece of work. But, so far as my own impressionistic comparisons of the treatment of very young children in Kalabari households in the Niger Delta with the treatment of their counterparts in English middle-class households are concerned, it certainly 'rings a bell'. And it is the more plausible because, given the differences in adult perceptions of the various sectors of the everyday world discussed above, these differences in the treatment of children are of just the sort that we should expect to flow from them.

We must hope that Rabain-Zempleni's very suggestive thesis will soon be further tested by parallel studies in other African cultures. Meanwhile, if the differences in early upbringing which she postulates *are* generally operative, they must have a strongly reinforcing effect on the divergences already described. They must tend to make the member of a traditional culture in Africa even more adept in the realm of human relations and even less adept in the realm of non-living things, and the post-mediaeval Westerner even more adept in the realm of non-living things and even less adept in the realm of human social relations. In short, two sets of 'vicious circles' must be operating.

The interpretation offered here is essentially Strawsonian in character: for it assumes the operation of a universal, everyday, cognitive framework in two different socio-economic (or historical) settings.

(2) In attempting to account for differences of theoretical idiom as between African and Western cultures, I postulate a 'logic' of theory-building which is common to both. It goes as follows:

(a) In theory-building, we use schemas of 'underlying' reality to introduce order, regularity and predictability into areas of experience in which these qualities are not apparent to the everyday eye.

(b) The only way in which such schemas can be built up is on the basis of analogies drawn from the everyday level of experience.

(c) Given the aim as described in (a), and the limitation of means as described in (b), the only *rational* move is to draw one's analogies from those areas of one's everyday experience maximally associated with order, regularity and predictability.

(d) Given the differences described in (1), the areas of everyday experience maximally associated with order, regularity and predictability differ radically as between African and Western cultures. In the former, it is the area of human social relations that is maximally associated with these qualities. In the latter, it is the area of non-living events and processes.

(e) Given all of the above, the rational move for the theory-builder in the African context is to draw his analogies from the area of interpersonal relations, whilst the rational move for the modern Westerner is to draw his analogies from the area of non-living events and processes.

Note once again that the interpretation is essentially a Strawsonian one. For it is based on the assumption of a universal logic governing the 'stretching' of the resources of the everyday material-object language: a logic which produces different results when it operates in different socioeconomic (or historical) settings.[36]

(3) In attempting to account for the differential development of a scientific attitude toward theory, I start with the question of whether or not a given culture lacks or includes

competition between different basic views of the world. I suggest that, in the traditional cultures of sub-saharan Africa, this kind of competition by and large did not arise, but that, at certain crucial periods in the history of Western culture (notably in the post-mediaeval period) such competition became a salient feature of life.

There are a number of fairly humdrum social and historical factors that can serve to bring about the replacement of a single, over-arching world-view by a multiplicity of competing world-views: the amalgamation of culturally heterogenous populations into commercial 'cross-roads' communities; the development of long-distance trade, travel and exploration as a salient feature of a country's way of life; the influence of increasing occupational specialization within a culture, and so on.[37] But although there is nothing particularly mysterious about the change, its consequences for patterns of thought are momentous.

Where there is a single over-arching world-view which has a monopoly of people's cognitive preoccupations, the main challenge to established theory comes from new patterns of everyday experience. In the normal run of things, such a challenge can be coped with by piecemeal adjustments *within* the framework of the theory; by introducing new auxiliary postulates, by challenging the validity of the experience, and so on. Though over several generations, such adjustments may change the framework itself, members of any one generation are characteristically largely unaware of such change, and tend to accept the main premisses of the established body of theory as having a timeless, absolute validity.

Where there is a multiplicity of competing world-views, the challenge to any particular body of theory comes from two sources. As ever, of course, it comes from new patterns of everyday experience. Now, however, it comes also from the adherents of rival world-views. And in order to ensure the survival of a particular world-view in the face of its rivals, its holders are compelled to deploy their intellectual resources in a manner for which there was no stimulus in the traditional monopolistic setting. Now, they search assiduously for inconsistencies in rival world-views, as ammunition with which to attack them; and they search with equal enthusiasm for inconsistencies in their own theory, with a view to eliminating those areas of weakness before their rivals get on to them. Now, they no longer wait for new situations to occur, adjusting theory to cover them as they arise. They actively devise and bring about new situations, either in order to show the imperfect explanatory coverage of someone else's theory, or in order to show the superior coverage of their own. Now too, faced with the multiplicity of answers to the same questions about the world, they are unable to sustain the conviction that their's is the only *possible* view of the world. Alongside the determined defence of their own body of theory, a certain undertone of doubt and reservation creeps in. Here, I think, we see the roots of three of the most important differential of the scientific attitude to theory: the systematizing tendency; the dedication to testing by experiment; and the spirit of scepticism which extends even to one's own preferred body of theory. Assessed by the pre-scientific yardstick, the intellectual resources involved in this setting are neither new nor strange. Nonetheless, they are deployed in new directions, and with a sustained intensity and forcefulness which almost turns a difference of degree into a difference in kind.[38]

Note that 'almost' is the key word here. For the theories involved in the competition are generated by the same 'stretching' process as are their pre-scientific counterparts. And when the chips are down, they are justified (and in this case attacked) in the light of the same 'stretched' versions of everyday criteria of truth and agreement with reality as reign in the pre-scientific world.

What I have tried to do here is show that Strawson's ideas about the relations between concepts and society are a viable starting-point for a full-blown cross-cultural sociology of thought. The scheme I have put forward by way of illustration is, admittedly, a tentative one. Apart from anything else, it deals only with African and Western cultures; and it may well prove inapplicable to yet other cultures. What I hope I have shown with its aid, however, is that (*pace* the current Winchian movement) it is possible in principle to construct a cross-cultural sociology of thought which is thoroughgoing *both* in its determinism *and* in its cognitive non-relativism.

As regards determinism, the scheme outlined above makes no concessions, leaves no area of thought 'sacred'. Thus it starts by giving a bio-social account of the universality and all-pervasive influence of the everyday, material-object framework. And it ends by asserting the socio-economic determination of the main differences between African and Western thought-patterns.

As regards cognitive non-relativism, the scheme is equally uncompromising. This is because it portrays the everyday, material-object framework as the ultimate source of criteria of truth and agreement with reality, both at the everyday and at the theoretical levels. Since this everyday framework is cross-culturally invariant, so too are the criteria derived from it.

How such criteria are ultimately to be justified is, of course, another question, and one which I leave to the philosophers.

Notes

1 On this see: Toulmin, S. 'Ludwig Wittgenstein', *Encounter*, Vol. XXXII, No. 1, Jan. 1969.
2 I say 'protagonists' rather than 'antagonists', since, as far as I know, they themselves have not engaged in debate. For representative work, see: Winch, P. *The Idea of a Social Science*, London, 1958; 'Understanding a Primitive Society', *American Philosophical Quarterly*, Vol. I, 1964. Strawson, P. *Individuals*, London 1959; *The Bounds of Sense*, London 1966.

3 Winch, *op. cit.* 1958, p. 126.
4 See for instance: Douglas, M. *Implicit Meanings*, London 1975 (especially the Preface).
5 Although I have talked about the everyday conceptual framework as Strawson's independent variable, his scheme, too, involves sociological determinism. For the everyday framework, in turn, retains its entrenched position because it is a crucial prerequisite to the survival of society. Later on in this paper, I shall try to see if we cannot improve upon the circularity implied here.
6 See: Lukes, S. 'Some Problems about Rationality', *European Journal of Sociology*, Vol. 8, 1967; 'On the Social Determination of Truth', in Horton, R. and Finnegan, R. (eds) *Modes of Thought*, London 1973.
7 Douglas, M., *op. cit.* 1975, pp. XV-XX.
8 For typical comments, see: Hesse, M. *The Structure of Scientific Inference*, London 1974, p. 291. Toulmin, S. *Human Understanding*, London 1922, p. 440.

    Yehuda Elkana, in a personal communication, says ominously of the Strawsonian everyday framework: 'History and Anthropology are knocking on the philosopher's door'.
9 For Lévy-Bruhl's early ideas, see his: *Les Fonctions Mentales dans les Societés Inférieures*, Paris 1910. For a summing up of fieldworking anthropologists' reactions to it, see: Evans-Pritchard, E.E. *Theories of Primitive Religion*, Oxford 1965 (especially Ch. 4: 'Lévy-Bruhl').
10 For this revised version, see: *L'Experience Mystique et les Symboles*, Paris 1938; *Les Carnets*, Paris 1949.
11 Even Mary Douglas seems to slip momentarily from her relativism when she recalls her days in the field. Thus she says disapprovingly of Durkheim: 'He really believed primitives are utterly different from us. A week's fieldwork would have shown him otherwise'. (Douglas, *op. cit.*, p. xi)
12 On this, see: Quine, W. V. *Word and Object*, Cambridge 1960 (Especially chapters 1-2); Hollis, M. 'The Limits of Irrationality' and 'Reason and Ritual' in Wilson, B. (ed.) *Rationality*, Oxford 1970.
13 See especially: Hintikka, J. 'Behavioural Criteria of Radical Translation' in Hintikka, J. and Davidson, D. *Words and Objections*, Dordrecht 1969.
14 The criticisms of these two schools are forcefully presented by an anthropologist in: Hallpike, C. 'Is There a Primitive Mind?' *Man*, 1976.
15 For a note of caution in this sphere, sounded by a psychologist, see: Wober, M. *Psychology in Africa*, London 1976.
16 Toulmin, S. *op. cit.*, 1972. Hallpike, C., *op. cit.*, 1976.
17 For recent discussions of the anthropocentric roots of the concept of causality in Western thought, see: Black, M. 'Making Something

Happen' in *Models and Metaphors*, Ithaca 1962; Anscombe, G. *Causality and Determinism*, Cambridge 1967. For discussions of the importance of spatio-temporal contiguity, see: Ducasse, C. 'On the Nature and Observability of the Causal Relation', *Journal of Philosophy*, Vol. 23, 1926; Michotte, A. *The Perception of Causality*, (Eng. trans.), London 1963. For a discussion of the everyday perception of causality in an African culture, see: Evans-Pritchard, E. *Witchcraft, Oracles and Magic*, Oxford 1936, pp. 33, 464.

18 On this, see: Skyrms, B. *Choice and Chance*, Encino 1975, p. 112-115.
19 Lukes, *op. cit.* 1973.
20 For a fuller discussion of this thesis, see: Horton, R. 'African Traditional Thought and Western Science', Pt. I., *Africa*, Vol. XXXVII, 1967.
21 Hesse, M. *Models and Analogies in Science*, London 1963. Harré, R. *The Principles of Scientific Thinking*, London 1970.
22 For an early discussion of this, see: Evans-Pritchard, *op. cit.* 1936, pp. 33, 464. For more recent discussions, see: Skorupski, J. 'Science and Traditional Religious Thought', Parts III-IV, *Philosophy of Social Science*, Vol. III, 1973, pp. 213-214; Horton, R. 'Paradox and Explanation', Part II, *Philosophy of Social Science*, Vol. III, 1973, pp. 293-312.
23 On this, see: Toulmin, S. and Goodfield, J. *The Architecture of Matter*, London 1962, pp. 194-197.
24 Born, M. *Natural Philosophy of Cause and Chance*, Oxford 1951, pp. 8-9, 16-17, 25-30; *Physics in My Generation*, London 1956, pp. 21-22, 96-98.
25 Quoted by Elizabeth Colson in: Middleton, J. and Beattie, J. *Spirit Mediumship and Society in Africa*, London 1969.
26 On this, see: Horton, R. 'Professor Winch on Safari', *European Journal of Sociology*, Vol. XVII, 1976.
27 On this, see: Elkana Y. *The Problem of Knowledge in Historical Perspective*, Athens 1973; *The Discovery of the Conservation of Energy*, London 1974.
28 See for example: Hesse, M. 'Models and Matter' in Toulmin, S. and Goodfield, J. (eds.) *Quanta and Reality*, London 1962; Born, M., *op. cit.* 1956.
29 For more on this, see: Horton, *op. cit.* 1973.
30 For a more detailed discussion of this whole question of contradiction in theoretical discourse, see: Horton, *op. cit.* 1973.
31 For a clear exposition of the way in which the infant develops its object concepts, without reference to the innate/non-innate controversy, see: Vernon, M. *The Psychology of Perception*, London 1962. For an exposition of this pre-linquistic development as evidence for innate pre-disposition, see: Chomsky, N. *Problems of Knowledge and Freedom*, London 1972, ch. 1 'On Interpreting the World'.
32 For this suggestion, see: Gregory, R. *The Intelligent Eye*, London 1970,

pp. 164-166, 179-180.

[33] For an assembly of some of the sources on the probable causal contribution of early hominid behaviour to genetic change, see: Geertz, C. *The Interpretation of Culture*, London 1975. (Ch. 3: 'The Growth of Culture and the Evolution of Mind'.) For the implications of such a causal contribution in the realm of innate predisposition, see: Monod, J. *Chance and Necessity*, London 1971. More generally, for jogging my thought on to this biosocial track, I am grateful to Vernon Pratt. In several recent conversations, he has made me increasingly sympathetic to the view that the sociologist in general and the sociologist of thought in particular, must come to terms with the work of the biologists concerned with primate evolution.

[34] Hopkins, A. *An Economic History of West Africa*, London 1973.

[35] Rabain-Zempleni, J. *Quelques Reflections sur les Modes Fondamentaux de Relations chez l'Enfant Wolof*, Paris 1965. Discussed at length in: Bruner, J. *Beyond the Information Given*. London 1974. (Ch. 21 'Culture and Cognitive Growth'.)

[36] This is slightly different from Hesse's 'inductive logic' of theory-building. But it might usefully supplement it.

[37] For more on these factors, see: Horton, *op. cit.* 1976.

[38] For a convincing advocacy of the view of science as licensed competition between alternative world-views, see: Lakatos, I. 'Falsification and the Methodology of Scientific Research Programmes' in Lakatos and Musgrave (eds.), *Criticism and the Growth of Knowledge*, Cambridge 1970. For a development of Lakatos' ideas in the service of definition of the traditional/modern divide, see: Horton, R. 'Understanding African Traditional Religion', *Second Order*, Vol. 5, No. 2, January 1976.

12. The Epistemological Unity of Mankind
by Martin Hollis

IN Norwich Castle there hangs a paper dragon which used to
be filled with hot air on carnival days and paraded round the
streets to be mocked by apprentices. Philosophers have too
often made such a dragon of the sociology of knowledge. At
interdisciplinary feasts it is puffed up by ascribing to all prac-
titioners a crass distinction between language-or-thought
and society and a brutal insistence that the latter produces
the former. It is then deflated with cries of 'genetic fallacy'.
Robin Horton, however, gives no excuse for such frivolities.
Having long admired his writings, I subscribe readily to
much of his present paper. But to spare him a bland eulogy
in return for his splendidly provoking thoughts, I shall claim
that he is right for the wrong reasons. In particular I shall dispute the origin and import of the philosophical ideas which
he commends and shall doubt his account of the relation of
theory to experience. Yet I do so in support of the intellectualism which he brings to bear on our understanding of social
life.

Horton's central proposition is, I think, that human life is
itself an attempt to understand human experience. Hence,
as he has argued skillfully elsewhere,[1] science, religion and
other intellectual endeavours are alike extensions of everyday life in search of order and meaning. There is no warrant-
able concept of reality or explanation peculiar to science,
setting the modern above the traditional. This attitude contrasts sharply with the orthodox, Positive sociology, which
still characterizes science, in Comtean spirit, as the replacement of metaphysical prejudice by empirical testing. Horton retorts (rightly I submit) that religion and science are
both theoretical activities and, ultimately, in the same way;

both are designed to remedy the disconnectedness of experience and both extend beyond what experience can verify. At the same time experience is not an independent realm of brute facts. The mundane and the profane are occasions of theorizing, but not prior to it. Just as theorizing permeates interpretation, so ideas about human life permeate social relations. The sociology of thought must start by recognizing 'the circular dependency linking thought/language and society'. In his present paper Horton calls on philosophers to endorse his 'Strawsonian' approach.

It would be sad if his overtures were rebuffed because the philosophers did not recognize themselves in his sketches. Having briefly pointed the danger out, I shall try to separate the ideas from the men. Horton says (or seems to say) that the new English contribution sprang from Wittgenstein, who begat Strawson, Winch and other Oxford philosophers; that Strawson begat Lukes (a healthy line); that Winch begat Douglas (a line not without merit but wrong in supposing society prior to thought); that too many of the rest were either infertile pedants or misallied with the tribe of Quine to produce an outcast relativism. Even allowing for compression, I can accept none of this genealogy. Wittgenstein has found his way into the English mainstream only recently, I think, and then, not by way of Oxford. Strawson's *Individuals* and *Bounds of Sense* were not typical of the conceptual analysis which so many of his colleagues were noted for and I cannot myself see Strawson in Lukes' writings. Winch is indeed a scion of Wittgenstein but not of Oxford philosophy and Mary Douglas tips her philosophical hat to Quine. There is at least room for dispute about the pedigree of the ideas which Horton asks us to consider.

Nor are Strawson and Winch, to my mind, properly dubbed sociological determinists. *Individuals* is erected on the reflection that

> there is a massive central core of human thinking which has no history . . . there are categories and con-

cepts which, in their most fundamental character change not at all... They are commonplaces of the least refined thinking; and are yet the indispensible core of the conceptual equipment of the most sophisticated human beings. (p. 10).

Horton notes the Kantian tenor of Strawson's arguments, yet, to the question of why there is this core, has him give a 'decidedly sociological answer'. Admittedly Strawson (like Kant) seems uncertain what sort of answer he is giving. The introductory chapter of *Individuals* presents it as a fact of descriptive metaphysics that all human beings organize their experience in the same way, whereas other chapters appear to make the core constitutive of all intelligible thought, a Kantian precondition *a priori*. But neither version smacks to me of sociological determinism, except in the too mild sense that the argument starts from linguistic transactions between speaker and hearer. His business is epistemological, not sociological — a contrast I shall exploit in a moment.

Winch does indeed say that 'logical relations between propositions depend on social relations between men'. But, having started by making epistemology queen of the social sciences, he treats social factors as neither independent nor causal. They are not independent because the social world is constituted by rules and inhabited by agents whose deeds and relationships are what they are by virtue of the rules they instance. 'Social relations are expressions of ideas about reality', he writes, on p. 23 of *The Idea of a Social Science*. Social factors are not causal because the form of life to which causal explanations belong — that of the practice of natural science — is inappropriate. Human action is to be identified and understood by finding the rules which agents follow. Admittedly Winch regards social rules as the explanations of the last resort and, in the curious absence of an account of freedom, cannot easily stop us inferring that men follow the rules because they are the rules. But even if he is thus more sociological than Strawson, no orthodox, deterministic sociology of thought seems to me implicit in his idealist notion of social structure.

Separating the ideas from the men, then, we have two views of the social world and of how to understand it. One, the 'Strawsonian', sees societies as groups of individual persons surrounded by objective particulars which they identify and theorize about in basically the same way. Understanding an alien culture is initially a matter of discovering how to perform the tasks of the universal conceptual scheme in another language. The other, 'Winchian', view sees societies as differing sets of institutions, each constituting its own rules to determine what counts as doing whatever actions comprise the social life of that culture. Understanding here is a matter of identifying the rules, and hence, in coming to know how to go on, of grasping the meaning of actions and interactions. These two views are not exhaustive nor wholly exclusive but they differ crucially about ontological and epistemological priorities. The 'Strawsonian' takes the massive central core as given in advance and relies on it in finding first how to use the language mundanely and then how members of the alien culture stretch the language in trying to make sense, after their own fashion, of their experience. For the 'Winchian' there is no given core and no theoretical limit to the possible peculiarity of each culture. Enquiry starts by detecting the constitutive rules and thence determines what is real and rational from within.

With time for discussion Horton and I could no doubt agree on how these views and priorities are best picked out. At any rate, we certainly agree that there is a crucial contrast to draw and one which captures an urgent dispute in current social theorizing. But we shall not agree, I fear, on how to set about deciding the issue. Horton says that if Strawson wants his armchair thesis accepted as valid for mankind at all places and times, then 'he has got to agree to its treatment as a theory, which can be confirmed or falsified by .the findings of historians, social anthropologists, ethno-scientists and cross-cultural psychologists'. Against the prevailing run of investigators, Horton himself finds it confirmed. His own experience points to a universal core of human thinking, whose existence, he hints finally, may have a bio-social, deterministic explanation. The method of decision proposed is thus to see which of the rival paradigms better fits the facts. It is not, I shall reply, that sort of issue.

I share the belief, well-entrenched among philosophers, that epistemological questions are not empirical. The problem of other minds, for instance, is one of the relation of intensional states to manifest behaviour and no amount of field work will settle it. The reason is not that, as used to be said, philosophy starts only after the facts are in. Philosophy has already started before the first fact is gathered, since no enquirer can be a camera, a *tabula rasa*, in making the interpretations which even the first facts embody. In gesturing to a 'bio-social account' and to the 'socio-economic determination' of thought-patterns, Horton is not retracting his earlier remarks about the pervasiveness of theorizing. He treats the dependency linking thought/language and society as circular, and Quine has stated that the puzzle of the indeterminacy of translation is a linguistic version of the 'other minds' problem. It looks as if Horton should have more in common with Quine than his passing swipe suggests.

The common ground may become visible, if we distinguish Quine's strictures on traditional empiricism from his case for pragmatism. That rational belief about the world is underdetermined by experience is a point made in the context of the traditional definition of 'experience' as direct, uninterpreted observation. Insofar as knowledge is treated as a warranted extension of this direct experience, translation and understanding depend on concealed *a priori* postulates and arbitrarily-established equivalences. The problem is then to see what other rational determinants of belief and understanding there are. But this is simply to state the problem and I would expect Horton to find it a genuine problem.

The pragmatist solution is altogether more contentious. It is to make elegance, economy and suggestiveness the arbiters of acceptable translation. When, moreover, we ask what justifies these tests as arbiters, there can be no answer, except perhaps one which explains the choice of them by refernece to our bio-social endowments. For pragmatism denies that there are givens not only in experience but also among the principles by which we organize it. In the seamless web of what we count as knowledge, there are no absolute or external constraints on possible revisions. There are not even independent 'non-linguistic, behavioural criteria' and the anthropologist is left with internal arbiters and, ultimately, faith.

Like Horton, I reject the solution. It is not enough to show how equivalences are unarbitrary within a whole scheme, if the principles for organizing the scheme are themselves arbitrary or bio-socially determined. But I respect the problem. What most threatens to reduce the entire, soul-rending struggle for correctness to a delusion, in my opinion, is the contention that it is entirely an empirical struggle. Winch, for instance, cannot easily prevent us from inferring that what is rational and real for members of a culture is wholly an empirical matter, determined from within by whatever criteria the culture happens to have. There is then no test of an interpretation other than whether it reflects the particular native understanding, and no way of knowing whether it does without first establishing enough correct interpretations. It is an indispensible merit of the Strawsonian view that the anthropologist can tackle other cultures armed with truths which he knows in advance that he will find embodied in the scheme he seeks to understand. Without concealed *a priori* postulates he could produce and justify no interpretations at all.

Any field-work is thus bound to confirm the epistemological unity of mankind. But so abstract an argument gives no hint of the content, and there is at least one large conundrum. However massive the central core, it has its limits.

Mankind does not subscribe to a single set of beliefs about what is real and what is rational. How then are we to decide whether a form of words is rightly interpreted to express a peculiar and local metaphysic or must be recast as a belief which any functioning human is bound to hold? When, in other words, is the belief the test of the translation and when is the translation the test of the belief? I leave it to Strawson to answer. My point in asking — apart from an honest desire to admit a difficulty — is that this too is an epistemological question, illuminated perhaps but not settled by experience. It is no slight on Horton's professional skills to conclude that, when he goes on safari, he takes his philosophy with him. That is why I allege that he is right for the wrong reasons.

Granting that he is right, however, it remains only to speculate on the shape of a sociology of thought grounded in everyday living and a core of human thinking which has no history. One surprising implication seems to be that structural functionalism is true after all. For, at least in Horton's rendering, the core is linked to ways of achieving social coordination and these ways should be as specific and permanent as the content of the core itself. There is a Kantian duty to find the corresponding set of social functions which have no history. The task of reviving this sociological corpse would hardly be a pleasure but, as Kant maintained, the more unpleasant the duty, the greater the merit in doing it.

The implication can be avoided, I think, since it depends on there being a bio-social explanation of the Kantian categories. I said earlier that Strawson's business was epistemological, not sociological. Communication is possible not because persons stand in specific social relations but because they share particular ideas. Social relations come into it secondarily and because they are expressions of ideas about reality. The implication now seems to be that there are no peculiarly sociological explanations but that, in return, the sociologist has his part to play in all explanation of belief and action. For instance there will no longer be a sociology of religion, still less one cast in terms of socio-economic status or secular power, but it will be crucial to understanding religion that believers stand in social relations which in part express their religious beliefs. The central fact of social science will be that man is located essentially, but under protest, in society, and lives an everyday life which makes imperfect sense to mortals.

Intellectualism has many other implications, which there is no time for. But Horton's own writings need no bush and philosophers can scarcely resist his call to study society through an understanding of the mind. If I think the epistemologist's armchair of more strategic use than he, it is not because the minutiae of English usage are sufficient unto themselves. Is a reasoned voice from the armchair universal or parochial? Let us give T.S. Eliot the last, ambiguous word:

> We shall not cease from exploration
> And the end of all our exploring
> Will be to arrive where we started
> And to know the place for the first time.

Note

1   Besides those of his writings he mentions himself, I am especially struck by his article 'Levy-Bruhl, Durkheim and the Scientific Revolution' in R. Finnegan and W.R.G. Horton, (eds.) *Modes of Thought*, London, 1973.

13. Reply to Martin Hollis
by Robin Horton

SINCE brevity is required, let me confine myself to comment on what seem to be the main points of misunderstanding and/or disagreement between Martin Hollis and myself.

1. Hollis takes the aim of my paper to have been that of securing endorsement of my approach by *philosophers*. In fact, my aim was the very different one of persuading *sociologists of thought* that, in their search for theoretical inspiration, they might do well to turn to a new source. In particular, I was suggesting that they stop their unfruitful gazing into the Teutonic mists of the Schutzian *Lebenswelt*, and turn instead to the clear Anglo-Saxon landscape of the Strawsonian 'central core'. True, I presented this paper to a symposium organized by philosophers, primarily for philosophers. But this, I have to admit, was largely because it just happened to be the paper I was working on when the invitation to participate came through! Of course, I hoped that criticisms from the philosophers would help me tighten up my argument. (And in this respect Hollis' contribution has been invaluable; though here I have hardly been able to make more than a start on the tightening-up.) Nonetheless, the ultimate aim was that of converting sociologists, not philosophers.

2. I do not find Hollis' criticism of the intellectual genealogies I sketched at the beginning of my paper very cogent. First, since he has brought Oxford and Cambridge into the discussion (I didn't), let me suggest that, in the post-war decade, Wittgensteinian influence was about equally strong in both places. When I was struggling with undergraduate philosophy at Oxford from 1954 to 1956, Wittgenstein's

233

name was invoked with reverence on all sides and in almost all debates, and possession of the newly published *Investigations* was considered a 'must'.

It seems we agree on Winch's debt to Wittgenstein. As regards Douglas' debt to Winch, I concede that it is not a direct one. Rather, it is the product of an atmosphere of respectful attention to certain aspects of Wittgenstein's dicta about the relations between thought and society — an atmosphere which Winch did much to create. (As for Douglas' 'tip of the hat' to Quine, I would suggest it is little more than that.)

Clearly, we don't agree on Strawson's debt to Wittgenstein. However, apart from clear continuities of interest discernible in his work, Strawson himself has made explicit statements of his Wittgensteinian allegiance in some of his more recent pronouncements.[1] It could of course be that these represent retrospective piety rather than valid statements about actual formative influence; but one would have to ask him if one wanted to get this clear. We seem to disagree also on Lukes' debt to Strawson. Again, however, I don't see any reason to change my mind on this, since Lukes acknowledged the debt in the seminal article in which he first sketched his basic position.[2]

3. Hollis says that I misrepresent the views of both Winch and Strawson. As regards Winch, he complains that I leave out of account his idealism and his exclusion of causal talk from sociology. I am aware of both these aspects of his thought. Indeed, I once criticized them, albeit somewhat amateurishly, in an article.[3] But Winch, like most seminal thinkers, is far from being a paragon of consistency. His official philosophical position does not prevent him from lapses into realistic and quasi-causal talk; and I would argue that such lapses have been as influential as his official line.

As regards Strawson, Hollis complains that I misrepresent him by characterizing his business as sociological rather than epistemological. Here I feel I am on very strong ground. In the first place, Strawson has aligned himself with those who can't be bothered with basic scepticism; and such scepticism seems to me almost definitive of the dedicated epistemologist.[4] Second, he has steadily increased his emphasis on explanation of basic categories, of thought and language in terms of social function in the context of communication. This emphasis was perhaps only implicit in his earlier work.[5] Lately, however, it has become more and more explicit;[6] and he now uses the labels 'semantico-functional' and even 'structural-functional' to characterize his explanations.[7] Whatever Hollis may say about the 'mildness' of the sociological emphasis in all this, it is clear from Strawson's more recent definitions of his position that he sees it as constituting a sharp divide between himself and certain other notable modern philosophers: e.g. Russell, Popper and Chomsky. The latter certainly have the same feeling.[8]

In the case of Strawson, indeed, I would say it is Hollis who does the misrepresenting. According to Hollis, Strawson's central message is: 'Communication is possible not because persons stand in specific social relations but because they share particular ideas'. In putting it this way, however, he is leaving out one half of Strawson's pregnant circle. To do the latter justice, he would have to say: 'Communication is possible because persons share certain basic categories of thought and language; and these basic categories are entrenched because they are vital to communication'.

4. All this leads up to the most substantial issue dividing us: the issue of whether the Strawsonian thesis is at bottom a sociological/sociolinguistic theory which must sooner or later be exposed to empirical testing in the cross-cultural arena, or whether it is an epistemological thesis for which such testing would be logically inappropriate. I favour the first answer, Hollis the second.

To start with, it seems worth pointing out that Strawson himself talks rather as if he, too, favoured the first answer.

Thus in one recent article, whilst describing himself as engaged in the discipline of 'non-empirical linguistics', he nonetheless concedes that the empirical value of his constructions 'is finally subject to the checks of psychologists and linguists, working separately and in combination'.[9] In a yet-more-recent interview, he prefaces the suggestion of the universality of his basic categories with a big 'if', and admits the possibility of a 'huge mistake'.[10] At this juncture, one feels tempted to bring the argument to a close by saying that, since Strawson himself regards his thesis as a theory potentially confirmable or falsifiable in the cross-cultural arena, an empirically testable theory it must *really be*.

But this would be too easy. After all, Strawson may be mistaken about the status of his own thesis.[11] Stranger things have happened in the history of ideas. So let me go a bit further, and see if I can't resolve our difference in a more constructive way.

First, I agree with Hollis that there is one key point which *can* be decided on *a priori* considerations, and to which empirical testing is irrelevant. The social anthropologist aims at a very special kind of cross-cultural understanding, which one might appropriately call 'translational understanding'. Given the character of this special kind of understanding, it is I think *necessarily* true that certain Strawsonian categories must be present in the thought/language of the 'other' culture if the enterprise is to succeed. And if, despite currently fashionable Winchian manifestos, anthropologists have always in fact gone to the 'field' assuming the existence of Strawsonian universals, this may be held to show a sound intuitive awareness of the *necessary* pre-conditions of their particular art.

However, to stop at this point, as Hollis does, is to stop short of a full delineation of the anthropologist's predicament. For in so doing, he fails to take account of the ever-present eventuality that one day, an anthropologist may go into the 'field', only to find himself thwarted by the fact that the vocal noises made by the particular group of human beings he has chosen to get involved with simply do not jell into a translatable language. In such a situation, though the necessary pre-conditions of his art remain unchanged, hard fact will drive him home. And if he has nothing else to present on his return to campus, he *will* have one very precious item: some empirical evidence against the universality of the Strawsonian 'central core'. That such an eventuality has not yet arisen in the history of social anthropology seems to me to constitute rather strong empirical confirmation of the Strawsonian thesis.

If Hollis has overlooked this scenario, it is perhaps because he has thought too exclusively in terms of orthodox social anthropologists operating in their normal adult human contexts, and has failed to consider the work of allied enquirers in more marginal situations. Here I am thinking of the research worker who goes out to engage in participant observation of a band of apes in the wild: of the student of human infant behaviour: and of the student of the behaviour of young apes brought up in human families. Such an enquirer cannot go to *his* field armed in advance with a single, specialized technique for the achievement of understanding; for he simply does not know what kind of technique is going to be appropriate. This of course is because, in the kind of situation into which he is advancing, it is a blatantly open question as to whether the 'others' have a language at all, let alone one translatable into his own. Here, then, a structure of necessary preconditions never gets a chance to build up; and the empirical element is over-riding. Indeed, the question of whether or not the 'others' have a language can only be decided in terms of evidence of a strictly 'behavioural' kind: evidence based on individual patterning and inter-individual co-ordination of vocal noises and bodily movements. Hence, of course, the likelihood of it's being from this kind of research, rather than from within social anthropology itself, that we shall eventually get an explicit formulation of the behavioural criteria of which the anthropological field worker unconsciously avails himself, in order to assess the translatability of an alien language.

5. Finally, I would like to allay what seems to be a suspicion in Hollis' mind that I reject inspired advice from the armchair. No social anthropologist with a sense of tradition would be likely to reject such advice; for, as Evans-Pritchard once pointed out, the greater part of our discipline's intellectual capital was supplied for years from the armchairs of the *Année Sociologique* group.[12] And now that this capital has almost drained away, I feel we should be as openminded as possible about where we look for our next injection. In this context, I think I have made my admiration for Strawson plain enough. It is just that, unlike Hollis, I see his armchair as being more sociological than epistemological.

I would go even further, and concede it is a sad truth that our anthropological excursions are not as generative of fundamental new insights into the human condition as they ought to be. Too often, they are Winchian safaris, in which we go out with our preconceived frameworks and mangle our 'field' experience to fit them. One might indeed despair altogether of the inspirational potential of 'fieldwork', were it not for those occasional great monographs where the reality of human interaction on an alien shore comes through all the more dramatically for being so obviously in conflict with the scholar's own pre-conceptions, and for the beautiful moments, in one or two such monographs, when the scholar comes face to face with such conflict in mid-exposition, and ruefully admits that he doesn't quite know what to do about it.[13]

It is these rare moments that encourage one to continue to insist that the 'field' is a vital complement to the armchair, and to claim Eliot's lines for our own. I wonder why no anthropologist has got on to them before!

Notes

1 See for instance: 'Wittgenstein's Philosophical Investigations', *Mind*, Vol. LXIII, 1954; *The Bounds of Sense*, London 1966, p. 151; *Meaning and Truth* (Oxford Inaugural Lecture), London 1970; statements of position in Magee, B. *Modern British Philosophy*, London 1973.

2 Lukes, S. 'Some Problems about Rationality' in Wilson, B. (ed.) *Rationality*, Oxford 1970. (See p. 209).

3 Horton, R. 'Social Science: Logical or Psychological Impossibility?', *Man*, Vol. LXI, Jan. 1961.

4 On this, see his remark in Magee, *op. cit.*, p. 177.

5 Even at the beginning of *Individuals* (London 1959), however, Strawson is emphasizing the importance of the criterion of 'identifiability' in determining the kinds of entities picked out as basic particulars by a language. So here already, explanation in terms of the context of communication is on the scene.

6 The following are two typical statements:
'We should remember that all Kant's treatment of objectivity is managed under a considerable limitation, almost, it might be said, a handicap. He nowhere depends upon, or even refers to, the factor on which Wittgenstein, for example, insists so strongly: the *social* character of our concepts, the links between thought and speech, speech and communication, communication and social communities.'
(*The Bounds of Sense*, p. 151.)
'Here (in the question of the role of proper names) . . . we have to bear in mind that an understanding of linguistic function pre-eminently involves *an understanding of the* UTILITY *of linguistic forms in communication between human beings variously circumstanced and variously equipped.*'
(*Subject and Predicate in Logic and Grammar*, London 1974, p. 42. Phrase in brackets is mine. Underlining and capitals are Strawson's.)

7 See for instance: *op. cit.* 1974, chapter 5.

8 In his Oxford Inaugural (*op. cit.* 1970), he talks of a 'Homeric Struggle' over this issue. For an equally strong reaction, see: Chomsky, N. *Reflections on Language*, London 1976, pp. 64-77.

9 *Op. cit.* 1971, p. 148.

10 Strawson in Magee, *op. cit.* 1973, p. 162.

11 In one respect, this may actually be the case, though in a manner that favours my answer rather than Hollis'. Here I am referring to the fact that Strawson maintains *both* that he is conducting a 'non-empirical' enquiry, *and* that the constructions which result from this enquiry are empirically testable theories. I don't really think he can have it both ways. If the results are testable, then the enquiry can't be non-empirical.

12 On this, see his introduction to: Hertz, R. *Death and the Right Hand* (trans. Needham, R. and C.), London 1960.

13 There are moments of this kind in Evans-Pritchard's great monograph on Zande thought. (Evans-Pritchard, E. *Witchcraft, Oracles and Magic among the Azande*, Oxford 1937.).

PART FIVE

THE RELATIVITY OF POWER

14. Power in Social Theory: A non-Relative View

by Michael Bloch, Bryan Heading, Philip Lawrence

THIS paper is inspired by Steven Lukes' recent work on power. Our intention is to offer a specific critique of Lukes' views and also to make a contribution to the wider methodological debate in social theory about essentially contested concepts.

Lukes starts his discussion, as any analyst of power must do,[1] by pointing out that different theorists conceptualize power in radically different ways, and the crux of his argument rests on the claim that this is not simply a consequence of a present lack of agreement about how an agreed primitive notion of power should be operationalized but a result of power being an 'essentially contested concept', a status that it shares with other basic concepts in the social sciences such as structure.

He takes the idea of an essentially contested concept from Gallie but, as he admits, there are differences between his use of the idea and that of Gallie.[2] Our concern will be with Lukes' position on such concepts. For him, a concept is essentially contested when it is 'ineradicably evaluative' in the sense that particular interpretations of it, which determine its empirical application, necessarily embody particular value assumptions of which the user may or may not be aware. As he states, when summarizing his discussion of the three views of power which he considers and which will be discussed later:

> One feature which these three views of power share is their evaluative character: each arises out of and operates within a particular moral and political perspec-

243

tive. Indeed, I would maintain that power is one of those concepts which is ineradicably value-dependent. By this I mean that both its very definition and any given use of it, once defined, are inextricably tied to a given set of (probably unacknowledged) value-assumptions which predetermine the range of its empirical application.[3]

Our strategy will be to spell out what we see as the implications of treating power or any other concept as essentially contested and then to examine Lukes' analysis of power in such terms to see whether he accepts these implications fully or whether there are apparent inconsistencies in his analysis. In short we shall be making four points. First, that, if power *were* an essentially contested concept, it would imply a relativism that would make it impossible for Lukes to substantiate the superiority of the particular conception of power he advances. Second, that the dispute over the nature of power as it is waged between proponents of different sociological metatheories must be distinguished from the disputes that arise within particular meta-theories. Third, that within a particular metatheory it cannot be simply assumed that different conceptions of power are incompatible rather than complementary. And, fourth, that, if Lukes is to avoid the problem of moral relativism, he requires a theory of real interest with which to justify his conception of the third dimension.

1. The implications of treating power as an essentially contested concept

To treat a concept as essentially contested involves a quite different claim than saying that different theorists happen to disagree upon its usage. Lukes is very careful to make the distinction between the empirical thesis that there is a diversity of views on a given subject and the philosophical thesis, with which he is concerned, that there are no criteria by which some can be judged right and others wrong.

In his article, 'Relativism: Cognitive and Moral',[4] he argues on well-established grounds for 'conditions of truth, rules of logic and criteria of rationality which are universal and fundamental', and which allow us to judge the truth claims of purported knowledge about the world, while, at the same time, opting for the position taken by 'both Max Weber and most contemporary Anglo-Saxon philosophers'[5] that there are 'no extra or trans-systemic grounds for criticizing moral beliefs and actions or systems as a whole'[6] and hence meta-ethical relativism (as he calls it) must be accepted. He finds this double claim uncomfortable 'because . . . it appears to rest on too simple a distinction between fact and value'.

The implications of this statement are crucial for his argument because he adopts a complex position on the relationship between theory, fact and value. He rejects the standard positivist line that drives a wedge between theory and fact, and consequently grants concepts validity only if they are amenable to validation through sense experience. In this account concepts are purely passive, like filing systems that can be re-arranged to fit altered empirical states of affairs. Here conceptual disputes about the nature of power can supposedly be settled by recourse to 'the facts'. This position is obviously untenable, for, as Lukes demonstrates, what counts as a factual instance of power must depend on the particular conception with which the theorist starts. Hence the apparently straightforward question: 'Is this an exercise of power?', cannot be answered independently of a particular conception, and different conceptions will provide different answers. Moreover, the conception of power is not an isolated one; it is inter-related with other concepts in a set of conjectures which mark the starting point of research, and Lukes specifically mentions 'interests' in this respect.

Thus, the identification of facts is inherently theory-laden, or, to use the philosophical jargon, there are no theory-neutral facts. More radically, the component concepts of the theory are value-laden. If different conceptions of 'interest' and 'power', which in his interpretation are crucially inter-related, are necessarily contested because people starting with different moral perspectives are bound, consciously or unconsciously, to define them in different ways, then 'every identification of a social fact will be value-laden, at least in the sense of ruling certain moral and political evaluations out of court'.[7] The argument is that the theoretical premises which play a crucial role in empirical research are themselves value-laden and that the most such research can conceivably do is to help to resolve certain disputes *within* a particular moral framework.

We can now summarize the implications of accepting crucial concepts as essentially contested.

(i) There are no theory-neutral facts which can arbitrate between theories containing different conceptions of power (or of any other concept?).

(ii) The theory-dependence of facts derives, at least in some cases with undefined scope, from the value-dependence of the basic theoretical statements which introduce the primitive concepts, i.e. no distinction can be drawn in such cases between theory-neutrality and value-neutrality.

(iii) The results of research embodying different conceptions of an essentially contested concept necessarily have ethical implications which derive from the values built into them.

If these are accepted as the implications of Lukes' portrayal of essentially contested concepts, as they surely must be, then we are left with a conceptual and theoretical relativism that he had apparently wanted to avoid and which reduces social science to more or less sophisticated ideology. The first implication does not by itself imply relativism as long as a distinction can be drawn between facts being theory-laden and being value-laden; but Lukes denies that such a distinction can be made in the cases that interest him. The first two implications do not by themselves imply relativism if we have good grounds for regarding one set of values as correct, but again he cannot take this way out of relativism precisely because he claims that the values that determine the varied conceptions are essentially contestable.

2. Does Lukes accept these implications fully in his analysis of power?

Despite the brevity of his book, *Power: A Radical View*, and the limited additional treatment in his article, 'Power and Structure', Lukes' conceptual analysis of power is impressively wide-ranging, and includes enough discussion of what we regard as the major competing conceptions of power to enable us to judge the position that he takes, not only on the conceptions proposed by Dahl and by Bachrach and Baratz, with which he is primarily concerned, but also on those of the structural Marxists, particularly Althusser and Poulantzas, and value consensus theorists, such as Talcott Parsons.

Lukes sets boundaries for his examination of power as an essentially contested concept in a manner that excludes alternative conceptions which have their strong supporters. Although he shares with the structural Marxists a primitive concept which sees power as being exercised when one party affects another against the interests of the latter, he does not accept the structurally determined conception of power relationships that follows from their theoretical premisses. The Parsonian conception is excluded because it does not contain the idea that the exercise of power involves parties with conflicting interests, which is built into his primitive concept. This exclusion must be arbitrary, given his claim that he is dealing with an essentially contested concept; indeed he explicitly recognizes this when he states that 'there are, however, alternative (no less contestable) ways of conceptualizing power',[8] when introducing his discussion of Parsons. It would appear that the only ground on which he is entitled to reject the conceptions of power developed by the structural Marxists and Parsons is that their value implications conflict with his own. But his analysis appears inconsistent when he offers alternative reasons for rejecting them, reasons which suggest that in significant respects he does not want to treat power as essentially contestable. His arguments will be examined in some detail because we believe that most theorists who start with a similar commitment to conceptual relativism tend, in practice, to employ somewhat similar strategies in the attempt to avoid the relativism which, on their own terms, they are forced to accept. If such strategies are logically sound then in certain respects at least the concept in question is not essentially contestable; if they are not sound they are simply attempts to make a particular conception appear 'rationally defensible'[9] by means that have no warrant at all, i.e. they are simply attempts at persuasive definitions.

(i) The structural Marxists are committed to a structuralist meta-theory which involves an ontological claim that human behaviour is totally causally determined by the structures within which men are located. They are the passive 'bearers' (*Träger*) of structurally-determined inputs rather than being capable of exercising, in thought or deed, a degree of free will. The exercise of power is, then, a particular kind of causal relationship at most (some might argue that it is indistinguishable from any causal relationship), that is, in Poulantzas' words, 'the capacity of a social class to realize its specific objective interests' and 'an effect of the ensemble of the structures'.[10] Lukes puts the key premiss of the structuralist meta-theory particularly clearly when he states: 'One can see (individuals or collectivities) as wholly determined, acting out roles and indeed being not merely influenced but actually constituted by ever pre-given structures of a system that operates upon them and through them'.[11]

This view of the determinants of human behaviour, and of power relationships in particular, is rejected by those who are committed to an Actionist[12] meta-theory, with its ontological claim that humans are qualitatively different from other subjects for science because they are agents who always have the potential, which may not be realized in practice for a variety of reasons, to exercise a degree of free will in thought and deed. For those who exercise power over others, in the sense of getting them to act against their interests, which will be accepted as the primitive concept of power for the present, but will be reconsidered when we discuss Parsons below, it can then be said that they *could* have acted otherwise, and it becomes possible to assign responsibility to them for their acts.

It is obvious that the different conceptions of power held by the structural Marxists and those like Lukes who wish to include within it the idea that the agent could have acted otherwise derive from the different models of man with which they start, models which are central to the two meta-theories. If human agency is an essentially contested concept, then it will follow that these two views of power will be essentially contested, there being no grounds other than the theorist's values for preferring one model of man and the conception of power that follows to the others. Alternatively, an attempt might be made to argue that human agency is not essentially contestable, there being epistemological grounds for resolving the apparent dispute between the two models of man. Either it could be claimed that they are compatible, in which case the two conceptions of power are compatible, or that they are incompatible, and one can be shown to be right and the other wrong, in which case the contest between the two conceptions of power will be properly resolved in favour of one of them.

Those, like Lukes, who see the two conceptions of power as incompatible, have to face the full implications of their position. It is not enough to argue that they are entitled to tie their conception to an Actionist meta-theory because everyday usage treats power in this way. Definitional *fiat* based on a theorist's understanding of such usage is hardly an adequate foundation for setting uncontested boundaries to a conception of power (boundaries within which it *may* admittedly still be essentially contested), when the real issue is that of a properly justified decision about which is the correct meta-theory. Stipulative and persuasive definitions will not help at all, because they too fail to resolve the crucial issue.

The crux of the problem is that we have two meta-theories, Structuralist and Actionist, both of which provide a conceptual map of what must be taken into account in any substantive social theory. It should be pointed out as an important aside that, although these are the dominant meta-theories in current debate in social theory, they are misleading in the sense that they involve ontological claims on two different issues, free will versus causal determinism, and individual versus structure as the basic unit of social life: it should be readily apparent that there are four, logically possible meta-theories which follow from the combined resolution of these issues. These meta-theories provide their own conceptions of human agency, of power and of other concepts employed in the development of substantive theory. If the meta-theories are incompatible so will be the conceptions of power and other concepts derived from them.

In his essay on 'Power and Structure',[13] Lukes claims that he wishes to develop a substantive theory of the relationship between power and structure and he seems to believe that power is located in the Actionist meta-theory, while structure is located in the Structuralist one. If this is the case and the meta-theories are incompatible, he obviously cannot develop the substantive theory that he desires. But he is quite wrong, because both meta-theories provide their own distinctive conceptions of power *and* structure. In the Structuralist account, as we have already shown, power is simply a particular kind of structurally determined relationship; in the Actionist account, it is *possible* to treat them as distinct concepts, allowing the theorist to address himself to what Lukes regards as 'the very problem at issue, namely, that of

the relation between (them)'.[14] This does not follow automatically from the Actionist metatheory, since, as he
rightly points out, some exponents of this position (he cites
the early Sartre) deny the existence of structures altogether.
We shall address ourselves to this problem briefly, after we
have shown the strategy which a theorist who wishes to
claim that there is *a* correct conception of agency, and hence
of power, which is Actionist, should adopt.

He cannot argue his case with the aid of an empiricist epistemology, since it is clear that we are not dealing with theory-neutral facts; what is to count as factual evidence can be
interpreted without difficulty in the terms of each meta-theory. The only available alternatives are to argue either that
the Actionist meta-theory embodies the right values or that
there are logical grounds for preferring it. The first alternative collapses into the second if we require 'right' to involve
more than personal preference, as we must in order to avoid
an essential contest.

It is not our intention to spell out in detail the argument
that should be used since our purpose is simply to show that
the issue can be resolved, if at all, only on *a priori* grounds.
One such argument that has many proponents takes the following form:[15]

(a) the Structuralist metatheory makes the claim that all
behaviour is determined by nomological causal laws;

(b) if some behaviour can be shown to be not determined
in this way, it must be wrong;

(c) if the Actionist meta-theory is the only meta-theory
to claim that at least some behaviour is not causally determined, then, if some behaviour is not so determined, it must
be right;

(d) explanations in terms of reasons are genuinely explanatory and not reducible to explanation in terms of nomological causal laws;
therefore (e) the Actionist meta-theory is correct.

If such a case can be successfully argued, then the

conception of power derived from the Actionist meta-theory is correct, though there might still be scope for it to be essentially contested within this meta-theory. What are the further implications of working with Actionism? It certainly does not imply the claim that all actions are completely voluntary and that there are no social structures, as in the position ascribed to Sartre. Its sole claim is that man is always potentially a free agent in thought and deed; this does not mean that man always thinks freely or is able to convert his thoughts into effective action. There is room within Actionism for (i) a conception of structures which are treated as either facilitating means or constraining conditions of action, and both means and conditions may be external or internal to the agent, and (ii) a conception of *social* structure that is compatible with the Actionist ontology, i.e. one that is the intended or unintended outcome of interaction. On *a priori* grounds, again, a strong case can be made against the antistructural and extreme voluntaristic position. Not only are human agents necessarily faced by structures in the form of their bodies and their natural environment, but social life necessarily involves some degree of structuration in such forms as language, more or less shared beliefs and values, patterned methods of exchange, and access to scarce resources, and such structures are bound to be constraining as well as facilitating for most actors most of the time. The writings of authors like Sartre, even at their most voluntaristic, should provide ample ammunition to substantiate this argument.

(ii) We now turn to the relationship between a conception of power, lodged in the Actionist metatheory, which involves A being able to make B act against his interests, and compare this with the Parsonian conception. First, we must state that for the purposes of this discussion we intend to regard Parsons' work on power as located within the Actionist meta-theory too, so that we are concerned with a different conceptual relationship from the one already discussed.

This is certainly contentious, as we readily admit, since Parsons as system theorist (i.e. post 1950) often appears to be committed to ontological premises radically different from those in his earlier work, where voluntarism was stressed (especially *The Structure of Social Action*, 1937).[16] He often presents himself, and is seen by others, as a Normative Structuralist, i.e. committed to Idealism within Structuralism, but we believe that his work can still more plausibly be examined in Actionist terms, and that his conception of power in particular makes best sense if understood in such terms.

For Parsons, power is an essentially symbolic system resource which is available to those in positions of authority and is the means by which they can take effective initiatives in setting goals for a collectivity, and secure the performance of binding obligations by units in the system in the pursuit of such goals.[17] While the authority to do certain things is a necessary condition in explaining the amount of power available, it is not a sufficient condition, a point not understood by those who treat authority and power in Parsons' work as synonymous. Power can increase (or decrease) to some extent independently of authoritative entitlement, as a result of such factors as generating and sustaining support for new ventures and the available services and other resources that can be counted upon.

Lukes is quite right to recognize that this conception of power 'ties it to authority, consensus and the pursuit of collective goals, and dissociates it from conflicts of interest and, in particular, from coercion and force'.[18] He claims that it is stipulative, persuasive and contestable and that it can only be understood in terms of Parsons' theoretical premises. He regards it as 'reinforcing' those premises. We, however, see it as following logically from them. It is undeniably theory-dependent but it does not follow that either the theory itself or the conception of power that it embodies is thereby value-dependent. It is most reasonable to interpret Parsonian theory as an attempt to set up a theoretical model of a consensual and fully integrated, structurally complex social system, in which power is the mechanism by which collective goals are pursued. There seems nothing inherently value-dependent in this, though there admittedly might be in its application if a broader empirical scope is claimed for it than is justified.

Lukes, despite claiming that the Parsonian conception of power and his own are equally contestable, in practice argues against it and decides to exclude it from further discussion because it is 'out of line with the central meanings of "power" as traditionally understood and with the concerns that have always centrally preoccupied students of power'.[19] We argued earlier that supporting one's own position by everyday definitions in use is an unjustified exercise when the problem is one of a choice of the right meta-theory. Is Lukes entitled to employ this argument in this case when the two conceptions are located in the same meta-theory?

The two conceptions of power refer to different types of social relationship, both of which are possible within the Actionist meta-theory. It would be tempting to treat the one as capturing 'power over' and the other 'power to'. However, both involve 'power to' in the sense of enabling those with power to do things that they would otherwise be unable to do, and they both also involve 'power over', since authority is always exercised over others. These are significantly different conceptions and we require different labels to distinguish them, but we do not need to choose between them as they are compatible, indeed probably complementary. Thus, what we must decide is which conception is most appropriate to call 'power', and here ordinary language considerations are important. Wherever possible we should use ordinary words as they are ordinarily used and, as we endorse Lukes' point that his own conception of power is closer to that of ordinary usage than Parsons' conception, there is some justification for calling Lukes' conception 'power' and that of Parsons, perhaps, 'authoritative initiative'.

(iii) Even if we have provided good logical grounds for establishing uncontestable boundaries around a primitive concept of power as A affecting B against the latter's interests, it could still be argued, as Lukes does, that various interpretations of it are possible, and appear in the literature, that each has value implications which, consciously or unconsciously, determine its choice, and that selection between them is essentially contestable. Clearly there are significant differences in defining power in terms of a conflict of perceived interests and A's ability to make his interests prevail in actual overt conflict, whether on the battlefield or in parliament (the conception of Dahl which Lukes calls 'one-dimensional'), or in terms of the ability of A, again in a situation of conflicting perceived interests, to prevent B's challenge from entering the formal decision-making arena (the main point in the conception of Bachrach and Baratz which is described as 'two-dimensional'), or in terms of the ability of A to manipulate B into a state of 'false consciousness' in which he fails to recognize that his 'real interests' run counter to his perceived interests which pose no threat to A (the neo-Marxist conception which Lukes calls 'three-dimensional' and which he prefers). They are not simply different definitions but they provide quite different answers to the question: 'Is this an exercise of power?', and their varied answers can doubtless be used to support different values.

If these varied developments of the primitive concept are essentially contested, stipulative or persuasive definitions, no more needs to be said. But Lukes says considerably more when he claims that the third conception is 'superior to the others, where this apparently does not simply mean that it happens to fit in with (his) own values or moral and political perspective'.[20] The basis of the alleged superiority of the two-dimensional view over the one-dimensional, and of the three-dimensional over the two-dimensional, is that they permit the range of what is regarded as power 'to extend further and deeper'.[21] We find ourselves in complete agreement with the claim of Hollis that, 'Lukes' book makes sense, to my mind, only as an attempt at a real definition of 'power-over' and I see no other way to read a claim that a three-dimensional view goes deeper than the others'.[22]

Lukes is 'not trying to engineer the consent of his readers by any old means but leading them by reasoned argument to see that his account extends the range of the concept's application "further and deeper than others"'.[23] His argument, we suggest, should take the following form:

(a) If our primitive concept of power is that A affects B against his interests, then clearly one way in which this can occur is by readily visible (i.e. overt) conflict over a difference in perceived interests. This view of power suggests the behaviourist operationalization of Dahl, in which the concern is with victors and vanquished in some clear decision-making process.[24]

(b) Without doubt, Dahl's conception of power is *a* legitimate interpretation of the primitive concept and one that any theorist of power should take into account, but it is not the only possible legitimate interpretation and significantly it involves a failure to recognize other possible ways in which A can affect B against his interests. This means that Dahl's interpretation fails to do justice to the full implications of the primitive concept. Moreover, this failure *may*, consciously or unconsciously, reflect the values of those who define power in this narrow way and it certainly has moral and political implications.

(c) It is logically possible that A may also affect B against his perceived interests 'covertly', i.e. in a manner that is not readily visible to B nor perhaps to an observer unless he has methods of probing the covert aspects of power. He will not attempt to do so unless he acknowledges, as surely he must, that this is a possible method of exercising power. 'Covert' is a difficult concept because it has no absolute empirical connotations; what is covert to some people might be overt to others. If hypotheses embodying the idea of covert power are proposed, the theorist must find some method of making overt to himself what would otherwise remain covert.

(d) There are various ways in which power could be exercised covertly.[25] It could occur with issues that have already reached the decision-making arena, either in the form of effective 'behind the scenes' pressure by the powerful or through the 'anticipated reactions' of the formal decision-makers who propose only those policies which they regard as safe, given their assessment of the likely response of those whom they regard as powerful. It would also occur in the form that Bachrach and Baratz stress, i.e. by keeping certain issues out of the political arena.

(e) Lukes' extension of the concept of power into a third dimension depends critically on developing a viable theory of real interests, and, as he recognizes, such a theory would have to distinguish between genuine and manipulated consensus as 'to assume that the absence of grievance equals genuine consensus is simply to rule out the possibility of false or manipulated consensus by definitional *fiat*'.[26] Furthermore, Lukes is aware of the risk that the theorist will be merely imposing his own values on the object of study in attempting to pursue the third dimension. Indeed, this is the charge habitually made by members of the empiricist camp against any exponent of critical sociology.

In his book Lukes attempts to deal with the dilemma by arguing that a type of empirical evidence can always be adduced to lend support to a claim that actors' real interests are being subverted. The approach he suggests requires us to consider what would have happened if certain actual circumstances had been different, the assumption being that where consensus has been manipulated the consent would be revoked if the agents in question could be made aware of their real situation and of what their consenting involved. The example he gives is taken from Crenson's study, *The unPolitics of Air Pollution*,[27] where it is presupposed that policies which preclude a 'clean air' programme are against the real interests of the citizens involved, and that if the citizens had been fully aware of their alternatives they would not have accepted the loss of 'clean air' as they, in fact, did. Lukes treats such cases as relatively unproblematic as they rest on such generally accepted human values as the value placed on life itself. However, he accepts that other cases may be more difficult and that he needs a firmer basis to ensure that he avoids the danger of an ethnocentricism of values.

In our view the quasi-empirical counter-factual method cannot provide the basis required. The counter-factual situation may in fact involve a regression for particular agents, or, more plausibly, it could generate a circular process where agents reject or accept particular political policies according to the particular information and presentation that confronts them at the time. At best it can reveal their preferences, and, although reflective preference has been taken as the basis for a theory of real interests, the project remains to be made out, even if it is not, as we believe, ill-judged. It may be true that the content of real interests is given in reflective preferences and that these may be investigated empirically. Yet, no amount of empirical endeavour can show that this is so. The procedure must itself first be justified by *a priori* argument.

Lukes' exploration of the possibility of extending the concept of power into the third dimension presents a challenge to social and political theorists. It is a challenge that we have not met, but hope to have clarified. In particular, we have distinguished the inter- and intra-metatheoretical controversies, and we have sought to identify where different conceptions of power reflect irreconcileable differences and where such conceptions may be complementary. The difference between Lukes and the structural Marxists is an inter-metatheoretical dispute of which differing conceptions of power are but one aspect. Within Actionism, on the other hand, although there are many basic variants, much of the dispute over power can be viewed as a dispute about what we should pick out as significant rather than about the basic description of what is going on. This seems to be the real focus of Lukes' interest, although the issue cannot be sensibly posed in terms of essentially contested concepts, as it depends on the rejection of the relativism that essentially contested concepts imply. The challenge is to justify a substantive theory of real interests, but the present lack of such a theory should not be treated as an invitation to sloth. Less ambitious conceptions of power, such as those of the first and second dimensions, are not without significance, and, given the understanding of their limitations that Lukes provides, they may be used without apology. Indeed, as long as the conception of power it presupposes it not treated as normative, there is no reason to ignore Lukes' own counterfactual method. Its results will be of interest in their own right, even if we cannot immediately turn them into substantive political theory.

Notes

1   See S. Lukes, *Power, A Radical View*, Macmillan, 1974.
2   Admitted by Lukes in 'A Reply to K.I. Macdonald' *British Journal of Political Science* VII, 1977.
3   S. Lukes, *op. cit.* p.26.
4   S. Lukes, 'Relativism, Cognitive and Moral' *Supplementary Proceedings of the Aristotelian Society*, 1974.
5   *Ibid* pp. 167-8.
6   *Ibid* pp. 175.
7   *Ibid* pp. 185-6.
8   S. Lukes, *Power, A Radical View* p. 27.
9   *Ibid* p. 30.
10 S. Lukes, 'Power and Structure' in *Essays in Social Theory*, Macmillan, 1977, p. 17.
11 *Ibid*, p. 17.
12 A. Dawe, 'The Two Sociologies' in J. Thompson and J. Tunstall (eds.) *Sociological Perspectives*, Penguin, 1971.
13 S. Lukes, 'Power and Structure' *op. cit.*

14 *Ibid* p. 18.

15 See D. Beyleveld, 'The Epistemological Foundations of Sociological Theory' unpublished PhD thesis, University of East Anglia, 1975.

16 T. Parsons, *The Structure of Social Action*, McGraw-Hill, 1937, also see J. Finlay Scott, 'The Changing Foundations of the Parsonian Action Scheme' in W. Wallace (ed.) *Sociological Theory*, Heineman, 1969.

17 T. Parsons, 'On the Concept of Political Power' in *Sociological Theory and Modern Society*, The Free Press, New York, 1967.

18 S. Lukes *Power, A Radical View, op. cit.*, p. 28.

19 *Ibid*, p. 31.

20 B. M. Barry, 'The Obscurities of a Power', *Government and Opposition*, X, p. 252.

21 S. Lukes, *Power, A Radical View, op. cit.*, p.21.

22 M. Hollis, *Models of Man*, C.U.P., 1977, p.178.

23 *Ibid*, p. 177.

24 R. Dahl, 'The Concept of Power' *Behavioural Science* 2, 1957, pp. 201-205 and R. Dahl 'A Critique of the Ruling Elite Model' in A. Pizzorno (ed.) *Political Sociology*, Penguin, 1971.

25 These distinctions are explicitly made by K. Davis, 'The Politics of Planning in Norwich', unpublished M. Phil thesis, University of East Anglia, 1977. The ideas of P. Bachrach and M. S. Baratz appear in 'Two Faces of Power,' *American Political Science Review*, LVI, 1962, pp. 947-952, 'Decisions and Nondecisions: An Analytical Framework', LVII, 1963, pp. 641-651 and *Power and Poverty, Theory and Practice*, O.U.P. 1970.

26 S. Lukes *Power, A Radical View, op. cit.* p.24.

27 M. Crenson, *The Un-Politics of Air Pollution*, Johns Hopkins, 1971.

15. On the Relativity of Power
by Steven Lukes

In their paper 'Power in Social Theory: a Non-Relative View', Michael Bloch, Bryan Heading and Philip Lawrence pose a general challenge. How, they ask, is it possible to reconcile a certain kind of cognitive non-relativism, which holds that there are conditions of truth, rules of logic and criteria of rationality which are universal and fundamental, with what they see as the 'conceptual and theoretical relativism' entailed by the view that concepts such as 'power' are 'essentially contested'? Negatively, they maintain that such relativism makes it impossible to 'substantiate the superiority' of any particular conception of power over others, reducing 'social science to more or less sophisticated ideology'. Positively, they claim that the rationally-grounded (indeed *a priori*) resolution of such conceptual contests is possible, both at the meta-theoretical and at the theoretical levels. More specifically, they claim that it should be possible rationally to resolve the (inter-metatheoretical) contest between what they call the structuralist and actionist conceptions of power (which I shall henceforth call Contest 1) and the (intra-metatheoretical) contest between the one-, two- and three-dimensional conceptions of power, seen as involving conflict of interests (henceforth Contest 2). On the other hand, they see the contest between the last conception and the Parsonian conception of power (henceforth Contest 3) as no real contest: 'we do not need to choose between them as they are compatible, indeed probably complementary'.[1]

'Power' is, I take it, if anything is, a 'theoretical term'. Bloch *et al.* recognize this when they state that 'what counts as a factual instance of power must depend on the particular conception with which the theorist starts, hence the appar-

261

ently straightforward question: 'Is this an exercise of power?' cannot be answered independently of a particular conception and different conceptions will provide different answers'.[2] Its definition and criteria of application are subject to seemingly endless dispute in the social sciences. Why? I suspect that a full answer to this question will tell us a great deal about the central differences between the natural and the social sciences. I have claimed that power, like other concepts in the social sciences, is 'essentially contested'. By this I meant to suggest that any given interpretation or conception of it is inextricably tied to further background assumptions which are methodological and epistemological, but also moral and political assumptions, which themselves partly govern which reasons count in favour of one conception rather than another. Thus it is that there can be disputes about the proper use of the concept of power which are both 'endless' and 'perfectly genuine', different uses serving 'different though of course not altogether unrelated functions' for different social groups, and contending positions 'sustained by perfectly respectable arguments and evidence'.[3]

'Power' is, therefore, self-evidently not part of what Robin Horton calls the 'everyday, material-object framework' which he sees (as I do) as 'operating at all times and places, in conjunction with one or more theoretical frameworks' and as 'the ultimate source of criteria of truth and agreement with reality, both at the everyday and at the theoretical levels'.[4] (I would put this differently: the fact that this everyday framework is universal and fundamental does not mean that it is not 'theoretical', only that for the kinds of reasons he suggests and for others, it is invariant across human communities). On the contrary, I claim that identification of cases of power — like those, say, of justice and freedom, or of inequality or deviance or alienation or anomie[5] — is always theory-relative in a deep and complex way: that is, that it is relative to a whole web of theories and positions which include what are commonly called value-positions. One central difference with theoretical terms in the natural sciences is that the history of the latter reveals what one might call a 'filtering process' by which contending theories and positions are filtered out, leaving one, or in some few cases, a small number of contenders in the field. Perhaps the reason for this is that they, typically, share background assumptions in a way the social sciences do not, because they have in common a cognitive interest in the prediction and control of the object world.[6] If this is so, then the absence of such a filtering device in the social sciences cannot be attributed to their 'immaturity'. Rather, it may be explained by the fact that the interest-relativity of all explanation entails continuing disagreement in the social sciences, given persisting differences among students of social and political life as to what requires and what constitutes explanation.

Consider the following questions about power. Is power a property or a relationship? Is it potential or actual, a capacity or the exercise of a capacity? By whom or what is it possessed or exercised: by agents (individual or collective?) or by structures or systems? Over whom, or upon what is it exercised: agents (individual or collective?) or structures or systems? Is it, by definition, intentional, or can its exercise be partly intended or unintended? Must it be (wholly or partly?) effective? What kinds of outcome does it produce? Does it modify interests, options, policies, preferences or behaviour? If a relation, is it reflexive or irreflexive, transitive or intransitive, complete or incomplete? Is it asymmetrical? Does exercising power by some reduce the power of others (is it a zero-sum concept?)? Or can it maintain or increase the total of power? Is it demonic or benign? Must it rest upon or employ force or coercion, or the threat of sanctions or deprivations — and, if so, what balance of costs and rewards must there be between the parties for power to exist, and how is this to be measured? Does the concept only apply where there is a conflict of some kind? If so, what is the conflict between, and must it be manifest or may it be latent: must it be between revealed (how revealed?) preferences or can it involve real interests (and how are these to be defined?). Is it a behavioural concept, and, if so, in what sense? Is it a causal concept?

My central claim is that alternative answers that have been given to these and similar questions derive from alternative and contending answers to other, background questions, including methodological and epistemological but also moral and political questions. John Rawls writes of alternative conceptions of justice that they are 'the outgrowth of different notions of society against the background of opposing views of the natural necessities and opportunities of human life'.[7] The same seems to me to apply to alternative conceptions of power, as to many other concepts in the social sciences. Unlike Rawls, however, I see no conclusive reason to believe that all differences between the underlying notions and views must be finally eliminable by rational means, especially where these include moral and political notions and views.

With respect to contending conceptions of power, Bloch *et al.* suggest that there are only two possibilities: that there is a real contest, which is rationally resolvable; or that we have a case of meaning-variance, and thus no real contest. Contests 1 and 2 exemplify the first possibility, Contest 3 the second. By contrast, my claim is that the background assumptions are such as to lead different thinkers in some cases to different conclusions about what it is rational to believe, and that these contests are such that in such cases no way may be found rationally to resolve them in a conclusive way. On the other hand, I also claim that, in practice, the area of irresolvable disagreement is likely to be much narrower than one might, given that my first claim is true, suppose. For such contests typically test the implications of the contending positions against one another, in a way which makes plain the costs of holding certain methodological views.

Let me try to illustrate this in respect of the three contests in question:—

Contest 1

Whether power is a form of structural determination or a concept tied to the notion of human agency (whether individual or collective) hinges on whether the alleged holder or wielder of power is correctly claimed to be able to act otherwise than he does. Whether that claim is correct or not depends on the truth or otherwise of a set of counterfactual claims (and indeed the prior question of whether counterfactual claims *can* be either true or false). Even supposing (what, in fact, I maintain) that there is a right answer to this question, in any given case, there is no way to establish the correctness of such a claim other than by the adducing of relevant indirect evidence and (where it is available) of relevant general theory. But what counts here as relevant, and when does such support of such counterfactual claims become rationally decisive? It seems that the most we can do is to produce plausible cases for one or another view about what agents could or could not have done in specified counterfactual circumstances, which will entail alternative views about how those very agents are themselves to be conceptualized.[8]

What *counts* as plausible — that is, rationally persuasive — here is a theory-dependent matter (in a very wide sense). A hard-line 'structuralist' (to use Bloch *et al*'s terms) will simply discount what their 'actionist' (whether he be an extreme or a moderate voluntarist) sees as grounds for his counterfactual claims; and indeed different kinds of actionist will discount one another's grounds. Thus what the actionist sees as a ground for postulating real but unrealized possibilities the structuralist sees as a challenge to show that there are no such possibilities. The latter can say of the former that his account is no explanation until all possibilities but one (and thus the existence of human agency) can be excluded, while the former can say of the latter that his elimination of possibilities fails because of the non-replicability of initial conditions (in particular) and the self-monitoring character of human actors.

Among other things, what is in dispute here is different cognitive interests leading to alternative notions of what requires and what constitues explanation — and, in particular, where explanations should stop. What Professor Apel calls 'the interest in controlling an objectified environmental world' leads to the search for 'isolated systems of causal or statistical connections'[9] — to the idea, in short, that to explain an outcome is to establish the structure of causal relations among the factors which jointly act so as uniquely to determine, or perhaps over-determine, it. The central rationale of such an approach is (as Habermas[10] and Apel plausibly argue) prediction and control: the theorist wishes to know how to bring about or avoid the *explanandum*.[11] Accordingly, he will aim at replication of data and generalization of theory. The so-called 'structuralist' (there are many varieties, from B.F. Skinner to Louis Althusser) takes this programme to imply the elimination of the agency of the human subject, and the non-explanatoriness of concepts tied, closely or loosely, to it (such as reason, choice, want, intention, preference, purpose, interest, strategy, rule, norm, 'freedom and dignity', etc.). Indeed, his strategy is to evacuate all such concepts from the *explanans*, on the assumption that, for so long as they remain there, a proper explanation is yet to be achieved. It will only be so when the agent as subject becomes an object.

The so-called 'actionist' may well share this interest in prediction and control and the tracing of causal relations. But, insofar as he uses agency concepts, he is, implicitly or explicitly, committed to the idea that the power of human agency involves the power to act otherwise, that is, the capacity to perform voluntary actions, in the presence of (variably) open alternatives.[12] If he does *not* hold this, then his use of agency vocabulary becomes redundant at best and misleading at worst. From the actionist point of view, the point of identifying the power links in the chain or structure of causation is to identify, within (variably) structural limits, which (individual or collective) actors are responsible for which outcomes. Such an inquiry would lose its point if their beliefs, desires, aims, interests, etc. and actions were themselves seen as totally determined by other causal factors. One might, for example, seek to establish the structure of causal relations (e.g. by path analysis) between actors' preferences and a given outcome,[13] but that very explanatory aim itself presupposes a view of actors able to act and think otherwise than they do.

I think that Professor Apel is right to suggest that there is a complementarity between what he calls 'quasi-naturalistic' explanation, of a causal and nomological kind, and the interpretation of meanings, as governed by 'the interest in communicative understanding'.[14] Indeed, the actionist, seeking to establish causal relations between, say, preferences and outcomes, has no other access to data than through such interpretation. Such interpretation, of the self-understanding of agents, will involve the interpreter in answering the question why they select some among a (variable) range of perceived alternative possibilities of action. Or, alternatively, if governed by what Apel calls 'the interest in critically-emancipatory self-reflection',[15] he may focus on the question why possibilities of their changing both their structural contexts and themselves in certain postulated emancipatory directions are precluded from being realized, or even perhaps from being perceived, by the agents themselves. (The answer to which, of course, involves both causal analysis and the interpretation of meanings).

I conclude that these interests dictate distinctive modes of explanation — distinctive views about both what is to be explained and how it is properly to be explained — and that these involve different views about what it is most plausible to suppose that the agents could have thought and done otherwise, and thus different ways of conceptualizing the agents. They are thus inseparable from differences as to how human beings should properly be conceived — as, say, the 'bearers' of structurally determined forces, as 'personality systems', as clusters, or bearers, of roles, as rational choosers, as self-interpreting, purposive beings, as repressed and alienated but potentially self-determining actors, and so on.

How, then, are such differences to be resolved? My purpose in stressing 'essential contestability' is to emphasize, first, that the contending positions are not morally and politically neutral and, second, that they dictate contending views as to what constitutes plausible, that is rationally persuasive, explanation. On the other hand, *this* relativism need not entail non-resolvability in any given case — and, indeed, I believe that many such contests *are* resolvable. For the adherent of each position has, after all, to make out his case, by the adducing of evidence and arguments. If the structuralist, in relation to any given area of social life, continuously fails to develop theories which exclude the possibilities the actionist insists upon, that surely counts against his position (which, however, he can maintain, by claiming that such theories could 'in principle' be generated — though, as Putnam has shown, if this could not be done in 'real time', this claim loses much of its force).[16] If, however, he *succeeds*, and comes up with theories which are both general and successfully predictive, then the actionist is in trouble — which he will probably recognize by declaring that we all are, that is, as Apel might say, human subject-objects have become objects merely, and the iron cage has closed in upon them.

Contest 2

Whether the one-, two- or three-dimensional view of power is adopted depends, among other things, on the view one takes of what constitutes 'interests'. On the first view, power is only exercised when individuals act in such a way as to prevail over the revealed perferences of others. On the second view, the concept extends more widely to cover cases where such actions prevail over the concealed or semi-articulated preferences of others. On the third view, the concept is further extended to cover cases where the actions and inaction of individuals and groups have the effect of shaping the beliefs and desires of others in such a way as preclude options which they would have chosen and preferred to those they actually prefer.

Now, these differences in extension of the concept of power (understood as being exercised when A affects B in A's but against B's interests) stem from underlying differences which themselves dictate different views about what needs to be explained and what constitutes a good explanation. These are partly epistemological and methodological. According to the first (empiricist and behaviourist) view, we can only know what we can observe at the level of overt behaviour. According to the second (empiricist and quasi-behaviourist view, we can only know what is observable at the level of overt and covert behaviour. On the third view, a wider notion of the scope of knowledge is allowed, bringing in the effects of both individual and collective action (including inaction) and relevant counterfactuals. (Actually, the first and second views are also, necessarily, committed to bringing counterfactuals within the scope of knowledge, but only deal in 'obviously plausible' ones, namely, those for which currently observable preferences provide the evidential grounding).

However, this methodological disagreement is hardly dissociable from a further practical, moral and political one. Proponents of the first and second views take the position they do about the scope of knowledge — what can legitimately be claimed to be knowable — because of their exclusive interest in predicting and retrodicting what actually happens. On the third view, the interest shifts to also identifying what prevents what could, but does not, happen from happening. On the first and second views, such an interest is both unscientific and dangerous. Unscientific because, it is argued, there is no way to single out relevant counterfactuals; dangerous because it licences talk of 'real interests' and 'false consciousness' in a way which disregards people's actual desires, discounting them in the light of their future and more enlightened selves.[17] But from the standpoint of the third view, it is clear that the exclusive focus of the first two views on the actual preferences of individuals in conflict is not morally and politically neutral, since their explanatory interest excludes consideration of the ways in which power is used to close off possibilities of action and self-development. In other words, the apparently 'scientific' focus on revealed preference itself reveals a moral and political preference for seeing human beings in one way rather than another. Conversely, the three-dimensional view is moral and political not only in taking another view, but also in offering one among a number of possible accounts of 'real interests', namely, one which relies on the notion of greater relative 'autonomy', a notion which itself requires (among other things) criteria specifying what constitute 'significant' choices.

None of this, however, prevents me from arguing that the three-dimensional view of power enables us to see further and deeper than the other two, and to adduce arguments and evidence to support this claim. If that evidence and those arguments are rejected as irrelevant by one- or two- dimensionalists, they have to show why. Thus, for example, they have to show why they allow some counterfactual knowledge claims and not others, why they suppose that there must be a behavioural component to the exercise of power, why non-events can constitute neither the source nor the result of an exercise of power. My case for essential contestability suggests merely that they do indeed have 'perfectly respectable arguments and evidence' to appeal to. But this does not prevent me from claiming that, despite its deep difficulties, especially in relation to research methodology, my own view enables us to capture relations which are of the same kind, but deeper and less visible, even invisible, to researcher and participant actors alike. The intuition that lies behind this idea is that power is unique among social phenomena in its self-concealing tendency; in many situations, its observability correlates inversely with its effectiveness, which cannot, therefore, be measured only by techniques of direct observation. I believe that any theory of power which fails to incorporate this intuition into its theoretical structure and its research methodology must be quite inadequate.[18] Considerations such as these are, I have found, capable of determining the intellects of some, if not others. The only possible strategy in these circumstances is to bring out the full implications of failing to be thus persuaded. Such a strategy cannot 'substantiate the superiority' of one position against others in the manner of a knock-down proof. But why should we suppose such a proof to be available?

Contest 3

With respect to this contest, Bloch *et al.* claim that what is involved is just meaning-variance. What for Parsons is 'power' is for others 'authoritative initiative'; and what for them is power is for Parsons, say, 'compulsion', 'coercion', and so on. But more than a mere difference of labelling is involved here, as can be seen from reading Parsons' debate with C. Wright Mills. For Parsons is offering a theoretical term to make sense of observable phenomena which, according to Mills, are to be otherwise explained, by using the same term, understood quite differently.

In part, this is a dispute about whether power is an agency or a system notion, an attribute of social actors or a system resource. In part, it is a dispute about whether power is asymmetric or not.[19] This difference is, of course, partly a difference about what requires explanation: for Mills, the élite theorist, it is the control and manipulation of the many by the few; for Parsons, the structural-functionalist, it is the ordered functioning of the social system. Partly it is a difference about what constitutes a good explanation and where such an explanation should stop — for Parsons with analytically defined elements of the system, for Mills with the actions and failures to act of the responsible, or rather irresponsible, 'men of power'. Parsons himself sees this difference as relating to differences of interest: Mills, he writes, 'is interested only in *who* has power and what *sectoral* interests he is serving with his power, not in how power comes to be generated or in what communal rather than sectoral interests are served.'[20] And Parsons further observes, perceptively, that Mills' conception of power has a normative dimension, pre-supposing what he calls 'a utopian conception of an ideal society in which power does not play a part at all', while he himself sees it as 'an essential and desirable component of a highly organised society.'[21]

Many different questions are at issue between Parsons and Mills, but one central question — which kind of conception of power offers a superior basis for theorizing about American society? — is still unresolved, not least because it is inseparable from so many other issues. Among other things, this contest, like the previous one, involves competing explanations of certain kinds of apparent consensus or non-conflict. I believe that this sort of contest partly turns on a further dispute about the role of external causes as against that of internal reasons. However, I am concerned here to do no more than suggest that this is a real contest. A translation manual of their respective power terms would not make it go away.

These are all contests in which the question of how power is to be conceptualized is traceable back to background positions whose role is in part to specify what requires explanation and what constitutes a good explanation of it. But from none of this does it follow that reasons cannot be given for one view rather than another, and, in particular, for the claim that one view enables one to see further and deeper than another. Such a claim can only be made out by bringing out both the implications of alternative views and their unacceptability. That they are unacceptable can always be denied: hence essential contestability. But the contending positions are not incommensurable: the contests are real ones. I have, as a matter of fact, been pleasantly surprised at the extent to which it is possible to appeal to the proponents of contending views in this area by calling their background assumptions into question in this way. Foreground battles may, after all, be won by stealthy rearguard action.

Notes

1 Michael Bloch, Bryan Heading and Philip Lawrence, 'Power in Social Theory: A Non-Relative View', above, p. 254. Bloch *et al.* see this contest too as intra-metatheoretical, stating (but not arguing for) the view that Parsons' 'work can ... more plausibly be examined in Actionist terms and that his conception of power in particular makes best sense if understood in such terms'. (p. 253). For reasons which will become clear, I disagree with this view. Anthony Giddens seems to me to be exactly right when he observes that '*There is no action in Parsons' 'action frame of reference'*, only behaviour which is propelled by need-dispositions or role-expectations. The stage is set, but the actors only perform according to scripts which have been written out for them' (Anthony Giddens, *New Rules of Sociological Method*, Hutchinson, London, 1976, p.16).

2 Bloch *et al.*, *art. cit.*, p. 245.

3 W.B. Gallie, 'Essentially Contested Concepts', *Proceedings of the Aristotelian Society*, N.S., LVI 1955-56, pp. 168-9.

4 R. Horton, 'Material-object Language and Theoretical Language': Towards a Strawsonian Sociology of Thought', above, p. 221.

5 See my *Essays in Social Theory* Macmillan, London, 1977, Ch. 4.

6 I owe this idea to Mary Hesse: see her paper, 'Theory and Value in the Social Sciences' in C. Hookway and P. Pettit (eds.), *Action and Interpretation* Cambridge, 1978.

7 J. Rawls, *A Theory of Justice* Clarendon, Oxford, 1972, p.9-10.

8 The argument for this is in my 'Power and Structure' in *Essays in Social Theory*, Ch.1.

9 K.-O. Apel, 'Types of Social Science in the Light of Human Cognitive Interests', above, p. 6.

10 See J. Habermas, *Knowledge and Human Interests* Heinemann, London, 1972.

11 This formulation echoes that of Hilary Putnam: see his *Meaning and the Moral Sciences* Routledge and Kegan Paul, London, 1978, p. 43.

12 See A. Kenny, *Will, Freedom and Power* Blackwell, Oxford, 1976.

13 See Jack Nagel's fine book, *The Descriptive Analysis of Power* Yale Uni-

versity Press, New Haven and London, 1975.

14   *Art. cit.,* p. 7 f.

15   *Art. cit.,* p. 8

16   *Op. cit.* p. 41 ff.

17   See, for example, Nelson Polsby, *Community Power and Political Theory* Yale University Press, New Haven and London, 1963.

18   Reading Nagel's, *The Descriptive Analysis of Power* has convinced me that his very general definition of a power relation as 'an actual or potential causal relation between the preferences of an actor regarding an outcome and the outcome itself' can be used to develop testable theories which incorporate this intuition and are not vulnerable to the criticisms levelled against the one- and two-dimensional views. But their adherents might (though they might not) object to such theories on the same grounds that they object to alternative definitions and conceptions.

19   For a fuller discussion of what is at issue between Mills and Parsons, see my 'Power and Authority', to appear in T. Bottomore and R.A. Nisbet (eds.), *History of Sociological Analysis* Basic Books, New York, forthcoming.

20   Talcott Parsons, 'The Distribution of Power in American Society' in G.W. Domhoff and H.B. Ballard (eds.) *C. Wright Mills and 'The Power Elite'* Beacon, Boston, 1968, p. 83.

21   *Ibid.*, pp. 84, 87.

Index

Actionism, 249ff., 254, 256, 258f., 265.
Adorno, Theodor, 89, 104.
African (vs. Western) cultures, 215ff., 218ff.
Althusser, Louis, 266.
Apel, Karl-Otto, viii, x, 45, 51-70, 140ff., 266f.
assertability condition, 167f., 171.

Bartlett, F. C., 186f.
behaviourism, 269.
belief, casual antecedents of, 160ff., 173,
see also under knowledge, social determination of
Bloch, Michael, x, 261ff., 273.

capitalism, 89ff., 92, 96f.
categories, 199, 226f., 235f.
causality, 206f., 208f., 227.
causal necessity, 131.
Chomsky, Noam, 18f., 46., 213.
cognitive development, 213f.
cognitive interests, 3ff., 51f., 93, 111, 266ff: complementarity of, 9, 12ff., 23, 28ff., 36, 52, 128.
communication, 69f.
communicative understanding, cognitive interest in, 6, 7f., 11f., 29, 132.
construction, social construction of reality.
see under reality.
contradiction, 208, 212.
control, cognitive interest in, 6f., 21f., 28ff., 93., 140f., 266.
'core statements', 157, 163, 165, 168f., 177f., 185ff.
critically-emancipatory self-reflection, cognitive interest in,

8f., 14, 36ff., 43, 85, 267.
critical-reconstructive social sciences, 37ff., 42ff., 40f., 111ff., 136f.
see also under critical theory.
critical theory, 90f., 112, 124, Ch. 6.

Dahl, R., 255, 260.
determinism, sociological, 151f., 199, 221, 226f.; casual, 250.
Dilthey, W., 10, 40f.
Douglas, Mary, ix, 151ff., 156, 159, 162, 172ff., 188ff., 200.
Dray, W., 25ff.
Durkheim, Emile, ix, 151ff., 158ff., 172, 175, 180ff., 184ff., 192, 194.

Easlea, Brian, 99f., 104.
epistemology, 151, 227, 229f.
explanation (nomological), 10ff., 19f., 25f.

falsification, 120.
Fay, Brian, 93, 97, 104, 112.
forms of life, 84f.
Frankfurt School, viii, 89, 95ff., 101ff., 102f., 120, 124, 127, 137.
Freud, Sigmund,
see under psychoanalysis.

Gadamer, H. G., 79.
Gallie, W. D., 243.
Gellner, Ernest, 173.
Gettier, E., 160, 176.
Giddens, Anthony, 273.
Ghandi, 59ff., 63ff., 85.

Habermas, Jürgen, 6, 44f., 52, 74, 93ff., 102ff., 105ff., 108ff., 112, 119, 127, 138f., 266.

Halbwachs, M., 183, 187.
Harvey, David, 96f., 99, 104, 112.
Heading, Bryan, x, 261ff., 273.
Hempel, C. G., 19, 27, 45.
hermeneutic circle, 33f., 121.
hermeneutics, 30ff., 40ff., 46, 132f., 160.
Hertz, Robert, 183.
history, 20f., 25f., 31, 34.
history of science, 11, 32f.
Hollis, Martin, Ch. 13 *passim*.
Horkheimer, Max, 89, 91f., 98, 104, 109, 112, 128.
Horton, Robin, ix, 173, 182, 192, Ch. 12 *passim*, 262.
Hopkins, Antony, 215f.
Hume, David, 131.
hypostatisation, 104f., 111f., 124f., 137.

idealism, 155, 167, 189, 191, 228.
ideology, 90, 106, 112, 159; Marxist critique of, 37ff.
induction, eliminative, 207f.
interests, 244, 245, 257, 264.
see also under cognitive interests.
irreversibility, 20.

Kant, Immanuel, 5, 129, 131, 172, 199, 213.
Kenysian economics, 100f.
knowledge, as a casual concept, 160ff., 178f., 193; social determination of, 151ff., 170; sociology of, 174, 180.
see also under cognitive interests, sociology of thought.
Kuhn, Thomas, 57, 120, 184.

language, 18
Lawrence, Philip, x, 261ff., 273.
laws (scientific), 160ff.
leading knowledge-interests, *see under* cognitive interests.
Lele, 157, 159, 161f., 170, 174f., 178f., 180.
Lessnoff, Michael, viii, 117ff., 124ff., 127, 130f., 133ff.
Levy-Bruhl, Lucien, 202.

Lobkowicz, Nicholas, 101.
linguistics, generative, 18f.; 'non-empirical', 236.
Logical Empiricism, 5, 6.
Lukes, Steven, x, 182, 200, 207f., 234, 243.

Marcuse, Herbert, 96f., 98ff., 108ff., 132.
Marx, Karl, 92, 97, 138, 184.
Marxism, 37ff., 41, 92, 112, 127f., 246; structural, 247f.
material-object language, 202ff., 205f., 211ff., 262.
meaning, 180f.
see also under realism, semantic.
Merton, Robert K., 47, 184.
Merton's theorem, 21, 22.
Mills, C. Wright, 27f.
natural science, 15ff., 20ff., 98, 102f., 119f.
nomological-deductive model, 38ff., 45f., 251.
see also under explanation.

objectivity, viii, 118f.
objectification, 15, 21ff., 31.
open society, 139.
operationalism, 131.
Orwell, George, 59ff., 63ff., 85.

pangolin, 174f.
Parsons, Talcott, 246, 253f., 271f.
Peirce, C. S., 16, 56f., 93, 130.
physics, 13, 15.
Plato, 53.
Popper, Karl, 20, 39, 47, 97, 103, 113, 139.
'positivism', viii, x, 90, 101, 104, 108f., 119f., 137.
Poulantzas, Nicos, 247f.
power, 243ff., 252ff., 268ff.; as an 'essentially contested concept', 243ff., 261ff., 268, 270.
praxis, 7f., 29, 128.
predictability, 20f., 25.
psychoanalysis, Freudian, 37ff.

Quine, W. van O., 153, 192, 203, 229.

Rabin-Zempleni, J., 216f.
'rationalisation' (Weber's sense of), 91.
Rawls, John, 264.
realism, 156, 170; scientific, 166, 173, 211; semantic, 166, 171f.
reality, social construction of, 151, 153ff., 159, 179ff.
reification, 138f.
relativism, ixf., 54, 152ff., 163ff., 166ff., 168ff., 176, 184ff., 188ff., 192ff., 199, 200f., 226, 244, 246f., 261ff.; self-referential, 156ff.; transcendental, 154ff.
religion (and science), 225f.
Ricoeur, Paul, 41, 50.
rules, 17ff., 29f.

sacred/profane distinction, 182, 185.
Scheler, Max, 102f.
Skinner, B. F., 266.
Skorupski, John, 176, 177ff.
social engineering, 125, 138f.
social sciences, as distinct from natural sciences, 17ff., 29, 262f.
sociology of thought, 197ff., 200ff., 206, 233f.
spatio-temporal contiguity, 208ff.
spirits, 210f.
Strawson, P. F., 197f., 200f., 205., 212f., 226f., 230f., 234f., 239.
structuralism, 248ff., 253, 265.
subject-object relation, 15ff., 22ff., 138.
systems-analysis, 48f.

technical interest, 140ff.
'technique', 91f., 100f., 106f., 124. *see also under* control.
theoretical language, 206, 208ff., 218f., 262f.
transcendental pragmatics, 54, 127, 133f.
translation, 203f., 206, 236f.; indeterminacy of, 206, 229.
truth conditions, 166.

underdetermination of theory by data, 163ff., 171, 229.
understanding, communicative, 10ff., 17, 40, 76f.; of the universe, 101ff., unity of science, 3f., 10, 52, 54f., 74, 128.

value judgments, 29ff., 34f., 90, 93, 95, 108ff., 133, 136f., 243f.
verificationism, 168, 171ff., 176.

Weber, Max, 28f., 89f., 95, 108f., 123, 133ff., 159.
Williams, Bernard, 154f.
Winch, Peter, 74ff., 198f., 200f., 203, 262ff., 230, 234.
Windelband, W., 133.
Wittgenstein, Ludwig, 56, 63, 68, 155, 157, 165, 169, 172f., 192, 197f., 226., 233f.
world view, 157ff., 162ff., 177, 188ff., 191ff., 199, 200f., 219f.
work, 92, 97.
Wright, G. H. von, 27., 131.